The Standard Bearer

The Standard Bearer by Van Dyck

PETER VERNEY

The Standard Bearer

The story of Sir Edmund Verney
Knight-Marshal to King Charles I

HUTCHINSON OF LONDON

HUTCHINSON & CO. (*Publishers*) LTD
178–202 Great Portland Street, London, W.1

London Melbourne Sydney
Auckland Bombay Toronto
Johannesburg New York

First published 1963

*This book has been set in Garamond type face. It has
been printed in Great Britain by The Anchor Press,
Ltd., in Tiptree, Essex, on Antique Wove paper.*

'Once to every man and nation
  comes the moment to decide,
In the strife of Truth with Falsehood,
  for the good or evil side.'
                              LOWELL

Contents

Illustrations

Introduction

'For my Part, I do not like the Quarrel, and do heartily
wish that the King would yield and consent to what they
desire; so that my Conscience is only concerned in Honour
and in Gratitude to follow my Master. I have eaten his
Bread, and served him near thirty Years, and will not do
so base a Thing as to forsake him; and chuse rather to
lose my Life (which I am sure I shall do) to preserve and
defend those Things, which are against my Conscience to
preserve and defend.'

THESE WERE the words of my ancestor Sir Edmund Verney,
Knight-Marshal to King Charles I, who died as the King's
Standard Bearer at the Battle of Edgehill in 1642.

This is the story of Sir Edmund in the setting of his times. The
story of a man who, although believing wholly in the opposing
cause his eldest son and so many of his friends espoused, knows he
himself cannot desert the royal master whom he has served for so
long, and for whom he eventually dies.

It is the story too of Sir Edmund's family, and his many friends;
old Lady Sussex, an indefatigable correspondent; John Leeke his
brother-in-law; James Dillon, the dashing Irishman; and many
others. Above all, it is the story of a man who, although never at
the head of affairs, was close to their heart for perhaps the most
momentous period in our history—the years before the outbreak of
the Civil War.

Much of the material for this book is taken from the Verney Papers, a vast collection of documents and letters, nearly 30,000 of them covering the whole of the seventeenth century; these which are still housed at Sir Edmund's old home at Claydon in Buckinghamshire. Of the many collections of seventeenth-century manuscripts in this country the Verney Papers provide one of the most absorbing domestic records of the times. They cover the life-span of two generations, of Sir Edmund and his four sons: Ralph, the eldest, a conscientious stay-at-home, writer of the Notes of the Long Parliament; Tom, the spendthrift vagabond; Mun, the gallant cavalier; Henry, the sporting-man.

The letters present a fascinating picture of the serenity of the country and family life in the period before civil war broke upon the nation. In them, too, can be read the despair of a man who, finally disillusioned and dispirited, throws his life away rather than serve a cause which he could not wholeheartedly support.

This book closes at Edgehill with Sir Edmund's death. The further fortunes of the family were then inextricably tied to those of the eldest son. Unfettered by personal loyalty to the sovereign, Ralph was able to follow the dictates of his own principles and come out against his King. But two years after his father's death, when extremists were by now in power, he preferred to go into voluntary exile and see his estates sequestered rather than sign the hateful Covenant which it was against his conscience to sign. Eventually, eleven years later, after the death of his wife and two of his four children, Ralph, now fully restored to favour, comes back to a forlorn and deserted Claydon 'to keepe company with the ghostes', as he put it.

Of the other sons only Mun distinguished himself. And he, after a short but successful military career, was slaughtered in cold blood by Cromwell's express order after the fall of Drogheda in 1649, when commanding one of Ormonde's regiments of foot.

The first attempt at sorting and cataloguing the Verney Papers was undertaken by John Verney, first Viscount Fermanagh, Sir Edmund's grandson, at the beginning of the eighteenth century. Later, almost exactly 100 years ago, Parthenope, Lady Verney, and her step-son's wife, Margaret, set about the mammoth task of re-cataloguing and properly storing the collection of manuscripts which in the intervening years had become mixed, mislaid and were in some cases rotting away. Fascinated by the material unearthed, they decided to write a history of the Verney family in the seventeenth century. The product of their labours was published in a very comprehensive and widely acclaimed four-volume work entitled *The Memoirs of the Verney Family*. This was reprinted and re-edited three times, the final edition being published in 1925.

The centrepiece of this book is the Standard Bearer's home at Claydon. Situated four miles from Winslow in Buckinghamshire, it has been transformed from the Stuart mansion of Sir Edmund's day by succeeding generations of the family. Now a classic example of a small Georgian country-mansion, it was given to the National Trust in 1956. Here are still kept, besides the boxes containing the original manuscripts of the Verney Papers, the ancestral portraits from which all but one of the illustrations for this book have been taken. Also at Claydon are various family relics dating from the period covered by this biography, including Sir Edmund's staff of office and a ring with a minature picture of King Charles which the Standard Bearer always wore and which was returned with his severed hand from Edgehill, all that was found of Sir Edmund's body.

It is self-evident that without the co-operation and hospitality of the present owners of Claydon this book would never have been written—and I am extremely grateful. I am also deeply indebted to Miss Mary Coate for her help over the 'Trip to Spain', Brigadier Peter Young for his advice on the Battle of Edgehill and Maurice Ashley for all his suggestions; as well as to the many people who have been kind enough to read the manuscript in its various stages, particularly Miss Ruth Verney and Miss Violet Needham. Largely instrumental in encouraging me to produce this book in its present form was Mrs. Elizabeth Whitley, without her help the task would have been immeasurably harder. However, my greatest thanks must inevitably go to Dr. C. V. Wedgwood for her great personal kindness in shepherding a totally ignorant author in the right direction.

P.V.

Author's Note

I hope that this book will draw attention to the still unworked riches in the Verney Papers. These have now been micro-filmed in their entirety and copies are available at Yale University, Dartmouth College in New Hampshire, the British Museum and the Buckinghamshire Records Office in Aylesbury.

To my mind much of the charm and colour of these letters is in the spelling and punctuation—I have religiously preserved both. And I have indexed at the end of the book those letters from which I have taken extracts.

When starting work on the letters I made the mistake of trying to decipher and translate word by word; later I found it not only easier but more satisfactory to tackle them phonetically, and I pass this on in the hope that it will be of help to the reader.

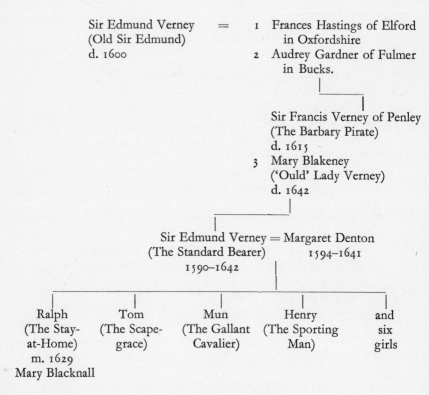

Sir Edmund Verney   =   1 Frances Hastings of Elford
(Old Sir Edmund)   in Oxfordshire
d. 1600   2 Audrey Gardner of Fulmer
                            in Bucks.

                            Sir Francis Verney of Penley
                            (The Barbary Pirate)
                            d. 1615
                         3 Mary Blakeney
                            ('Ould' Lady Verney)
                            d. 1642

            Sir Edmund Verney = Margaret Denton
            (The Standard Bearer)   1594–1641
                1590–1642

Ralph   Tom   Mun   Henry   and
(The Stay-   (The Scape- (The Gallant (The Sporting six
at-Home)   grace)   Cavalier)   Man)   girls
m. 1629
Mary Blacknall

A more comprehensive genealogical table may be found on p. 206.

I

The Half-brothers

'. . . And each the other's difference bears. . . .'
MARVELL

A<small>T THE</small> the time of the Spanish Armada one of the five captains
chosen to command musters in the County of Hertfordshire
was a certain Edmund Verney. Old Sir Edmund, as he was known
(he was knighted in 1597 or 1598), married three times: by his first
wife he had no children, but his second wife, daughter of a Buckinghamshire squire, produced one son—Francis. On her death he once
again remarried. His choice this time was Mary Blakeney, herself
twice a widow though still under forty, and daughter of a William
Blakeney of Sparham in Norfolk. She produced a son, Edmund,
and it is he who is the central character in this story.

Edmund was born in 1590 on New Year's Day at his father's
house in Drury Lane. Not a great deal is known about his father
except that he did a certain amount of public business in both Hertfordshire and Buckinghamshire, where he was variously sheriff
from 1577 to 1591; and that he evidently suffered from a poor
digestion, for there is a licence from the Archbishop of Canterbury
about that time which permits him to 'eat flesh on days forbidden,
with a good conscience for the term of his life', because, 'that the
eating of fish was injurious to his health by reason of the great
weakness of his stomach'.

B
17

Old Sir Edmund was also a large landowner, having considerable property in Buckinghamshire, Hertfordshire and Lincolnshire. The proportioning of this between his widow and two sons entailed some difficulty and eventually necessitated a special Act of Parliament. He died at Chalfont St. Giles in 1599 at the Stone House, which was afterwards sold to the Hampdens. The funeral was occasion for 'great pompt of streamers, heralds, etc.', and he was buried in a private chapel in the ancient church of Albury. The portrait of old Sir Edmund at Claydon—by an unknown artist—shows him wearing doublet and hose, with a heavy gold chain round his neck and a black skull-cap on his head. His face appears stern but kindly, with piercing eyes and a firm mouth. He was forty-nine when this picture was painted.

After the death of old Sir Edmund his son and namesake, who was then only nine, continued to live with his mother, Dame Mary —'ould Lady Verney', who was a person of considerable intelligence and business acumen, and there is no doubt that much of the credit for Edmund's highly reputable behaviour later in life was due to his mother's influence and guiding hand. She died aged ninety-five only two weeks after the battle of Edgehill.

The sole reference we have to Sir Edmund's education is mention of his graduating from St. Alban's Hall, Oxford, in 1604. Prior to this he doubtless had some schooling in which religious study and languages played no small part. However, from an early age it was planned to fit him for a life of both public and private duties, and after his graduation from Oxford he was sent abroad to see something of foreign countries and gain some knowledge of the world. In a book of short biographical notes on the men of the day it is said that 'after some time spent with my Lord Goring to see the armies in the Wars in the Low Countries, and some sallies out with my Lord Herbert and Sir Henry Wootton to see the Courts of France and Italy, he goeth with my Lord of Bristol into Spain'.

Presumably these travels were successful in giving him that essential polish to be acquired only through frequenting Court circles, for in 1606, when he returned 'his mind accomplished in all active, useful and manly knowledge', Edmund was taken as Chief Sewer,[1] with the salary of £20, into the household of Prince Henry, King James's eldest son, where his uncle was one of the chief falconers, and Sir Thomas Challoner, who lived near the Claydon estate, was

---

[1] A sewer was a form of steward, food-taster cum server.

the young Prince's tutor and chamberlain. It was probable, too, that his mother was largely instrumental in Edmund being given this appointment. Lady Verney continued to live at Drury Lane and was evidently known to James's consort, Anne of Denmark, for there is record of her attending the Queen's funeral as a Lady of the Privy Chamber. This honour was assigned to her specially for the day and placed her above the wives of baronets—'not without repining', adds the chronicle.

While Edmund was on the threshold of his long career at Court, his elder half-brother, Francis, was setting out on a career of quite a different sort. Six years older than Edmund, he was a totally dissimilar character; where Edmund was high-minded, conscientious and generous to a fault, Francis was utterly self-seeking, idle and pleasure-loving. And whilst Edmund was a most affectionate father and husband, not in any sense could Francis be called a family man.

From the first Francis seems to have been a constant source of trouble. Unfortunately he had no parental discipline, for at the age of five he lost his mother and eleven years later his father died too. His step-mother, Edmund's parent, appears to have had nothing to do with his upbringing and he seems to have been under no control, leading a thoroughly wild life and doing much as he liked. When fifteen he was married to his step-sister, Ursula St. Barbe, daughter of his father's third wife by a former husband, but she had no influence over him and had little effect on his career, which pursued a rapid and dissolute course.

First mention of his misdeeds is in 1604 when one of his servants was killed in a drunken brawl in Alsatia, a notoriously unsavoury district in the backwash of London, and the home of thieves and vagabonds of the worst sort. Francis was still under twenty when this happened, and evidently had already taken to his evil ways.

By the terms of his will old Sir Edmund had left the main part of his property to his third wife for her lifetime, and thereafter to their son Edmund. Francis was thus deprived of his rights as eldest son during his minority and had considerable grounds for grievance. Having quarrelled with his step-mother all his life, when he came of age he determined to have set aside the settlement which had been made to her. He petitioned Parliament, but after 'much dispute and argument' the Bill was rejected. Stung to desperation by the sense of injustice he felt after his treatment, the family quarrels, and most probably his gambling debts, he determined to sell all and 'forsake the friends who had injured him and the country which had refused him redress'.

In high dudgeon he took himself off to Palestine and from there returned to England some time later. Apparently he came by way of Paris, for there is a letter from the then ambassador talking in very favourable terms of Francis whom he recommends to 'my very good Lord the Earl of Salisbury, principal Secretary of Estate at Court'.

Soon, however, Francis is up to his old tricks again, and the good impression he created in Paris did not survive long in London. Heavy debts and bad company forced him once more to leave England and, while his half-brother Edmund was completing his education on the Continent, Francis set out on that downward path which was to end only with his death seven years later. He had sold most of his own property before the trip to the Holy Land, so there was little left for him to dispose of. But, determined to sever his connections utterly, he sold his remaining belongings, gave an authority to an uncle to look after his few surviving interests and left the country in 1608 never to return.

Tales of the excitement and adventure to be had on the Barbary coast must have been common talk amongst the sort of company Francis kept. Doubtless, too, the example of the many Englishmen who were then seeking their fortunes in the service of the Beys of Tunis and Algiers was an added attraction to a young man determined to rid himself of family counsel and live an independent life. So it was to the home of the corsairs, who ravaged the Mediterranean shipping of Turk and Christian alike, that Francis made his way.

In the days of Queen Elizabeth there was a subtle distinction between privateer and pirate. It had frequently happened that the Queen had found it expedient not to notice too closely how her captains interpreted their orders. But when James came to the throne one of his first acts was to try to lessen the scourge of these privateers by withdrawing their commission and offering a free pardon to those who had transgressed in any way. Some accepted the gesture, but others, taken with the adventurous life they were leading and loth to give up so profitable a profession, ignored the royal command and carried on their activities with unrelaxed zeal and a growing disregard for the niceties of nationality or the abuse of flag.

The rough Barbary coast afforded an ideal lair for these pirates

IN ÆTATIS SVÆ: 5 9 : 1 5 9 4

Old Sir Edmund, the father of the Standard Bearer
ARTIST UNKNOWN

'Ould' Lady Verney, the mother of the Standard Bearer
ARTIST UNKNOWN

—its narrow inlets protected them from prying eyes, and the dangerous shoals and reefs prevented pursuit from heavier-draft vessels. Thus, from the safety of their havens, the corsairs sallied forth in search of merchant ships to rob them of their riches and sell their crews to slavery. Not content with these exploits, they made forays to pillage and carry off the inhabitants of the villages on the Spanish mainland, and as success bred boldness they cast their net wider and attacked the southern coast of Ireland where, amongst other things, they found a 'good store of wenches'.

Nor was the coast of England itself safe from such depredations. So extreme had the threat become that the Lizard Light was extinguished for fear it would 'conduct pirates', and worshippers on Sundays were asked to pray for those taken by the galleys. James's policy of peace at any price had cost London dear, for in the twenty years of his reign the City merchants lost more ships than in the whole of the late Spanish war. Moreover, the now small navy was powerless to put an end even to the piracy off their own shores; so much so, that in 1611 the Dutch asked leave to enter English ports and capture any pirates who might be sheltering there.

But it was the trade in the Mediterranean which was the corsairs' chief objective. The fat, slow merchant ships of the period made ideal targets for their own swift galleys and galliasses. After a time many of the merchant ships came to be armed, particularly those of the East India Company, which were well able to look after themselves in the event of trouble; nevertheless there was prey enough and a booming slave market existed.

Of the pirates themselves, although many were Algerians or Turks, many more were Christian renegades of mixed nationality— English, French, Dutch and others, owning allegiance to no one and surpassing one another in brutality. In addition were the ships of the 'Religion' from Malta and Tuscany, many of them manned by a barbaric and fierce tribe, the Mainotes from ancient Sparta.

Most main Mediterranean ports were in collusion with the pirates to a greater or less degree, providing either a haven for their ships or an outlet for their ill-gotten goods. Of these Algiers and Tunis are popularly supposed to have been the greatest 'nests of piracy', but at this period they were comparatively law-abiding. Situated astride the east–west routes of both the sea and land trade they were thriving cities in their own right, yet loyal subjects of the Ottoman Empire. Each had a law and government, both strict and just, which compared very favourably with that enjoyed in supposedly more civilized countries. In fact it was reputed safer to walk abroad in Algiers than in many parts of London itself. Even the captives were well treated, and on many occasions released or ransomed slaves preferred to remain rather than to start life anew in their native countries.

The towns along the coast were ready purchasers of prizes and slaves. But, equally, much honest shipping plying its trade treated them as normal ports of call, and many nations considered it worth while to keep a consul in residence to represent their interests. So, in fact, many of them presented a strange anomaly—on one day a prize would be brought in and her cargo and crew sold; on the next a ship of the same nationality would call, carry out her business and depart unmolested. As the politics of the period fluctuated, so would the warmth of the reception given to a visiting ship. The task of Consul was extraordinarily difficult—granted few funds from home, he never knew from one day to the next if his intercessions would end in success or his own death. On the whole, however, there was remarkably fair play from the ruling authorities in the ports; and this despite the frequent exhortations from European governments for 'a common resistance of the Turk, the common enemy of Christendom'. The Turks, on their part, seem to have despised the machinations of the European, and their attitude to Christianity was that they would 'rather be transformed into dogs than embrace a religion which practices so many abominations'.

Much of the barbarous treatment that was common must be attributed to the European: either the free-lance pirate operating on his own behalf, or the one-time captive now 'turned Turk' and in the service of an infidel master.

James's decision to maintain a small navy had meant that many experienced mariners, now no longer offered lawful work at sea, turned to piracy as their only opportunity to practise the one profession they knew. This overflow, together with those privateers who had refused the pardon extended in 1603, gravitated naturally to those haunts of their kind in North Africa where they sought and found congenial employment. Their new masters discovered that the Englishman, above any other, made an excellent pirate. He was a bold and resilient fighter, not unduly troubled by the legality of his deeds, but loyal in adversity and, above all, knew and did not fear the sea as did so many of their own countrymen. He was the ideal choice to lead the forays on the rich commerce passing so peacefully and temptingly past their very doors.

So it was that we find many English names amongst those of the rogues who plundered and menaced the shipping in the Mediterranean in the seventeenth century.

These adventurers 'doubting their offences to be unpardonable by law and nature, became runagates, renouncing Christian faith, exercising all manner of despites, and speaking blasphemingly against God, their God, their King, and country; and taught the infidels the knowledge and use of navigation, to the great hurt of Europe'. To their own countrymen, though, it was the traitorous act of 'turning Turk' that was a greater crime than of piracy itself.

It is very probable that Francis had met some of these renegades before he took up his new profession. In particular the Giffards, who were distant cousins and the then lessees of Claydon, the largest of his father's Buckinghamshire estates.

The Giffard family had been implicated in North African affairs for many years. The first was John Giffard, who found himself involved in a war of succession for the Moroccan throne. At that time there were three claimants, each with a band of followers. Giffard backed a gentleman called Muley Sidan, and although this turned out to be the right choice, the Englishman never lived to see his faith justified. Muley seems to have had high regard for Giffard and he gave him command of a portion of his army, which included a small English detachment.

'Ouer the English and all the Christians was a generall captaine John Giffard, a gentleman of worthy spirit, and descended from the auncient and honourable stemme of the Giffards in Buckinghamshire. Upon his first entertainment and welcome into the countrey, Sidan bestowed upon him a rich sword, valued at a thousand marks, and a scarlet cloake richly embroidered with pearle. . . . With him as secondarie men in charge, was one maister Philip Giffard, his neare and verie deare kinsman, captaine Jaques a verie vailiant souldier, captaine Smith one of the most exquisite engineers in Europe . . . men evrie way able to undergoe their severall commands.'

Unfortunately, the war started badly for Muley. His forces were routed in a skirmish and he himself was driven back on to his provincial capital, whence he eventually emerged victorious. But his English contingent were annihilated to a man in the preliminary clash. Muley had realized their plight and, before quitting the field himself, had 'sent to the English captaines to be gone, and to captaine Giffard a good horse'. Despite this, as the chronicle says, 'Few of al the English nation was left alive'.

The example of John Giffard was taken up by another member of the family, Richard Giffard. He was one of the most notorious of the English corsairs and many are the complaints of his depredations. He had a remarkable career, for, after achieving fame as a pirate, he was granted a complete pardon by the King and became a member of the Admiralty Board, one of whose tasks was to put down the selfsame outrages of which he himself had been such an able exponent.

It is probable that Francis joined Giffard's band until he gained enough experience to venture in his own ship. However, we know little of Francis's exploits in his new profession except that in 1609 he is credited with the taking of 'three or four Poole shipps and one of Plymouth'. He was probably one of the captains in Ward's fleet of corsairs, for it was said that 'no English nobleman kept such state as Captain John Ward, who is called their chief with whom were associated Sir Francis Verney, Granvile, and others'. John Ward, once a Faversham fisherman, was the acknowledged leader of the English band of corsairs. Originally, he had operated on his own but later turned Turk and received a commission from the Sultan of Tunis under whose orders he thereafter operated. At one time he had under his command a greater fleet than King James himself, but lost twenty ships in one disastrous action. He lived in incredible splendour and was reputed to dine from gold plate. He died of the plague in 1622, having settled down in Tunis and occupied himself ashore with training gunners and casting cannon.

What then happened to Francis can only be a matter of conjecture, for nothing more is heard of him until 1615 when an inveterate traveller called Lithgow in his *Most delectable and true discours of an admirid and painful peregrination* describes how he came across:

'the sometime great English gallant, Sir Francis Verney, lying sick in a Hospital, whom six weeks before I had met at Palermo, who after many misfortunes, exhausting his large patrimony, abandoning his country and turning Turk in Tunisis, was taken at sea by the Sicialian galleys, in one of which he was two years a slave, whence he was redeemed by an English Jesuit upon a promise of conversion to the Christian faith. When set at liberty he turned common soldier, and here in the extremest calamity of extream miseries entreated death. Whose dead corps I charitably interred in the best manner time would afford me strength.'

How much of this is true no one knows. The only thing that can be verified is that Francis indeed came to the Hospital of St. Mary of Pity in Messina and did eventually die there. Whether he was in 'extream' poverty as Lithgow relates, however, is open to doubt for, after several years, through the kind offices of an English merchant, together with Francis's death certificate, the family received a parcel containing a turban, a kind of dressing-grown trimmed with silk to look like fur, two pairs of slippers and a strange pilgrim's staff inlaid with mother-of-pearl crosses—all that remained of Francis's personal belongings.

At some stage in his life, before he abandoned his native country, he had a truly magnificent portrait painted in Spain. In it he is wearing a costume typical of a gallant of the period with quilled ruff, striped Spanish jerkin, trunk hose and loose boots of light-brown Cordovan leather; in his hand is a black-tipped gold cane which was returned with his effects from Messina and to this day hangs below the picture. He is an impressive and dignified figure and shows none of the despair that he must have felt.

So ended the brief, inglorious but romantic career of the Barbary Pirate—he was only thirty-one when he died.

Francis's death left Edmund undisputed head of the family. As Claydon was still let and the other houses had been sold by Francis before setting out on his travels, Edmund and his mother were forced to live in their town house which was in Drury Lane and much too near the Market.

Covent Garden in the seventeenth century was a thoroughly unsavoury place. There were no sewers and the refuse from the Market, flourishing even then, was merely thrown into the street, where it rotted and stank. The Market itself 'was held close to the dwellings of the Great. Fruit-women screamed, carters fought, cabbage stalks and rotten apples accumulated in heaps at the threshold of the Countess of Berkshire and the Bishop of Durham', says Macaulay. The noise must have been unbearable, quite apart from the stench and indescribable squalor.

In January 1611, when he came of age, Edmund was knighted at Whitehall and the same year he visited Madrid where Lord Digby was ambassador, apparently on some public business, possibly connected with the projected marriage between Prince Henry and the Infanta of Spain. It must have been shortly after his return from this trip that Prince Henry gave him his portrait. This is mentioned in a later will, but seems to have completely disappeared; although the portrait facing page 29, and depicting King Charles the First when Prince of Wales, was until recently considered to be the one concerned.

Prince Henry was seventeen when Sir Edmund returned from Madrid, but, when only little older, he was taken ill with a sudden attack of fever. No one could diagnose this strange illness which caused him to grow daily more pale and emaciated. Initially it was attributed to the 'continuance of his violent exercises, or too frequent indulgence of himself in eating grapes or other fruits'. But as time passed and he grew no better his doctors became seriously alarmed. Cures from simple physic to the application of pigeons and cupping-glasses to his shaven head were tried, but all to no avail. At last, after nearly six weeks of sickness, the Young Prince died—he was not yet nineteen.

The tragic event shocked all England—there was widespread grief, for the Prince was universally loved and already his bearing and counsels were winning him praise from those many years his senior. It seemed a tragedy beyond measure that a life so full of promise should be so prematurely ended. In a tract written seventy years later it is said: 'when women in England do lament the death of their dearest children, to comfort them it is ordinarily said, and is paste into a proverbe, "Did not good Prince Henry die?" ' Such was the esteem in which the young Prince was held.

For six years Sir Edmund had served his Prince, and, in common with all who came in contact with the heir to the throne, he had developed a close friendship and immense respect for him. Twenty-seven years later Sir Edmund alludes to Prince Henry's death as causing him the greatest sorrow he had ever known. They were about the same age and had the same interests; but what probably attracted the young courtier to the Prince more than anything else was their similar religious feelings and a shared liking for simplicity in worship.

The Prince's true Protestant belief was never more emphatically and popularly made clear than when he turned down the overtures to a Spanish marriage with the blunt declaration that 'two religions should not lie in his bed'. This echo of their own feelings heartened the English people to believing that here indeed was a true defender of their religion against the insidious encroachment of the Papists, and they gave him their complete trust. He was received like a hero wherever he went, and his every saying was widely quoted as showing a wit and wisdom far beyond his years.

Foreigners visiting England were advised to pay their respects to Prince Henry, for in the young Prince people said they saw a reincarnation of his illustrious namesake Henry V. The Court of the young Prince became the focus for many great men who waited there in preference to the Court of his father. Certainly the contrast between behaviour at the two could hardly have been greater. Protocol and etiquette before the Prince was strict in the extreme, and a box was kept to collect the fines of those who swore in his presence. In fact the eighteen-year-old Prince was considered a paragon of almost every virtue; his only acknowledged failing was an overfondness of fruit. It is astonishing that, in face of all this, he did not become spoilt, but such indeed appears to be the case and nothing can be found that does not praise the young Prince in the most fulsome fashion.

It was unfortunate for Prince Charles that he succeeded so outstanding a young man. He was compared unfavourably with Prince Henry in every action, and it must have been a constant source of annoyance for a man so duty-minded and sensitive.

In 1613 a household was formed for the new Prince of Wales, then aged thirteen, and Sir Edmund was placed in it as one of the Gentlemen of the Privy Chamber. This was the start of a long association for Sir Edmund with Charles whom, as Prince and King, he served devotedly for nearly thirty years. The fact that they had been together almost from boyhood immeasurably complicated the feelings with which Edmund regarded the proceedings of his master.

Shortly before taking up his appointment in Prince Charles's service Sir Edmund, then aged twenty-two, married Margaret Denton, the eldest daughter of a neighbouring landowner, Sir Thomas Denton, who lived at Hillesden, only three miles from Claydon.

The Dentons were a good county family 'of birth and estate' and the match was thoroughly suitable in every way. Indeed, Sir Edmund had found himself an excellent wife who possessed many attributes, not the least being the then sizable fortune of some £2,000.

In view of this fortune the question of a settlement was most serious. A meeting of the two families was held in order to come to terms and 'ould Lady Verney' was brought over to assist in the negotiations. A jointure of £400 was insisted upon by the old knight, this Sir Edmund was quite unable to secure, but his mother came to his assistance and the matter was settled amicably. The formal contract was drawn up and it was agreed that lands should be bought and included in the settlement. The meeting passed off to the satisfaction of all parties and culminated with a most generous offer from Sir Thomas Denton of 'four years boarde' for the young couple. They were married at Hillesden in December of 1612.

Margaret Verney was a good and clever woman, devoted to her husband and many children, gentle and retiring: 'the heart of her husband trusted in her', and, obliged as he was to be very often away from his home when in attendance at Court, most of the business of the family fortunes devolved upon her. Luckily, she had considerable money sense, which was as well, for Sir Edmund was sadly lacking in it, and much of the time his finances were in almost insoluble chaos. Had it not been for his wife's careful hand the family would have soon been in a state of near-penury. It says much, too, for Margaret's care as a mother that in those days of terrible infant mortality she succeeded in raising ten of her twelve children.

She was greatly attached to her own family and there are many portraits of the Dentons at Claydon. There is a particularly fine one of Margaret herself. This shows her 'with a tender sad face full of feeling and intelligence, in an undress "smock" trimmed with lace, and a large "jewel" hung round her neck, she is leaning on her left arm, held so as to show the marks of a burn'. There is evidently some story connected with this scar, but there is no mention of it amongst the Papers.

Some six months after his marriage Sir Edmund took up his new appointment at Court. From then on for some years he seems to have been particularly busy, sometimes staying with the Dentons at Hillesden, sometimes at his lodgings at Court and occasionally at his house in 'Coven Garden'—then a fashionable part of town. His mother still occupied part of the town-house, and another relation, Sir Nat Hobart, who married her niece, had a study there

Sir Francis Verney, the Barbary Pirate
ARTIST UNKNOWN

Charles I as Prince of Wales
ARTIST UNKNOWN

as well. Their nearest neighbours and most intimate friends, divided only by a 'fence wall', were Sir Edward Sydenham and his wife. So, in many respects, the London house was far more Sir Edmund's home than was Hillesden, where for the most part his wife stayed and looked after the children.

During this time the Claydon estate had been a source of great annoyance. The lease, which had been renewed to the Giffards for 100 years, had still fifteen years to run. As a result, the young couple had nowhere to live and the offer of 'boarde' extended to them by the Dentons was particularly welcome.

The Giffards were not ideal tenants and they had sublet the estate to a lessee who was a continual nuisance. He cut the timber, made himself disagreeable in many ways, but, above all, ploughed up the pastures, then a great crime in Buckinghamshire, where they were particularly good. In 1620 Sir Edmund decided to put an end to this unsatisfactory state of affairs. To fulfil the unexpired tenancy he agreed to pay £4,000 for the surrender of the remainder of the lease. To cover this sum he was forced to ask for a loan from Prince Charles, who promised to lend the money over a period of four years. As Sir Edmund put it:

'Heretofore my means being small I did, to my great charge attend the late most renowned Prince Henry and my ever most honoured and famous Prince Charles, my loving master, and for my better maintenance and supporting myself to do my best service to the said Prince, I did buy in a lease of my lands, and thereby I did become much in depte. . . . According to his princely woord and promis he hath paid unto me one thousand pounds of the same, and the said most worthy prince hath ever been so just of his word and promise that he will no doubt give order for payment thereof.'

There is, however, no record of any further instalment being paid and this rash loan was the start of Sir Edmund's more or less continuous financial difficulties for the rest of his life.

Having at last secured the lease of Claydon, Sir Edmund and his wife quitted Hillesden and took up the management of their own property. At last they were able to set up their own home, by themselves and away from the Dentons, who, kind though they were, must have become rather a trial to the young couple during the course of time since their marriage. It must have been an equal relief for the Dentons—because the family already consisted of four boys, Ralph, Tom, Edmund, who was always known as Mun, and Henry, as well as two girls.

The early years following the move to Claydon were spent in setting the estate to rights, whilst Sir Edmund, encouraged by the Dentons, who were among the leading people in Buckinghamshire, began to take his share in county business. He took his part as a Justice of the Peace, and his standing was enhanced by being created warden of the neighbouring Waddon Chase. This honour had been bestowed with regal munificence by Buckingham who, now King James was failing, curried favour with Charles and distributed his favours with a careless liberality to the future King's followers.

This wardenship gave Sir Edmund the right to hunt and kill deer in the Chase whenever he liked. The park was one of the largest in the kingdom and covered a large stretch of country some eight miles to the north of Claydon itself. In return for his sport the duties were not onerous, consisting as they did of seeing to the welfare of the commoners, whose land was continually being invaded by the deer, and ensuring that too much wood was not cut by the charcoal-burners. A certain amount of game preservation was carried on, but here deer were plentiful and Sir Richard Graham, Buckingham's Master of Horse, says of his master: 'hee will not lymmitt you in the allowance of a warrant, but gives you free leaue to kill what you will, both in the parke and the chase. You need not be spareing to pleasure yourselfe and your freindes also, for there are to many in the parke.'

There is a curious petition dated three years after this from a number of cottagers whose commons were on the Chase bounds. In it they complain that deer are injuring the common land and ask for redress of their grievances:

'Worthie Sr, we heare that Mr. Sandys did latelie writ to you about your deere lying on corn and grasse. . . . These are therefore to certifie that it is most true that the deere doe much oppresse us in most places of our feeld [common land], and we are continuallie damnifyed by them. Soe that we had a purpose to petition to the Lord Duke his grace, rather then to endure the injuryes that we suffer. Yet first we thought fitt to acquaint your worship with our grievances, humblie entreating that you would be pleased to thinke of some course whereby they may be remedyed. We have ancientlie used to cutte and fetch furzes from offe our sheep-comon for oir own uses. But now of late we have been forbidden and discharged as from you. We hope or gracious Lord will suffer us to enjoy or ancient rights and therefore we desire that you would not goe about to take them from us. And thus craving pardon for this or bold-nesse we take leave, resting your worshipp's in all duty,' and then follow eight signatures, five of them marks.

So followed a period of great happiness for Sir Edmund. Settled at last in his own house with his wife and family, he devoted himself to setting Claydon in order. Within a short time the estate showed ample evidence of his care and attention.

II

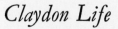

Claydon Life

'. . . Sufficiency, content,
Retirement, rural quiet, friendship . . .'

JAMES THOMPSON

LIKE MOST large houses of the period Claydon was, in effect, a small community. In a hard winter it was cut off completely from the outside world. Even in summer the roads were appalling and soon became impassable quagmires after a shower of rain. As a result, few provisions were imported and almost everything consumed was provided from the estate.

Here was produced the bread, the meat (slaughtered in their own slaughter-house), the beer, the butter—all the basic provisions they needed. Little came in from outside but wine, and luxuries such as salt, pepper and fish. Even some fish were to be caught in the stew-ponds in the garden, a relic of the time when fish-eating was decreed compulsory on certain days.

Dove-cotes were common throughout the country. The one at Claydon is reputed to have been particularly good, and there is frequent mention in the letters of a dozen pigeons sent to friends in London—where they must have been extremely welcome. Venison from Waddon and wild-fowl from a famous nearby decoy, helped vary the monotony of the fare at Claydon. A welcome change was also provided by game, which had to be captured by hawk or

32

net, for, as late as the reign of James I, an old law prohibiting the
use of the 'long gun' was occasionally invoked. It was not until the
turn of the century that it became the custom to 'shoot flying' in
England, although in Spain they practised the sport of shooting
'partridges flying and conies running'.

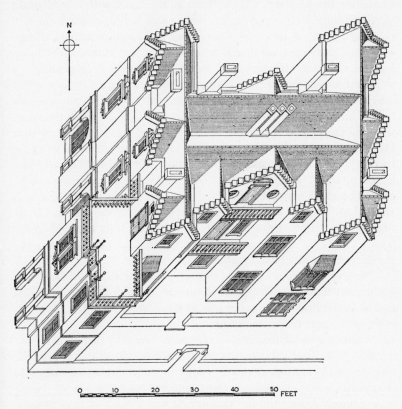

Claydon House in the Seventeenth Century, reconstructed by Peter
Pratt from contemporary elevations, using axionometric projection

The house at Claydon is believed to have been rebuilt in about
1500. Before that date there had been a mansion on the site which
had originally been bought by a Ralph Verney, Lord Mayor of
London in 1465, who was knighted in the field five years later,
after the defeat of Thomas the Bastard Fauconbridge just outside
London. To this day the ancient manor-house can be traced at the

C

core of the present building. The central narrow part, joining the two blocks, consisted until as recently as 100 years ago of two rows of rooms back to back, so that a whole suite of rooms had to be traversed in order to reach the ends of the house. None of the walls was at right angles; the floors rose and fell again in the same room to a difference of three to four inches in level; and the ceiling would vary in height by as much as six inches in a length of thirty feet.

When siting a house our ancestors possessed a strange dislike of wind, but none at all of damp, and as fuel was scarce a low-lying and thus warmer situation was often chosen. As a precaution 'to avoyde the inconvenience of moathes and moldinesse' the builder was encouraged to face the house towards the east. Some other beliefs and practices to do with the placing and siting of the mansions of the period may have been prompted by the effusions of a Dr. Andrew Boorde, who published his *Dietary of Health* in 1542. In this he says of the aspect and situation of a house: 'The air must be pure, frisky and clean; the foundations of gravel mixed with clay. The chief prospects should be . . . never south for the south wind doth corrupt and make evil vapours.' Claydon, however, is sited on ground that slopes gently to the west, fully exposed to the 'evil vapours' of the south wind, which, in this case, blows over the pastures of Buckinghamshire.

There were probably only two chimneys when the house was built: one, with chimney corners on the ground floor, ran up the centre of the house, the other was in what was called the 'Tenants' Hall' at the rear of the building.

In the houses of that period the main 'chimney places' achieved a colossal size and often at the back was a hiding place, a 'priests's hole', in which the persecuted Jesuits in the sixteenth century had sometimes hidden. One such was found at Claydon when the house was repaired during the last century. It was a small chamber in the central chimney in which 'ten men could stand upright'. The whereabouts of these secret chambers was a closely guarded secret passed from father to son, and it is said that many of the ghost stories handed down to the present generation may have originally been started in this way to prevent too much prying curiosity.

Four hundred years ago there would be little glass in the windows. Instead, linen steeped in oil or wooden shutters were substitutes, and those few windows which were glazed had small leaded lattice panes of inferior glass.

Within the rooms the walls would be covered with 'tapestry arras work or painted cloth, wherein either diverse histories or herbs, beasts or knots and such like are stained', or else they were 'ceiled with oak'. This panelling or wainscot was a prized possession, so it was that when Sir Edmund took over the lease of his house in Covent Garden he was specifically granted the 'use of wainscot'. In this lease there is mention, too, of 'stock locks' which were kept 'loose in the closet'. This same house was relet and it was then suggested, as quite a new idea, that these locks should remain on the doors as so much damage was done in pulling them off and on.

There is an inventory of the contents of Claydon made on the orders of Ralph, the eldest son, in 1645, three years after the death of Sir Edmund and during his own exile. This gives a good idea of the interior of the house in the early part of the seventeenth century. In this he mentions 'the odd things in the roome my mother keept herself, the iron closet, the little roome between her beds head and the backstairs'—probably a secret place—'the little and greate Fripperies, your owne greene wrought velvet furniture, the red velvet furniture, the looking-glasses (there should bee at least four), leather carpets for the dininge and drawinge rooms, the stooles with nailes guilt, the great cabanet like yours, the tapestry, the great branch candlestick, all such wrought worke as my mother had from London and was not finished, the booke of martirs and other bookes in the withdrawingroom, the preservingroom, the spicery with furnaces and brewing vessels, plat left for the children's use.' In another letter comes news of 'the feather bedds that were waled up are much eaten with Ratts . . . the spitts and other odd thinges are so extremly eaten with Rust thatt they canot be evor of any use againe . . . the cloath of the Musk-coloured stools, which is "spoyled" and the dining-room chairs which are "in Ragges".' At the same time Ralph is concerned lest the 'Moathes' destroy the 'Turkie worke cushions'.

By this time the early Tudor habit of throwing rushes on the floor was largely past. In most houses the floors were of polished wood or, in the case of the hall and some other rooms, of stone or tiling which was occasionally sanded. In public halls where rushes were still sometimes used it was the custom to add rue and other variously scented herbs.

A considerable number of English-made 'turkey-work' carpets

were now to be seen, also many rugs imported from Persia and Turkey, but these were expensive and therefore more frequently used as covers for tables than on the floor.

The general improvement in the standard of comfort was particularly noticeable in the styles of furniture. The heavy Tudor chairs and stools with their unyielding 'sturdy oaken' seats and backs were giving way to the more comfortable embroidered or cane-backed type of walnut or cedar so common later in the century. However, there were too few chairs for any but the elderly; the remainder of the household sat on stools.

Beds were the heavy four-poster type, often with an elaborately carved back fastened to the wall behind. The carving on the bed-posts was usually very ornate and they were often crowned with the Four Evangelists, who as time passed were supplanted by a kind of grinning monster, which was supposed to lull the unfortunate occupant into an untroubled sleep.

The best bed was invariably left to the widow, and there is mention among the papers of 'on fader bed' which was passed on in this way.

There was one other bed to be found in many of the larger houses, this was the 'greate black bed' which emerged from obscurity when any member of the family died. Mourning was a serious business and it was the custom to send it to all intimate friends as well as to close relations. The 'blake bed' at Claydon used to be lent out to members of the family as occasion offered. Indoors the death-room was swathed in black. Not only were the hangings black and the furniture shrouded in crape, but even the sheets on the bed were black. There is a list of thirteen 'pieces' which came when the bed was originally bought, these include: 'blacke cloathe hanginges three yardes deepe and foure and a halfe yardes longe', two others, 'three yards deepe and three yardes longe'.

The custom continued until at least the end of the century, when there is record of a young Verney widow being allowed a white coverlet because she is sick and cannot bear black. Old Lady Sussex, a close friend of the family, does not seem to have observed the custom as strictly as some, though in declining the offer of the black bed on the death of her old friend Dame Margaret Verney, Sir Edmund's wife, she cannot resist adding that she herself spent £400 on her husband's funeral in order to express her 'love and valy' of him. On another occasion the bed was returned rather hurriedly by this old lady after her second husband had died and she was contemplating marriage to her third. She felt the embarrassment caused by this article of furniture might have had a damping effect on the wedding festivities, and writes somewhat urgently that, 'the blacke bed and haninges your ante never sent for; if you would have me deliver them anywher i will'.

Outside the house mourning was carried to yet further extremes. The use of the 'blacke coche' was considered correct for some time after a death, and when Ralph, lately a widower himself, was travelling abroad even though a 'blacke bed' was quite impracticable he did what he could to preserve the proprieties. His methodical lists include: 'Two black taffety night-cloathes, with black nightcapps, and black comb and brush and two black sweet-bags to it, and the slippers of black velvet.'

Apart from black 'coches' and 'hanginges', the bereaved family, of course, clothed themselves in nothing but sombre black. Sir Kenelm Digby, a gallant of the period and very fond of fine clothes, never wore anything after the death of his wife but a suit of black worsted with a plain linen collar, a long cloak of black and a slouch hat. Widows were even less fortunate and custom compelled them to wear a long veil of black entirely over the head; they continued to wear this until released by death or remarriage.

Life at Court was expensive. The fashion set by the richer courtiers and the cost of keeping up appearances meant a considerable outlay on clothes—an expense Sir Edmund could ill-afford. The Elizabethan dress of a 'stiff ruffe, long peasecod-bellied doublet and stuffed hose' had by now given way to the richly coloured velvet doublet, the short cloak and small close ruff. Silks, satin, velvet, precious stones, gold and silver were all employed according to the taste of the wearer and the length of his purse. The Court of James I was renowned for the magnificence of the dress of its courtiers. The King's favourites were lavished with presents of gold and jewels and much of this wealth went to the adornment of their persons. There were ludicrous extravagances, of course, and satirists had ample scope.

Tight-laced whalebone stays were worn by men, and breeches were padded out; so too were stockings, and there is one story of a young gallant who had the misfortune to snare his stocking on a nail, whereupon to his acute embarrassment came out not blood but bran. On another occasion we read of a person arraigned on a charge under an Act of Parliament which forbade certain kinds of padding for the trunk-hose. However, he handsomely cleared himself and convinced the court by showing that the suspected stuffing consisted of no less than 'a pair of sheets, two table-cloths, napkins, shirts and nightcaps'.

Sir Edmund was not able to afford truly extravagant dress; nevertheless in 1632 there is mention of a 'crimson sattin dublit and scarlet hoase laced with gould lase', and a 'black velvet cloake lyned with plush'. While in 1633, when, as a Gentleman of the Privy Chamber in Ordinary, he accompanied King Charles to his coronation in Scotland, the tailor's bill for that one trip reaches the staggering sum of £260 and includes such clothes as the 'purple satten suite', the 'cloath-of-gold waiscote and cappe', and 'the willow colored satten suite and cloake laced all over doble'. This sort of outlay must have been a grave strain on his rather precarious finances.

The wearing of linen was tending to become a general practice by the middle of the century. The linen industry, long in abeyance, was starting a revival, although the English workers were far inferior to the craftsmen of France. The will of Dame Margaret Verney, Sir Edmund's wife, lists not only her jewels and possessions but also linen which, made of thread of her own spinning, was good enough to last for generations. The document is addressed to her eldest son, Ralph, who was her executor:

'Give to your wiffe . . . my sable muffe and six of my new greate smockes. . . . I dessier your father that he will not let anie of my Household linnen bee soulde. but that itt may goe toe you and your elldiste sonn and I hope to his sonn toe, only sum of my brodeste of my own makinge give toe your sisters. . . . There are 4 verry fine smokes in your father's little linnen tronke and one of my four breadthe Holland sheetes for your own gerle Pegge.'

There was nearly a disagreeable quarrel, as a result of this will, between Ralph and his sister Pen when she preferred to have money and he would offer only £8 for some sheets she had been left. By comparison, a good horse could be had for about £10 in those days.

Lace, too, was worn by everyone of rank, and Claydon was near the centre of the industry, for the art of lace-making had been introduced into Buckinghamshire by Catherine of Aragon, part of whose dowry was derived from Steeple Claydon. St. Katern's Day was long held a traditional holiday by the makers of pillow lace in the county, and not until the nineteenth century was this finally discontinued.

Catherine herself 'delighted in working with the needle curiously' and her example did much to promote the lace industry. However, lace-making did not really thrive until anti-Protestant excesses drove many skilled workers from France and the Low Countries. These fugitives, exiles from Lille, Mechlin, Flanders and other great lace-producing centres, for the most part settled in the midland counties. Olney, in Buckinghamshire, was their focus and there was a church dedicated to the patron saint of lace-makers, St. Rumbald, who in his three days of mortal life managed to perform a quite astonishing number of miracles.

The Elizabethan ruff saw to it that the lace-workers were kept in business, and afterwards the patronage of Anne of Denmark kept the industry alive. In every country-house of any size there were built 'fripperies' to protect beautiful clothes, and doubtless much Buckinghamshire and Northamptonshire lace found its way to those at Claydon.

The finery and magnificence prevalent at Whitehall was, of course, hopelessly out of place in the country and the men reverted to a style less picturesque but considerably more practicable. A coarse cloth suit with worsted stockings, leathern shoes and a broad-brimmed felt hat was the normal dress of the country-gentleman. The lady of the house, too, wore clothing of a nature more suited to the accomplishment of her many tasks about the home, which kept her occupied for the greater part of the day.

It was in the outhouses, as well as indoors, that the business of provisioning the house was carried on. Here was done all the baking and brewing, the churning and milling, the slaughtering of cattle and poultry. Here, too, were the blacksmith's forge, the sawpit, the carpenter's bench, the painter's shops. The timber for building and the wood for burning were collected there, together with the odds and ends of stone, iron and carved woodwork which accumulate as if by magic at the back of any house of any age. The country-house of the day was indeed as nearly self-supporting as it is possible to be.

One of the many important tasks that befell the housewife was the salting down of meat for the winter. The difficulty of keeping cattle alive when stocks of hay were scanty was so great that, until the middle of the seventeenth century, come the autumn, all animals were killed and salted down. This diet of salted meat, only lightly relieved by fresh vegetables, gave rise, not unnaturally, to skin diseases, of which there is frequent mention in the letters. The Dutch introduction of winter roots into the country was of inestimable value and enabled cattle to survive the winter. So, by the time that Sir Walter Raleigh's potato started to be seen regularly on the table, it was no longer necessary to depend entirely on spices to relieve the monotony of a changeless salted diet. Nevertheless, the variety offered by game and fish was very welcome.

Until the Restoration period there was no coffee, tea or chocolate, so the home-made wines and beer were of vital importance. Ale was the common drink for women as well as men, and on Ralph's marriage in 1629 the health of the bride was drunk by Sir Nat Hobart 'in cake and ale, my wife and ant will do the same'. Even the children were 'indulged full liberty of drinking small beer', and took their medicine concealed or diluted in ale.

The habit of drinking wine with or without 'water mixt' was common among the well-to-do. The staple wines were sack, sherry and Malaga or Canary, but there were importations, too, from France, or from the Rhine Valley by way of Holland. All these were drunk as new wines, for the habit of maturing wine could not be practised until the cylindrical bottle superseded the 'bulbous stand-up' shape of the period. For some time the cork had taken the place of the piece of oiled hemp which had previously acted as a stopper, but these corks were conical in shape and placed only loosely in the neck.

As yet only the better classes drank wine, that is, except on Coronation Days when the larger provincial towns caused the conduits to run wine instead of water. Whisky must have occasionally been drunk, as some 'Irish Usquebagh' was one time sent as a present with the following recommendation: 'If it please his lordship next his hart, in the morning to drink a little as it is prepared and qualified it will help to digest all raw humours, expel wind and keep his inward parts warm all day after without any offence to his stomach.'

In the fruit season the ladies were fully occupied. On one occasion Lady Gardiner, a friend of the family, is excused by her husband from writing to Sir Ralph . . . 'being almost melted with the double heat of the weather and her hotter employment, because the fruit is ripe and she is so busy preserving'. And at another time Mrs. Isham,

Sir Edmund's sister-in-law, sends word to Lady Verney in London:
'I pray tell yore mother I will doe oup hur sugar if she hath corrantes
a nowe, for this last wicke of windes hath bine so bige that most of
them was bloed off the treeses.'

The work of the still-room, 'preserving, conserving, candying,
making syrups, jellies, beautifying washes, pomatum essences and
other such secrets', was an important part of the business of the
ladies of the house. There were many queer tin vessels with spouts
at all angles in the cupboards of the old still-room at Claydon, and
the frequent recipes in the letters show how the 'decoctions, in-
fusions and essences of herbs and simples' were prepared. With the
prescription, the doctor produced detailed instructions on how to
concoct the medicine. The making of such obscure mixtures as
'Hiera Picra, the Mithridates, Orbiculi, Bezoartis', and the snail
water, are all thus explained.

Invalid and other recipes are legion among the letters and in the
many books on the life of the times. Sir Edmund's daughters seem
to have enjoyed concocting their own creams and 'messes', and they
recommend for a 'pimpled or saucy' face an ointment of roasted
eggs and white copperas, and to 'make on loke yonge longe' it is
suggested that myrrh water be used.

Among the draughts concocted at Claydon the housekeeper
evidently had one of particular potency, a 'purginge drink as she
made for the maids and the upholsterer'. This was treated with
great awe by the doctor, who recommends the addition of burdock
seeds or roots. The unfortunate upholsterer was given too much of
this brew at one time and was like 'to make a dye of it'; however, he
survived these ministrations but doubtless lived in considerable
dread of them thereafter. In many cases the ailment must have been
far less unpleasant than the cure: for the 'Frenzie of inflammation
of the Caules of the brain' the unhappy patient had to suffer the
ordeal of having the juice of beets squirted into his nostrils. A deaf
person had to wait for the oil which came out of a grey eel buried
in an earthenware pot in a dunghill.

The mistress of the house had a difficult and arduous task; thus
it was the practice to have a lady to help her in her multifarious
occupations. Often this companion was a poor relation, or an unmarried relative or friend, who had no home and accepted an offer
of this kind, all too frequently to find herself as little more than a
lady's maid. At Claydon, Doll Leeke, a daughter of an Irish friend,

helped the mistress of the house. She seems very popular and much liked by the family. Ralph does small errands for her and is constantly at pains to invest her small income to the best advantage.

As to be expected in a house so dependent upon its own resources, the garden assumed an especial importance. Sir Edmund and Ralph loved their garden at Claydon. The letters are full of references to presents of seeds and plants; of 'Persian tulips and ranoncules' sent from Holland, and other roots and trees sent specially from France, as well as full and detailed instructions on how to grow them.

The cultivation of herbs and flowers had received great impetus since Elizabeth's day. This revival was due in part to the publication of Gerard's *Herbal* in 1596, but more particularly to the influence of the royal gardeners Parkinson and Tradescant and to that of two enthusiastic amateurs Lord Bacon and John Evelyn.

The Italian style so prominent in seventeenth-century architecture had now begun to spread to garden design. John Tradescant, third in a line of royal gardeners and plant collectors, introduced the strictly formalized Italian layout which relied for effect on stone vases and terraced walks. Vastly more popular was the natural garden of Parkinson, who knew how to grow the old-fashioned flowers the English loved—the stock gilliflower, the violets, honeysuckles, columbines, the damask and other roses—and who viewed with disfavour the 'outlandish' foreign importations.

These importations were entering the country all the time from Africa and America, while Flemish and other refugees brought over many plants as well as an inborn skill and love of gardening. This was the day of the formal 'knot' garden, with pleached alleys and superb topiary. The Tudor habit of dividing the vegetables from the pleasure garden lived on, but strong French influence began to make itself felt in the actual planning.

The 'knots' were small beds often raised to a height of twelve or more inches. They were of such a size that 'the weeders handes may well reach into the middest of the bed'. The borders of 'roses, thorne, lavender, rosemaris, isop, sage or such like' were planted by Michaelmas and clipped at the top to form a level platform on which the housewife dried her washing. The greatest care was needed over the levels: 'you are to keep your level to a haire, for if you faill in it you faill in your whole work', instructed one expert.

Within the borders, flowers or herbs were planted, or, in a

French variation called a parterre, an inlay of coloured earths was used instead.

Gardening knowledge was still tempered by fantastic super-stition. Hail was feared, and to keep it off the gardener had either to enclose a speckled toad in an earthen pot, or else drag a marsh tortoise around the garden on its back, and then place it, still on its back, on a mound so the animal could not fall over or do anything but flap its legs. Even the most elementary aspects of horticulture were shrouded in mystery and it was evidently seriously believed that if you 'water your peach-tree with goats' milk three days running when beginning to flower it will bring forth pomegranates'.

A catalogue of flowers common in those days, and now, un-fortunately, lost to cultivation, makes formidable reading: the spotted-cranesbill, the old roses—Crystall, Frankford, Hungarian, Velvet, Cinamon, the Spanish Muske, the Apple Rose; the old varieties of gilliflower such as the 'melancholicke gentleman', the many different auriculas or 'beare's ears'. Fruit was popular, too, for strawberries were eaten with 'claret wine, cream or milke' and their praises were sung as being 'good for perturbation of the spirits'.

Herbs and salads were highly prized and much used. The gardening books of the day give a bewildering list, most of the contents of which appear to be possessed of near-magical properties. For instance basil is 'cordial, exhilarating, soveraigne for the braine, strengthening the memory, and powerfully chasing away melan-choly'. Borage, too, is 'an exhilarating cordial of pleasant flavour: the tender leaves and the flowers especially, may be eaten in com-position: but above all the sprigs in wine, like those of Baum, are of known Vertue to revive the Hypochondriac and cheer the hard Student'. The thistle seems to have been a useful plant, as it 'cures deafness, giddiness, loss of memory, the plague, ague, swellings, wounds, bites of serpents and mad dogs'. And the marigold, when steeped in vinegar, would cure toothache in some people or with others would make the hair yellow, they 'not being content wyth the natural colour which God hath gyven them'.

Flowers, above all, were grown for their scent. Bacon mentions 'what flowers and plants do best perfume the air' and lists in order of smell 'violets, especially the white double violet, musk-rose, dying strawberry leaves and vine flowers'. Even the paths of the flower and herb garden were covered with burnet, wild thyme or watermint.

Sir Edmund was very generous with his presents of plants and seeds, although these were sometimes received ungraciously, particularly by his brother-in-law, Dr. Denton, who, having just been sent a consignment of vegetables and salads, remarked caustically that he cannot see they are much better than the ones he already had.

Visits were few, and tended to last for weeks or months rather than days. In the country, where roads were both bad and dangerous, travel was reduced to the minimum, and the lady of the house seldom went far afield or to London.

The few odd items and letters coming to the house from outside were usually borne by carriers. This simple and effective method of transporting news and papers had been improving over the centuries, and by the 1630's the carrier system had reached a high state of development. At fixed times, and from well-known landmarks or inns, carriers left for their several destinations. Passengers were carried on these waggons for a consideration and they, in turn, were expected to assist when their waggon sank into the numerous ruts and seas of mire along the way. In 1635 this rather haphazard system of communication was officially recognized and a horse-post and a foot-post instituted. The horse-post rode from stage to stage, changing horses at each halt and handing on the packets entrusted to his charge to the respective foot-posts, who continued their onward transmission to an eventual destination. Evidently the foot-post also carried luggage of various sorts, for young Mun, the third son, on his move from Winchester to Oxford sent both his bed and his trunk by this means.

The *Carriers Cosmography* is a mine of information as to when and where the 'carriers, waggons, foot-posts and higglers do usually come from any parts, towns, shires and countries of the kingdom of England; as also from the kingdom of Scotland and Ireland'. There is no mention of how long a packet consigned to the care of these postmen took to arrive at its destination. This was a wise precaution, as the dangers of the journey were considerable—bad roads and desolate heaths made easy the task of the footpad and highwayman, especially as there was no efficient police force. The carriage of goods of value was a particularly arduous undertaking and needed special precautions.

Moving from one place to another was usually performed on horseback, even by women. When the man of rank left his house he was escorted by mounted servants armed with pistols to protect him on his way. Enormous distances were covered on horseback, and in 1639 Sir Edmund, in company with the King, covered 260 miles from Berwick in four days. Only the elderly or sick travelled by coach, as it was both uncomfortable and slow. Great lumbering coaches with no springs, and metal shutters in lieu of windows, can have offered little inducement to travel unnecessarily over the ruts and pot-holes of the 'noyous and foul' country roads.

This was a great age of letter-writing; huge families, few but close friends, and the impossibility of seeing any but the nearest neighbours more than occasionally, made this inevitable. But, lengthy as their letters were, there are few allusions to politics and political matters. This was a course of common prudence; with delivery so uncertain and transit taking so long the chance of letters falling into unfriendly hands was very great. Later, when times became more dangerous, systems of codes and cyphers were commonly used.

When Sir Edmund was away at Court, or with the King elsewhere, many of the letters between himself and his son deal almost exclusively with matters to do with the estate. These give insight into the immense care and consideration he afforded the labourers and estate workers at Claydon.

The country-labourer's home was still generally a hovel of mud and chopped straw built on a foundation of stone and with no chimney. Its one room was shared by both tenant and animals, and his fare for the most part was black bread and onions, with beer to drink—meat was an occasional treat. The better-off graduated to a building of wood of several rooms, according to need, sometimes with a second storey projecting over the lower. The fire hazard in towns with a high proportion of wooden houses was so fearsome that rings were attached to the walls ready to pull them down in the event of an outbreak.

The lot of the normal labourer, however, was in great contrast to the comparative luxury enjoyed by his masters. An average wage of 4*d.* a day, including food, was his income. Artisans received more, up to 8*d.* or 1*s.* a day; while a manservant in the country began at 20*s.* and eventually earned the princely sum of £5 or £6 a year. Women servants started at 14*s.* and advanced to perhaps 26*s.* a year when they were able to do plain cooking and could bake and brew.

But, though there was poverty, there were few beggars—the

Elizabethan Poor Law system saw to that. In the past it had been the prerogative of the Church to administer the needs of the poor and the destitute. With the weakening of ecclesiastical power in Reformation times, the Church was no longer able to perform this service, so, of necessity, some other means had to be found—and the parish was chosen as the instrument for poor relief. Administered by the Justices of the Peace and supervised by the distant Privy Council, the system worked well. In each parish the Overseers of the Poor supervised work and bought working materials for the poverty-stricken with money raised from the compulsory poor-rate levied on all landowners.

There was considerable local authority in other fields as well. The regulation of prices and wages, hitherto controlled by the local Justices, had for the most part passed from their hands except in municipal districts. Nevertheless, the administering of petty justice and the responsibility of carrying out government or royal decree on matters political or ecclesiastical was still theirs.

So, too, was the responsibility of ensuring that bridges and highways were kept in decent repair. In times of plague precautions were taken to prevent the infection spreading, and day and night watches were set up to stop any travellers who might bring the disease with them. When villagers fell sick, people were appointed to look after them and help was given from a county fund set up for the purpose. The constables and churchwardens were the instruments to see the Justices' instructions were carried out. It was their duty, also, to raise the compulsory levies for the County hospitals and the poor prisoners in the county gaol, King's Bench and Marshalsea Prisons.

Within the county the sheriff was the sovereign's direct representative, and was chosen for a term of one year by the King. His authority was limited to carrying out sentences passed on offenders and administering the county gaol—the true power in the county now lay with the Justices of the Peace.

Such degree of local autonomy tended to insulate the parish from the country as a whole. With news both irregular and slow, the only way the ignorant villager could judge the economic state of the country was from the effect on his own pocket. There had been a gradual rise in prices over the last 100 years. This, and the 'Monopolies' imposed from London, enforced by the Justices, and sometimes extorted by the petty official, affected the villager grievously. He could not understand the rising costs of a government becoming ever more centralized. Thus, as the King, of necessity, became more grasping, an economic discontent started to spread across the country and added fuel to the fire of political and religious unrest.

In the country districts the golden age of agricultural prosperity experienced under Elizabeth was not yet on the wane. Profiting from the new peace under James, business was good, and England, nearly self-sufficient, was still thriving. There were occasional periods of unemployment, particularly in the cloth industry, as the Continental markets closed one after another, but on the whole the economic health of the country seemed good.

By the end of the previous century the long-drawn-out demise of strip farming had started—not without opposition. Agriculturalists and landowners appreciated how uneconomic were the old methods, but they had difficulty in convincing the peasantry. Although the transition from common to individual ownership helped to set farming on a sound footing, still the villager fought stoutly for his commonland rights.

The manor-houses, on the whole self-farmed and carefully managed, were the backbone of good agriculture and a living example to the small yeoman and husbandman. Several agriculturalists had written of their experiences as practical farmers, and many of the Flemish refugees came over with years of farming behind them. But it was the realization by the gentry of the economic possibilities of their land which really extended the general knowledge of scientific farming in the country.

Buckinghamshire as an area of mixed farming was not as hard hit by rising costs as were some other parts of the country which relied on a staple crop for subsistence. Sir Edmund seems to have been a successful farmer, and reared sheep and cattle as well as growing grain and roots. He was fortunate in owning some land in East Anglia, and so was able to send his beasts away each spring to the fens 'where they could fatten at an easy charge'. However, he usually brought them back to Claydon to sell at nearby Northampton, where the cattle fair was famous, or at Aylesbury, a more local market.

Each spring, as soon as the weather improved, those riding horses and cart-horses, which had been in 'House all winter' and which could be spared, were sent to the fens 'where I shall fatt them for little and spare my own ground', as Sir Edmund writes; and he adds instructions to send 'a carefull messenger with them'.

The oxen get their measure of attention, too, and in another letter he writes, 'send all such oxen as are putt of from the wayne downe to the fenns, and give them a Horne Marke of myne owne'. Apart from pulling the 'wayne', they were used for ploughing.

Of the grain crops, wheat, barley and oats seem to have all been grown at Claydon, as well as some roots which were a comparatively recent introduction. 'Compostynge' was an important practice, and the old thatch from cottage roofs was carefully preserved and laid where it could make muck. In early spring this and other 'Dungg' was collected from the many yards and spread where needed. There was some attempt at rudimentary crop-rotation—although it was not until the Commonwealth that the four-course system was in common use in the country.

Sir Edmund, now increasingly away at Court, left the management of Claydon to his brother-in-law, Dr. William Denton, who had newly left Oxford and lived at nearby Hillesden. In conjunction with an invaluable steward, Roades, the doctor exclusively ran the estate until the eldest son, Ralph, was grown-up and able to take over its supervision.

Despite having these assistants on whom he could rely, Sir Edmund still tried to conduct affairs from London, and he could never bear to be away from Claydon for long. It must, therefore, have been with mixed feelings that he obeyed the summons to join Prince Charles, who was then embarked on his abortive trip to Spain.

III

The Trip to Spain

'Youth at the Prow, and Pleasure at the Helm,
Regardless of the sweeping whirlwind's sway.'
GRAY'S *Bard*

I N 1623 took place the strange and foolish episode of the journey
of Prince Charles to Spain to win the hand of the Infanta Maria.
Our chief knowledge of Sir Edmund's doings at this time is from
the letters of James Howell, merchant and self-appointed reporter,
and it is from these that many of the quotations in this chapter are
taken. Of the notable letter-writers of the period, Howell, who
happened to be in Madrid at the time, was admirably placed to give
an accurate account of the enigmatic fortunes of this match. His
critical and prolific letters to his many friends give a colourful,
though probably biased, picture of the progress and difficulties of
this curious interlude in British history.

The match, had it ever come to pass, would have linked the ruling
houses of two of the most powerful nations in Europe; the one
Catholic to the core, the other as adamantly Protestant at heart.
It had long been the dream of the feckless, changeable James I to
unite the two countries, and, originally, the infant Prince Henry was
promised in marriage to the young Infanta Anna, eldest daughter of
King Philip III of Spain. On the death of Prince Henry attention
had then turned on his younger brother, Prince Charles. It was he,
with a small band of faithful followers, who ventured into the very

D   49

maw of England's most feared and hated foe in search of his bride. Little the wonder that after nine months away from his native shores Prince Charles should receive a tumultuous welcome on his 'return out of Spain'.

Of Sir Edmund's adventures there is no mention amongst the Verney Papers. The sole relic of this formative period in his life is a portrait at Claydon marked, 'done in Spain, very unlike'. This depicts him as a youthful gallant with pointed beard and rich lace collar over breastplate and doublet—and bears little resemblance to what we can imagine he was like from later portraits.

'Blessed are the Peace-Makers' was the motto of King James, and it was a regardless preoccupation with this ideal that was the one theme recurrent in the foreign politics of that misunderstanding monarch. The religious and political vacillations and schemings of the King largely ignored the wishes and well-being of the majority of his unhappy subjects. They wanted peace indeed; but not at the price of becoming vassal to Spain and figure of contempt to the rest of Europe. Memories of the Armada were too fresh for any except the Roman Catholic minority to view the proposed Spanish Alliance with anything but extreme abhorrence. Nevertheless, the scheme progressed, despite protest and almost general disapproval.

With a nation of such missionary zeal as seventeenth-century Spain, the anticipated return of heretic England to the fold of Catholicism would lead one to expect that the proposed match would be welcomed, but the most curious of the many curious aspects of this episode is the strange, fluctuating enthusiasm shown by the Spaniards. So much so that when the match was first mooted in 1611 the contemptuous reply came back that the Infanta Anna was already betrothed to Louis XIII, but that the Prince of Wales might have her younger sister Maria, then aged nine, provided he would conform to the Catholic religion. Prince Henry died a year later and the proposal lapsed.

The following year James's only daughter, Elizabeth, was married to the Elector Palatine. This cemented England's already firm Protestant alliance with the Continent and at a blow gave heart to the anti-Spanish party in the country, and disillusion, if not despair, to their opponents. At the same time arrangements were put in hand to marry Prince Charles to the second daughter of King Henry of France. The danger to Spain of union between two such powerful nations, together with the existing one linking the Low

Countries with the German Protestant States, was a threat which could not be ignored. Reaction followed and once more marriage proposals were in the air.

The Spaniards offered a dowry of £600,000, and to James, ever in need of money, this was sufficient inducement to abandon the French match. In return, however, substantial concessions to the Penal Laws in force against Roman Catholics, and a considerable say in the future education of any children resulting from the marriage, were demanded of the English King. These conditions horrified the nation, and even James hesitated; cupidity overcame the King's scruples, however, and he empowered Somerset to treat with the Spanish ambassador whilst at the same time setting up a commission to study the matter.

As negotiations dragged on it became clear that the King was out of sympathy with the rest of Protestant Europe and no longer had even the support of his own government and people. The trouble came to a head in 1621 when Parliament endeavoured to present a petition complaining of laxity in prosecuting the laws against Popery and calling for war on Spain. The response was violent. His 'absence', said the King, had 'emboldened some fiery and popular spirits to debate and agree publicly in matters far beyond their reach or capacity'. The House was to be informed that no Member was to meddle 'with mysteries of state' and there was to be no speech of the Prince's match with the daughter of Spain. This direct assault on the rights of the Commons could not pass unchallenged and a protestation was prepared, reiterating that the 'arduous and urgent affairs concerning the King, State, and defence of the realm' were 'proper subjects and matter of counsel and debate in Parliament'. This protestation was not presented to the King, but was entered on the Journals 'there to remain as of record'. Parliament adjourned soon afterwards, and during this time the King deliberated on what he would do to punish the rebellious Commons; finally, shortly after Christmas, he called for the Journals of the House and in the presence of the Council and judges tore out the offending pages. Then, all discretion thrown aside, he dissolved Parliament. So ended the last legal opportunity of ending the headlong course to ruin the King had adopted.

In Spain, too, complications had set in. The congregation of the four cardinals formed to examine the Articles of the Marriage Treaty had sent to Rome for further advice. The reply they received confirmed their view that these articles as they then existed were totally inadequate, and that nothing less than complete freedom of worship for Roman Catholics in England would suffice. This suggestion was unacceptable even to James, and so negotiations wore on between London and Madrid. Finally, a compromise was reached whereby the Papists should no longer suffer persecution for their religion so long as they gave no scandal. The King and Prince Charles signed the document without demur.

Disgust at the sorry course the business was taking grew apace in England. Well might Buckingham write that the conditions set by Spain could 'tend to no other end but to bring his master in jealousy with the greatest part of his subjects'. Opposition spread. There were several anti-Catholic incidents and outspoken denunciations from the pulpit. Also certain scurrilous libels made their appearance, the chiefest of these was 'Tom Tell-Truth', a foul-mouthed missive produced in manuscript form and passed from hand to hand. This effusion denounced the sovereign as Defender of Popery, and suggested that the King's relationship with Buckingham was based on the distortion of all morals. The sermons were more veiled, but there was no disguising the country-wide feeling of very real apprehension over the King's conduct of affairs.

Throughout the course of the negotiations Prince Charles had shown little interest and no enthusiasm for his future marriage. So much so, that on one occasion, after a tedious audience in which he had had to pay gracious compliments to a portrait of his bride-to-be, believing he was out of ear-shot, he turned to a courtier and remarked that 'were it not for the sin, it would be well if Princes could have two wives; one for reason of state, the other to please themselves'. His views were gradually changing, however, and shortly before the departure of Gondomar, the all-powerful Spanish ambassador, the latter had drawn from the Prince a promise to travel to Spain to win the hand of the Infanta. To the Prince the trip increasingly assumed the guise of a romantic adventure, and in this he was doubtless spurred on by the thought that his father and grandfather had won their consorts in the same way. The dangers and implications for Protestant England of the course he was adopting bothered him not at all; only a selfish desire for personal glory and the romantic savour of the knight-errant held any meaning. In this he was ably abetted by the vain and shallow Buckingham, who had been recently created a marquis.

As proposal succeeded counter-proposal, it became clear that the headstrong Prince was fast losing patience with negotiation and wanted action. His guide and mentor, familiarly known as Steenie, by reason of some faint or fancied resemblance to St. Stephen, made no effort to restrain him from this folly, and together they concocted a plan. This first took the form of the Prince accompanying the Marquis, who was to go as Admiral of the Fleet to fetch the Infanta to England. But this exploit was far too mild for their fiery imaginations and they determined to travel incognito via France. After considerable demur, the King at last gave his assent and so preparations went forward under conditions of the greatest secrecy.

Accompanied only by Sir Richard Graham, Buckingham's confidential attendant, the pair set off wearing false beards and travelling under the names of Tom and John Smith. On the journey to the coast they ran into the party escorting the new Spanish Netherlands emissary to London. As it was the custom for the King to lend the royal coaches and attendants to newly arrived ambassadors, there was real danger of the Prince and Buckingham being recognized—however, they took to the fields and managed to avoid detection. Eventually they reached Dover, where a ship was standing by to take the small party, now swollen to five, across the Channel.

They arrived at Boulogne without further incident and on the 21st of February reached Paris. On the pretext that they were strangers there, they gained admission to a rehearsal of a masque in which the Queen and the beautiful Princess Henrietta Maria were performing. Seeing the Queen thus, only strengthened the Prince's resolve the sooner to see her sister the Infanta, and before dawn the party were once more on their way.

Meanwhile, in England the news that the Prince was en route, beyond recall, to Spain was received at first with incredulity and then with utter dismay. Prayers for his preservation and safe return were said in churches throughout the country, and even James began to fear for the safety of his 'Baby Charles'. Particularly virulent were the attacks on Buckingham, whom they declared was guilty of high treason in carrying the Prince from the realm, and who would one day answer for his conduct before Parliament.

Whilst England was fretting, the small party, the 'sweete boyes and deare ventrouse Knights, worthie to be putt in a new romanse', as the King put it, were speeding south through France. Despite an accident to Buckingham at Orleans, they covered the first 450

miles to Bayonne in under four days. Short of the Spanish border
they met with a courier bearing despatches to England from Lord
Bristol, the English ambassador in Madrid. These were for the most
part in cypher, but the few passages the Prince could read told of
more delays in the negotiations and were hardly reassuring. Nevertheless, they continued in their folly, and the Prince with Buckingham, having outstripped their companions, reached Lord Bristol's
'House with the seven chimneys' in Madrid on the 7th of March
just as night was falling. Leaving the Prince hidden in the shadows
of the street to guard the horses, Buckingham burst upon the
astonished ambassador and told him of the delivery of the heir to
the throne into Spanish hands.

Despite the utmost secrecy, the news of their arrival soon
reached the ears of the Spanish Court. At first there was amazed
stupefaction at so startling a turn of events, but this soon changed
to relief that the impossible had happened. To begin with only
Buckingham was admitted to the royal presence, whilst the Infanta
was ostentatiously driven up and down the Prado—described by
Bristol as 'a hole without the town, where men do take the air'—
wearing 'a blue ribbon about her arm, of purpose' so that Charles
might recognize his intended bride. Officially no one knew of the
coming of the Prince, but in fact it was common knowledge that the
son of the heretic King of England was in Madrid.

To the Spaniards there could be but one reason why Prince
Charles had come to Spain. His conversion was expected daily,
and when nothing happened towards this end they became increasingly perplexed. It was concluded that it was Bristol who was
holding back the Prince from his appointed course and they determined to separate the suitor from the ambassador. Equally, Philip[1]
could not forget his duty as a host and was at pains to entertain his
royal guest in a manner befitting the son of the King of England.
So it was decided that the Prince should be accommodated in the
palace itself, where a suite of rooms was completely redecorated.

The State entry took place nine days after Charles's coming.
Madrid was alive with excitement. The streets were swept clean,
the houses along the route richly decorated, petty prisoners were
released and a recent proclamation against extravagance in dress
was suspended so that the occasion could be suitably celebrated.

Philip treated his royal guest with the greatest courtesy. For

[1]Philip IV, who succeeded his father, Philip III, in 1621.

once Lenten restraint was abandoned. Fêtes, bull-fights and fire-work displays went on for three days and nights and, as few servants had by then arrived from England for the Prince, a household of Spanish noblemen was provided to ease his stay and make him as comfortable as possible. Moreover, in a grand gesture the King gave him a golden key which, as the locks were the same, opened all the doors in the palace.

From England, meanwhile, had set off by sea the main retinue of the Prince's servants and attendants, sixty in number, under Lord Andover, Charles's Master of Horse. In the party were eight Gentle-men of the Privy Chamber, among them the young Sir Edmund Verney and Sir Richard Wynne, author of the following extracts, which have remained largely unpublished[1] since 1729.

On the 3rd of April 1623 they left Portsmouth on board the King's ship *Adventure,* and in less than five days reached Spain. They anchored before the town of Santander but were hardly impressed: 'a very poor thing, having neither Glasse Windows nor Chimneyes'. However, the Governor himself came aboard and bade them welcome. They were lodged in the best houses in the town and 'wonderfull courteous' was their reception.

Sir Edmund was fortunate in having been in Spain before; nevertheless, the country struck them all as curious:

'Wonderfull populous the Town is, the Men from the highest to the lowest going in the habits of Gentlemen, ever in Cloakes and Swords. Drudgery they will do none at all. For theire Wives they make theire Slaves, which do not onely till their Ground, and plant and prune their Vineyards, but also carry all Luggage, as our Por-ters do in England. Wee have seen when these Women have come with great Trunks upon their heads from the Shoar, and ready to sink under the burthen, their own Husbands standing by. Their pride was such that they scorned to put their helping hands to help their Wives, when they were ready to fall under the burthen, and suffered our People to help them, when they stood by and laught. The meaner sort of Women that are unmarried, go all bare headed, with their Crownes shaved like Fryers. . . . They make dainty Chaines of young Orrenges, which they sold to divers of us. It seems they fast not over much, for they be plump and fat, though not handsome.'

[1] Hearne, Thomas, *Historia Vitae et Regni Ricardi I* (London, 1729).

They took, too, a highly cynical view of their hosts' religion and Wynne goes on:

'Upon Holy dayes all these People do but goe from one Crosse to another Shrine, with their Beades in their hands, praying in a Language they understand not, and adoaring of dumb Images. So much Zeal joyn'd with blind Devotion I never saw afore.'

Joy at their arrival was not universal either, for the 'Jesuites offerr'd us some Affronts', but these it was 'thought fittest not to take notice of'. However, after they had rested a week, some saddle-mules arrived and they set forth on their long journey 'every man with a Cloak-bag afore him'.

It was not long before their mounts started giving trouble, for on 'putting to Spurr's, the Beastes, instead of going forwards, kicked backwards, standing stone still, till the Toy [muleteer] took them to goe on, and then all they would do was, to walk. In this Equipage wee marched on, desireing our Friends in England had but seen us in these Postures. Thus travailed wee on a Carrier's pace.'

They had never seen such country:

'The most wicked Wayes and Country that ever Christians past. It was well wee were upon the backs of Mules. For I believe no other Beasts in the World could have past those Wayes. The terrible stony Hills wee climbed, and the steep Downfalls wee descended, are not to be believed, having for two Leagues together a narrow Passage of two feet broad, all made like Staires, lying a hundred Fathoms above a great River, whose Roaring amongst the Stones was such, that wee could not heare one another speak. The Hills for the most part, covered with Schrubs and Furrs; the Heat between these Hills was such, that wee thought our selves in Stoves. Yet all this while, upon the Topps of these Hills wee saw Snow in abundance.'

They must have looked forward to their arrival at the first night's stop, especially as the muleteers had regaled them with stories of how 'King Philip and his Queen had both layn in the House'. But they were to be soon disillusioned for:

'When wee alighted wee were brought up to this Lodging, which was a long Room, so much decayed, that wee expected hourly when it would fall upon us. Glasse Windows we had none, (for they were things not known in those Parts) yet wee wanted no Ayre. For there was not a Foot of that Royall Roome, that wanted Holes, which within few Hours after wee had a feeling of, the Night being very sharp and cold. There wee walked two Houres, whilset Supper was a preparing. When wee were ready to sit, there was no Table nor Stool, but with much adoe, wee got a peece of Timber, about which wee stood, and gave God thankes for what wee had.'

After all this it was fortunate that the 'Bread and Wine were both good'.

Perplexed as they were by the language, the customs, the people, now came another burden to add to their discomfiture—in the form of a letter from Prince Charles bidding them all to return to England by the ship they had come in. Fearful for the Prince's safety, yet equally fearful of disobeying his royal command, they were uncertain what to do.

At length it was resolved that the main party would return to Santander and re-embark, while Lord Cary, the Prince's Chamberlain, and Lord Compton, his Master of the Ward, who had been specifically summoned, were to continue to Madrid. However, rather than return by sea, six, among them Sir Edmund, resolved to carry on to Burgos, a day's march away, and from there take post and go home through France.

Here the author of the saga leaves Sir Edmund and his small party. After many vicissitudes and considerable inhospitality after returning to Santander, which is now described as being 'where the Divil himself doth inhabit, if he dwell on Earth', once more they were all reunited at Burgos, where further instructions from Prince Charles had stayed those that had gone ahead.

The journey on was not without its incidents. No saddle-mules were available, so they had to make do with pack-mules instead, with no saddles and no bridles, as the muleteers would not 'suffer us to put anything in their Mouthes, to guide them with'.

Before they had covered a mile there had been seven or eight falls. By the time they reached their lodging that night, where they slept in a 'Hay-loft upon the Boards', there were few who had not had 'suddain Overthrows' occasioned by the 'Spurrs, which the Jades not acquainted with, when they felt them, never left kicking, 'till they had overthrown their Riders'.

Some days later, as Wynne describes:

'Wee mett a Fellow leading of two Mares tied together. Our mules were all Horse Mules, as all Carriers have for the most part.

The foremost man . . . his Mule having discovered the Mares, began
to dance under him, so that he was forc'd (for his Safety) to hold
with one hand before, and the other behind, fast upon the Pack-
Sadle, his Mule going all upon Curvetts. The next my Man rid upon,
which was more unruly then his, who never left 'till he had tumbled
his Rider with his Heeles up, and so furiously pursued the Mares,
that he forced both the Leader and the Mares into the River, and
he upon them. The Fellow, to save himself, wades clear throgh,
and stands on the other Bank, to see what would be the end of this
Tragedy. Doctor Maw's Mule (undiscover'd of us) with our earnest
viewing this Disaster, was teaching the Churchman, how to prove
a good Horsman, with infinite Bounces beyond his Resistance. At
last backwards he comes, lighting full on Head and Shoulders, where
he lay groaning, and his mule went into the River, to make up the
Consort, where the Musick they made was so loud and schrill, that
it drew a number of Labourers to be Spectators. At last the Mares,
to save themselves from drowning, clamber up the Bank again,
and then to resolve to trust to their Leggs, which they did, and ran
over a fair Field in view, at least four Mile, my Man's Mule still
pursuing, the rest being taken by the Muleteers. Recollecting ourselves, and surveying our Troop, to see what hurt was done, wee
found this Tragick Beginning end in a Comedy. For all was well
again, onely the Mule still in view pursuing the two Mares, who with
their Heeles at every stand gave him sound Bangs, the Muleteers
(being put to their Footmanship) still following.'

So they continued on their way, greeted by pealing bells and
entertainment in every town they passed through. Their opinion
of the Spaniards was no higher, however, and they declared that
'they will do as many base things as any Nation, so their wives or
Servants do it by their direction, and they be not seen in it themselves. Divers little things wee had, they pilfer'd away. As for petty
things, they are the veriest Theeves in the World.' They were
astonished at the power of the 'Jesuite' who gets 'up upon a Stall,
and there preaches to the People, untill most of them drop away',
and who persuades them that if they 'contribute liberally at his
Shrine to defray the Charges of Lights and other Necessaries, that
then there is nothing they can pray for there, but they shall obtain.
. . . Thus they do fleece the People, whom they keep in Ignorance,
and so in more Obedience, then any Prince can do his Subjects.

All the Profit got this way, they convert to their own private benefit, living as plentifully and as easie as any. Studdy, I believe, they do little. For I finde them continually walking the Streets, and prying into every Corner.'

They were surprised, too, at the usual form of Sunday recreation:

'All the Men use, is to walk a slow pace up and down the Streets, with their Cloakes and Swords. The Women, some dance, and the Musick they have to it, is their Voices, and a thing like the head of a Drum, which they tamber upon with their Fingers. So holding hands all in a Circle, they go round without any other Variety, all sing together such Discord, as quickly wearied us all, that were Standers by.'

They were more taken by the great ear-rings which all the women wore 'bigger than those they hang at Curtaines by much', and by a 'Pancake of Eggs and Bacon, all fryed together' which they were offered at one inn they stopped at.

So, amazed at what they saw each day, from 'a Stork building of her Nest upon a Steeple' to a bride and bridegroom riding home 'according to the Custome of the Country, both upon an Asse', at last on the 29th of April they reached Madrid.

Their destination was as interesting as the rest of the journey had been and they likened the capital to Newmarket, 'both for the Country, and for the Sharpnesse of the Ayre'. They were fascinated by the brick or stone buildings 'all set forth with Balconies of Iron', and the streets 'wonderfull full of People and Coaches in abundance ... and more good Horses under Sadles, Foot-clothes, and in Coaches, then ever I saw in all my life'.

They came direct to the palace to pay their respects to their master, whom they found at dinner. They were very unimpressed by his apartments where he must 'mew himself up all day', or else walk in a small garden 'so nasty and ill favouredly kept, that a Farmer in England would be ashamed of such another'. They found also that Charles and Buckingham were wearing 'Spanish habits, such an Attire as will make the handsomest Man living look like another thing'.

Sir Edmund and another Gentleman of the Privy Chamber, Sir William Howard, were fortunate in remaining in attendance and living near the Prince. The remainder, to start with, had to fend for themselves and found to their cost that 'the worst chamber to be got was at forty shillings the week, a turkey at ten or twenty,

and a hen at five or six'. Later they moved to the palace of the Duke
of Montelo, a long way removed, and where they had nothing to
do but play cards all day.

Their opinion of the Spaniards was little heightened by what
they saw, and the behaviour of the women deeply shocked them:

'Through one Street I met at least five hundred Coaches, most
of them had all Women, in going into the Fields to take the Aire.
Of all these Women, I dare take my Oath, there was not one un-
painted; so visibly, that you would think they rather wore Vizards,
then their own Faces. Whether they be handsome or no, I cannot
tell, unlesse they did unmask. . . . The boldest Women in the World.
For as I past along, Numbers of them call'd and becon'd to me.'

They were equally struck by the number of people wearing
spectacles: 'You cannot meete tenne, but you shall finde one of
them with a pair of Glasse Eyes.'

Within a fortnight the bulk of Charles's servants were given
instructions to go home, either by the *Adventure* or by land through
France. Wynne chose to go by sea and on May the 9th left Madrid
with some fifty others. Sir Edmund and Howard were allowed to
remain with the Prince, who by now was growing impatient and
beginning to feel that events were not moving fast enough. For,
although Charles had managed to see the Infanta more closely on
several occasions, he had never yet spoken to his intended bride
alone, despite having been in Spain since March.

Nevertheless, the Prince was so taken by her charm that Buckingham was able to declare: 'without flattery, I think there is not a
sweeter creature in the world! Baby Charles himself is so touched
at heart that he confesses all he ever yet saw is nothing to her, and
swears that if he want her, there shall be blows!' 'And', Howell
writes, 'I have seen the Prince have his eyes immovably fixed upon
the Infanta half an hour together in a thoughtful speculative posture,
which would sure needs be tedious unless affection did sweeten it.'
That was one interpretation—the Spanish chief minister swore the
Prince watched the Infanta 'as a cat doth a mouse'.

The Infanta Maria was no great beauty, nevertheless, 'the
sweetness of her disposition found expression in her face, and her
fair complexion and delicate white hands drew forth rapturous
admiration from the contrast which they presented to the olive
tints of the ladies by whom she was surrounded', or so said Howell

in 1623. However, when the popularity of Spanish overtures had waned, he described her as being of 'fading flaxen hair, big-lipped, and somewhat heavy-eyed'. She was a devoted church-goer and twice a week went to confession. Her chief pleasures were meditating upon the Immaculate Conception and preparing lint for the use of hospitals. Any money she was given was carefully set aside for the poor, and she was 'model in righteousness'. Such was the lady it was intended should be the consort of the future King of England. Her own very evident dislike of the marriage was ably furthered by her confessor, who declared that a heretic was worse than the devil. 'What a comfortable bedfellow you will have. He who lies by your side, and will be the father of your children is certain to go to Hell.'

The confessor was removed after this outburst and every effort made to bring the Infanta to see the holy work she would do by marrying the Protestant Prince. For a short time she was persuaded by these blandishments, but her own good sense soon prevailed and she became once more adamantly opposed to the match. So much so, in fact, that she announced that rather than accept such a marriage she would 'enter a convent of barefooted nuns'.

The Prince's routine varied little. In the morning he studied Spanish, in the afternoons he was entertained by the King and in the evenings he often joined the Royal Family and was allowed to talk to the Infanta—but not alone. The formalities were never forgotten and as the days passed Charles found time hanging heavy on his hands, 'mewed up' in his apartments and getting nowhere in the matter nearest his heart.

It had been King James's intention that the Prince should carry on his own devotion without hindrance, and to further this two chaplains were despatched with the main party of the retinue with instructions to prepare a 'convenient room appointed for prayer'; but even this solace was thwarted by the Spaniards, and it was pointed out that any attempt by the chaplains to enter the palace would be resisted by force. On one occasion the Prince had indeed attended communion at the ambassador's residence, but this was so obviously unpopular that he never did it again. So, powerless, separated from most of his companions, and surrounded by an unyielding, tedious protocol, yet fêted to satiation point, the Prince spent his days hoping to catch a glimpse of the Infanta, who occasionally walked in the gardens beneath his window.

In late April the long-awaited dispensation had arrived from Rome. But the conditions it imposed were such as even the hopelessly infatuated Prince could not accept. Argue as he might, promise as he might, the Spaniards would not be swayed from the terms laid down by the Pope. On top of this, too, a further stipulation had been made that the Infanta was to remain in Spain until the conditions declared were put into execution; this might take nine months to a year.

In England the old King was growing fearful for the safety of his son. On the first news of his arrival in Spain he had ordered bonfires to be lit and bells to be rung; and, as the negotiations appeared to be proceeding satisfactorily, so were the preparations for the triumphant reception for the Prince and his bride pressed forward. First intimation that all might not be as well as expected came when Charles asked for a warrant to vouch for his own promises. The King gave this extraordinary *carte blanche* with no qualm of conscience, and promised 'by the word of a King, that whatsoever you, our son shall promise in our name we shall punctually perform'. After this the King's mood appeared to be changing, and at times he showed ill-humour and despondency. 'The King is now grown quite stupid', wrote one attendant, and on another occasion James burst into tears and asked: 'Shall I ever see the Prince again?' Nevertheless, the preparations continued, the fleet to bring back the Infanta was made ready under the command of Lord Rutland and the building of the oratory at St. James's hastened on so as to be ready for the triumphant homecoming.

It came, therefore, as a considerable shock when James first heard of the possibility of the Infanta's arrival being delayed. He poured out his heart to his 'sweet boys':

'Your letter . . . hath strucken me dead. I fear it shall very much shorten my days . . . come speedily away, if ye can get leave, and give over all treaty except ye never look to see your old Dad again, whom I fear ye shall never see if ye see him not before winter. . . . Alas! I now repent me sore that ever I suffered you to go away. I care for match, nor nothing, so I may once have you in my arms again. God grant it: God grant it: God grant it: Amen, Amen, Amen. . . .'

So the weeks laboured on. To the Prince's followers it was now abundantly clear that no good could come out of their trip to Spain.

Charles daily grew more melancholy, and only the all too rare sight of the Infanta would lift him from this despair. Once he scaled the wall in hope of meeting the Princess, who was walking in her garden outside Madrid gathering May dew, and only the earnest entreaties of the Infanta's attendant persuaded him to desist in his folly.

In the negotiations on the marriage terms, argument now turned on reducing the delay before the Infanta could follow Charles to England. Now, too, the voice of the Catholics at home was added to the Prince's infatuated entreaties. This body had viewed the apparent impasse in the negotiations with growing alarm, for although they had considered the full terms as far too sweeping ever to be fully carried out, at least there had existed some possibility of their being allowed freedom to worship without fear of persecution. Even this hope now looked like being dashed.

The theological arguments and discussions continued, but always with the same conclusion—the Pope's will must be fulfilled. At last the College of Theologians produced their final resolution: to the effect that the marriage could take place in September and the Infanta follow to England in March. Charles received the information quietly and asked for the arrangements to be made for him to depart, as they must consider the treaty at an end. His followers rejoiced and he prepared to take his leave of the King the following day.

But at this audience, far from bidding farewell, Charles announced that after due consideration he had decided to accede to all the requests, in his father's name. The ultimate degradation had been reached. Heedless of the views of his own countrymen, Charles had promised what he was totally unable to put into effect, and it was never forgotten of him.

For a time all was rejoicing. Philip embraced him as a brother, Madrid was gay with illuminations and the Infanta was openly spoken of as Princess of England. Since Charles's coming rain had broken a seven-month, and potentially disastrous, drought. This and other portents were produced as showing the Divine hand in the business of the match. The happy news was despatched to England and only the bare formalities seemed to be outstanding.

Meanwhile, in England the colossal perplexities of the problem were weighing heavy on the King. At first it seemed that only a royal connivance at a breach of the penal laws was required, but now it was becoming all too apparent that a major revision of

policy was necessary and James foresaw 'an infinite liberty and a
perpetual immunity granted to Roman Catholics'. To grant this he
had no power, but if it were not granted he might never see his
'darling boy' again. In common with most Englishmen, he was
convinced that if the articles were now rejected the Prince would
never leave Madrid. He summoned his principal counsellors and
lay the matter before them.

On July 20th the articles were sworn. But in England rumours
were rife. Quite what had taken place at Court no one was clear
about, but the general feeling was one of deep mistrust. Finally a
letter, purporting to come from Abbott, the Archbishop of Canterbury, was printed:

'Your Majesty hath propounded a toleration of religion. . . . I
beseech you to take into consideration what your act is, and what
the consequence may be. By your act you labour to set up that most
damnable and heretical doctrine of the Church of Rome, the whore
of Babylon. How hateful will it be to God, and grievous to your
subjects, the true professors of the gospel, that your Majesty who
hath often defended and learnedly written against those wicked
heresies, should not shew yourself a patron of those doctrines which
your pen hath told the world, and your conscience tells yourself,
are superstitious, idolatrous, and detestable. . . .'

The authorship of this effusion was denied, but in plain language
it told what the majority were thinking.

Though stringent were the articles sworn in England, yet more
so were those promised in Spain: secret clauses were included and
even these did the Prince vow to see obeyed: 'I Charles, Prince of
Wales, promise and take upon me in the word of a king, that the
things above promised and treated concerning those matters shall
take effect and be put into execution as well in the Kingdom of
Scotland and Ireland, as of England.' This included the abrogation
of anti-Catholic laws, the assurance that for twelve years the children of the marriage were to be brought up as Catholics and, finally,
the promise to 'give ear to divines and others whom her Majesty
shall be pleased to employ in matters of the Roman Catholic religion'.
All were promised freely, with no quibble, and with every intention
of deception. Condonation of such behaviour would be difficult at
any time; in the religious circumstances of seventeenth-century
England it was impossible . . . and Charles was never forgiven.

Sir Edmund Verney 'Done in Spain very unlike'
ARTIST UNKNOWN

Ralph Verney, eldest son of the Standard Bearer
BY JANSEN

His word no sooner passed to this binding agreement than the Prince again commenced entreating, wheedling, pleading, for a reduction in the time the Infanta was to remain in Spain. Once more the question was referred to the College of Theologians, once more they gave their answer that the Infanta could not go before the spring when the measures to relieve the Catholics had been given time to prove effective. They did, however, make one concession: namely, that the Prince could remain in Spain, marry at Christmas and carry back his bride in March. The implications of this were obvious to all but the Prince, for by then there was even the possibility of another heir to the English throne being in Spanish hands.

Charles could not decide. Still hopelessly in love, he vacillated. By now Rutland's fleet, sent from England in August, had reached Santander, and this chance of escaping the teasing problems must have weighed heavily with the Prince. Other factors, too, were helping him towards this decision.

The Prince's faithful followers led a difficult existence. Plagued with boredom, and met with contempt or open hostility by their Spanish hosts, this little band of Englishmen was fast losing hope that they would ever leave the Spaniard's clutches. The danger they were in was obvious to all but the persistently blind Prince, and their own conduct probably did little to endear them to the Madrileños. Sir Edmund was fortunate in knowing the Spaniards of old, but the others could not understand them, and perhaps made little effort not to offend them.

Unable even to practise their devotions without hindrance, they were assailed with religious propaganda wherever they went, without hope of retaliation. On their journey to Madrid they had heard a highly provocative sermon in Latin, in which Queen Elizabeth was called 'the daughter of lust and adultery, whose mother was begot by none but Satan', and which ended with a declaration 'that the Prince of England had doubtless come with the resolution to be a Catholick, and leave the damnable way he and his people were in'. This seems to have been the theme for other sermons in Madrid, and any outward display of Protestant teaching or belief by the Prince's attendants was frowned at.

On one occasion a Spanish courtier came upon a copy of the English Catechism, translated into his own language, lying upon the Prince's table and bore this example of English heresy triumphantly to Philip. This incident led to accusations that the Prince's followers

E

were striving to gain converts to their own religion and leading
Spanish citizens away from the True Faith. The trouble was with
difficulty smoothed over—after many harsh words on both sides.

A more serious incident occurred when Sir Francis Cottington,
one of the Prince's closest confidants, was suddenly taken seriously
ill. Believing himself to be dying, the old courtier summoned a
priest to reconcile him to the Church of Rome. Some days later,
however, the invalid started to recover and, when all danger was
past, once more declared himself a Protestant. These clashes can
have done little to help relations between the two parties.

The culminating incident concerned Washington, the Prince's
page, who as it happened was a native of Buckinghamshire. This
youth was taken fatally ill of a fever and was lying in his chamber
visibly weakening. As Howell relates: 'A little before his death one
Ballard, an English priest, went to tamper with him, and Sir Edmund
Verney meeting him coming down the stairs out of Washington's
chamber, they fell from wordes to blowes, but they were parted.
The business was like to gather very ill blood, com to a great
height. . . .', were it not for timely intervention of authority. As it
was, there were serious repercussions, the Spaniards demanding
that Sir Edmund be punished, and the Prince as adamantly demanding
that an officer of the watch who had manhandled Sir Edmund should
suffer equally. The unfortunate Washington was finally laid to rest
'under a fig-tree in Lord of Bristol's' garden, the only burial place
the Spaniards would allow.

The effect of all this was to give the Spaniards yet more cause to
suspect the religious integrity of their royal visitor. At last Charles
was beginning to appreciate the true nature of his position. The
failure to get any firm promise of political improvement for the
Palatinate, and the irreconcilable clashes between the two Courts,
decided his course of action. But he wrote to his father in different
vein:

'The cause why we have been so long un wryting to you . . . is
that wee would try all meanes possible, (before wee would send you
word) to see if we could move them to send the Infanta before
winter: they for forme's sake called the Devynes, and they stuke
to their owd resolution; but wee fynd by circumstances that Conscience is not the trew but seeming cause of the Infanta's stay, to
conclude we have wrought what wee can, but since wee cannot have

her with us that wee desyred, our next comfort is that wee hope shortlie to kiss your Matie's hands.'

Before finally taking his leave, Charles was obliged to swear solemnly to the marriage articles he had signed on August the 4th and promised: 'Even if all the world conjoined were to oppose itself and seek to trouble our friendship it would have no effect upon my father or myself.' With this solemn promise ringing in his ears, the Prince paid his last court to the Queen and saw the Infanta for the last time. With his parting words he once more vowed that the Catholics in England would suffer no persecution, and that he considered them under his own personal protection.

He made a liberal distribution of gifts, but finding himself running short was forced to buy 'a cross of ten thick table diamonds from his servant Sir Edmund Verney as a gift to Don Maria de Lande'. King Philip was as generous with his own presents, and on the 3rd of September Charles took his leave of his royal host. They parted with every expression of mutual esteem and apparent goodwill, the King wearing mourning as an expression of his grief. Only once did Charles betray his true feelings: when he was asked if he would prefer an open carriage, 'I should not dare,' he replied, 'to give my assent without sending to Madrid to consult the Junta of Theologians.' On this note the Prince and his retinue set out on their way.

The small party was met outside Santander by officers from the waiting fleet. Even then their troubles were not ended, for, windbound, they were forced to delay, waiting for a favourable breeze. The town gave them a royal reception, festivities on land and on ship-board were as magnificent as they were by then unwelcome. At last, on September 18th, they hoisted sail, bound for England.

Nearly three weeks later they reached their native shores, having experienced a rough and stormy crossing. The Prince straightway mounted horse and rode for London, where he arrived at daybreak on October 6th. News of his return had somehow preceded him, and it was to the joyous peal of bells and cheering throngs that he entered the capital. After a short pause he set out for Royston, where the King was residing. By this time the whole of London was in tumult. Never was such rejoicing. Delight at seeing their Prince once again, after so long in the hated Spaniards' clutches, was equalled only by universal satisfaction that he had not brought the Infanta with him.

Rich merchants brought out tables stacked with food and drink into the very street, debtors were released, felons pardoned and by nightfall the sky was aglow with bonfires lit to celebrate the good news.

Whilst Sir Edmund had been experiencing the rigours and danger of crossing the Bay of Biscay in winter, his wife had safely given birth to another daughter, Margaret. So it was with happiness and relief that he hurried to Hillesden, where the family had moved during the long separation.

After the initial joy on the return of the Prince the serious question of the terms of the match was once more in the air. Although leaving Spain with solemn promises to fulfil his part of the marriage agreement, Charles was no sooner out of reach than it became apparent that he had no intention of honouring his princely word. The matter, indeed, dragged on against quibbles of the most trivial nature; but by the end of the year relations between the two countries became so strained that the match was considered at an end, and the Infanta allowed to return her English books and grammars to the shelves whence they had come.

Thus closed this degrading passage in English history. The trip to Spain was an extraordinary episode viewed in any light, far more extraordinary considering the religious heat of the times. Seldom can any King or Prince of England have behaved with such utter disregard of the feelings of his people in the pursuit of his own selfish ends.

IV

The Family

'He was a verray parfit gentil knight.'

CHAUCER

ON HIS return from Spain Sir Edmund became Member of Parliament for Buckingham in the first Parliament since the 'Memorable Protestation' and the débâcle of the 1621 sitting. For Sir Edmund this was the start of a long association with the House of Commons, an association which, as time passed, became increasingly embarrassing. Although secretly sympathizing with and sharing the opposition views of many of his fellow Buckinghamshire gentlemen, yet Sir Edmund—closely connected as he was with King and Court—could not in all honesty of duty openly appear to agree. As the situation developed, he found his position growing more and more invidious.

One aftermath of the attempted Spanish match was a fresh bout of Roman Catholic persecution. A letter from the Duke of Buckingham to the Deputy-Lieutenants of Buckinghamshire about this time adjured them to 'disarm the Roman Catholiques', a task made no easier, so we are told, for the magistrates fearing 'being lawffed at'. Levying money fared no better, and constant are the complaints ... 'the multiplicitie of payments in maynetayninge of soldiers is very greevious'. The object of this particular grievance was the 'coat and conduct' money needed to equip and despatch men for

the current expedition against Cadiz, an expedition which like so
many of this time ended in procrastination, muddle and near disaster.

By 1630 the family are growing up and the letters become
more numerous and detailed. This is particularly so when Ralph,
the eldest son, starts taking an active interest in affairs. Hitherto,
Sir Edmund had kept only business notes or the occasional piece of
correspondence from his relations and closest friends; but now Ralph
preserved every scrap of paper and even scrawled copies of his own
letters. As he was always ready to help his many friends, and they
took every advantage of his kindness, the volume of these letters
reaches formidable proportions. Many extremely interesting letters
must have been destroyed as too dangerous to keep, nevertheless,
Ralph kept many that he was carefully adjured to burn after
reading.

Little is known of Ralph's childhood, but, as was so often the
custom, he was married at an early age. His father's choice for him
was a young heiress, Mary Blacknell, who had been left an orphan
when nine years old, both her parents dying of the 'great Plaage'.
Her father, described as 'affable and full of clemencie and curtesie',
was a rich landowner in Buckinghamshire whose estate included the
site of the Abbey of Abingdon. An unprotected orphan, Mary
came under the jurisdiction of the Court of Wards, and as such
could not marry without the court's consent. Four guardians were
appointed, and after one unsuccessful attempt by one of them to
marry her to his son, the child was offered to Sir Edmund for his
eldest son. Sir Edmund accepted the stipulation that she was not
to be forced in marriage but was to be well bred and 'allowed to
make her choice at years competent', and Mary went off to live with
relations until the time came for her marriage.

Unlike many girls in her plight, Mary fell into kind hands,
and at the age of thirteen, when Sir Edmund had obtained the
court's permission, she was quietly married to Ralph. Writing to
her aunt, she says: 'Good Aunt, besides the desire I have to heare
of your health and my uncle's, I thincke it fitt to acquaint you that
now I am married, in which state I hope God will give me his
blessings and make it happy to mee.' The couple did not live together for two years, Mary returning to her relations and Ralph to
his studies.

When nineteen Ralph went to Oxford. Magdalen Hall, his
college, had been called a 'very nest of Puritans' in the days of

James I, and thither still went the sons of many staunch Protestant families.

Probably Dr. Denton, a Magdalen man himself, was largely instrumental in getting Ralph there. But, doubtless, many other of Sir Edmund's friends encouraged the same course, for the Challoners, who lived only two miles away, were strong Magdalen supporters, while at Court and in Parliament were others.

Magdalen shaped Ralph's future. Here was one of the birth-places of the Puritan revolution, and very many of his contemporaries and friends found themselves on the same side as he during the memorable Parliaments before the Civil War.

In those days there was great difficulty in obtaining textbooks, and each student had more or less to compile his own. Ralph was fortunate in that Crowther, his tutor, had put together some as-trology and other notes for him, and also lent him books from his own quite extensive collection. Some of Crowther's advice, how-ever, must have grown more than a little tiresome at times, as his pupil is adjured to: 'Devote to Logic and Divinity from three to four houres a day', and at one time Ralph is advised not to give up his studies for Hymen's delights and is told that 'Pleasures are augmented through theire intermissions and the sweetnesse of a kysse will rellish better after the harshnesse of a syllogisme'. Yet Ralph appears to have taken it all with a good grace and to have stayed on the best of terms with his tutor, who indeed remains a firm friend of the family.

Whilst Ralph was at Oxford, Mary lived at Claydon, where her husband joined her whenever his studies permitted—regardless of weather—to the great amusement of his tutor. Old Crowther was evidently not as completely humourless as he first appears, for he writes to Ralph:

'To take soe wette a journey and find soe bad a successe. I had thought when you went out of Oxford you had beene steeled against any weather, but it seemes your courage was cooled . . . you a huntsman, to give of in the midst of the game, to turne soe faint hearted as not to persue it. I would have helped you here to dryer canvase at a cheape rate but to reserve my laughter till our next meeting.'

It is touching to see how affectionately her parents-in-law re-garded Ralph's wife. No letter, however brief, passes but that some kind reference is made to 'my sweetest sister' or 'my good daughter', while old Crowther refers to her as 'your sweetest comfort'. The brothers show real affection for their sister-in-law and her pet name in the family was 'Mischiefe'. An extremely capable woman, she made Ralph a good and loving wife on whom he could always depend. When both were exiled from England and living in near-destitution in France, it is she who crossed to London to fight the endless legal battles to regain the sequestered estates, and it is only thanks to her persistence that after long years abroad Ralph finally returns in 1645 to the ruins of his family heritage; it was hard, indeed, that the engineer of this never lived to see Claydon again.

After leaving Oxford, Ralph accompanied his father firstly to Edinburgh for the King's coronation, and then elsewhere on Court business.

Although life in London was pleasant enough, Ralph found himself more and more in the country, managing Claydon and his wife's estates. On one occasion he attempted to get abroad with Lord Arundel, who was going as ambassador extraordinary to Emperor Ferdinand of Austria. His father, though, is very reluctant, but writes cheerfully: 'My lord Marshall is goeing a fine journye, and noe man would bee gladder of such an opportunity to lett you see something abroad, then I should bee.' He then proceeds to give his reasons why it is impossible: 'In the first place you know I cannot settle my business without you'; secondly: 'That my Lord must be gone on Munday next att the farthest. If neyther of thes will sattisfy you, the third shall; that is, hee will take noeboddy with him, for hee has refused my Lord Russell, my Lord Grandison, my Lord Andrues, and in breefe all others, my Lord Dawbingny only excepted, and hee goes with him. Now I thinck your journey is att an end, and soe with my love to my daughter, I remain your loving father.'

Indeed, Sir Edmund could not settle his business without Ralph, for now the latter is grown up he takes over the supervision of the estate. Dr. Denton, however, still often tenders advice when he returns to the country from Court, where he is Physician in Ordinary to the King. Only seven years older than Ralph, he remained a close friend. He was very fond of horses and evidently had other attributes, for he was described as 'an ingenious and phasetious man, who for his Polite Conversation among the Ladies of the Court was called the Speaker of the Parliament of Woemen'.

Sir Edmund's confidence in his brother-in-law's handling of the estate did not evidently include the handling of horses, despite the doctor's reputed fondness for them, for he writes to Ralph: 'I thincke Doctor Denton has spoyled that nagg soe in the front that hee will not recover it for a good while, the pricking hurts him not but the bruise of his foote which was done with extreame riding in the frosts.'

Horses are a recurring subject in the letters of this period. Riding-horses were in heavy demand, as might be expected. They were considered valuable property, and their well-being was constantly watched, even the cart-horses receiving their share of attention and being sent with the riding-horses to the magnificent pastures on the fens. 'I am sorry to heare your horses thrive as ill as myne, I would send as many cart horses as I could', his father writes to Ralph. No detail is too small for Sir Edmund to give his instructions upon. 'Thos coalts that are att home', he writes, 'must not bee putt to grass yett for if they goe out before grass be well growne, they will be spoyled having been housed all this Winter.'

On another occasion:

'Forgett not to bidd John Black to take upp two of the fattest mares att Quarendon grounds [three miles from Claydon] on Tuesday next . . . ther is three other mares in some of those grounds, lett him see them and send me woard in what grounds they goe and in what case they are in; bidd him meat the mares well that hee takes to howse and after a few dayes to Ayre them morning and evening.'

Whenever he can, Sir Edmund writes to the long-suffering Ralph or Roades, or even sometimes to his wife: 'Good Puss, I pray desire my sonne when hee comes home to cause the coalts to bee putt to grass in the furry cloace assoone as the coalt that were geld maye bee putt out without Danger'; and again:

'I would not send my mare chamberlain [to the fens] because I will have hir coverd againe. Yor graye gelding and shee maye keepe company a while togeather but send away all the rest assoone as you can . . . I thinck it will doe the coalts noe Hurt to playe abroad in the Heate of the daye, but I heare the pied coalt gott his mischance by a strooke of one of the cart Horses, and that must bee by the carelessnes of servants.'

The dogs, too, were important and get their share of space in the letters: 'I have sent home a verry likely young Hound that was bred at Will Gerys his name is Gamboy I praye desire Thos Isham to take great care to order him well; the rest of the whelps I sent into this part are all lost.'

Sir Edmund employed a number of excellent servants. Apart from Roades, who increasingly came to be the financial manager of the estate, there was Raphael, who looked after the sheep, Tom Isham, who seems to have been in charge of the hounds, and John Black, who cared for the cattle. He nearly always sends personal messages to them, and in every case these are a model of consideration and kindness. Sir Edmund was also described as having 'a loving and sweet courtesy to the poorest', and this is amply borne out in his own letters to Roades, who, as often as he can, writes back to his master of what is happening on the estate. Constant concern is shown to tenants and dependants on every occasion. Writing of Roades's own father, Sir Edmund says: 'he hath sent to mee about that ashwood. The poore old man offers to pay for it: tell him I cannot wright to him now, but that I have sent to you to lett him have that wood to keepe him from coulde.' And, again, when a storm had blown down a cottage on the estate: 'I am glad my hovell fell upon noe Christian creature.'

In even the smallest matter concerning the estate Sir Edmund takes an interest; be it willows 'of the right kind' for one field, or a 'post and rale' for the 'rammcloace'. It is evident from one letter that the gardener is giving trouble and Sir Edmund advises: 'the Gardner shall pleach noe Hedge this yeare . . . if you fiende him idle about his woarke, agree with him by the great [i.e. piece-work] for trewly I will noe longer indure his daye woarke; it is intollerable to beare with his knavery.'

Getting 'home the coales' was another matter of concern and he is full of advice to Roades on obtaining 'as mutch stoane as hee can from Stratton Audly and other places', adding that the 'carrage maye well goe twice a daye for stoane if the men be well followd; otherwise the men will loyter, and saye it is to hard a labor for theyr Horses'. This last was from Theobalds—and it is clear that even when with the King, and closely involved in Court business, Sir Edmund's heart was still with his beloved Claydon.

There is little gossip or scandal in these letters; however, the occasional story or titbit of news is sometimes sandwiched between farm instructions or some item of family interest:

'To requite yor noos of yor fish, I will tell you as good a tale from hence as trewe. A merchant of lundon wrote to a factor of his beyoand sea, desired him by the next shipp to send him 2 or 3 apes; he forgot the r, and then it was 203 apes. His factor has sent him fower scoare, and sayes hee shall have the rest by the next shipp, conceiving the merchant had sent for tow hundred and three apes; if yor self or frends will buy any to breede on, you could never have had such chance as now. In earnest this is very trew.' Unfortunately, there is no record of Ralph taking up this offer.

Ralph was the pillar of good sense in the family, indefatigable in his kindness and consideration for others; nothing was too much trouble to him, and his relations came to rely increasingly on his judgement. Lady Sussex was loud in his praises and has the highest opinion of him. 'You ar so good a sone that I see your father can do nothing of bisness without you', she writes to Ralph; and to his father she says: 'you have a son truly good; i pray God make him happy every way for i thinke ther cannot bee a bettir younge man'.

Even Ralph's goodness was tested to the full by the behaviour of his younger brother Tom. Doubtless this scapegrace was an unmitigated nuisance to his unfortunate parents as a boy, but his misdeeds then are not recorded and there is no mention of Tom's schooldays or schooling. It can be deduced, however, that he absorbed none of the qualitites of honesty, truthfulness or gratitude, in fact about the only worthwhile legacy of this period in his life appears to have been a beautifully neat and readable handwriting.

Tom's real downfall started at the age of nineteen when he proposed to marry the 'good daughter' of a Mr. Futsin without so much as asking his father's leave. In an age of such strict parental control this was a most monstrous crime, and Tom did little to make it less so by saying: 'The thing was commonly spread about the house and I verily thought it came to my father's ears.'

For this behaviour many fathers would have driven their son from the house for good, but Sir Edmund was too kind-hearted and resolved only to send Tom to Virginia, where many Englishmen, long-dissatisfied with their lot at home, had gone to settle. Margaret Verney took it upon herself to make all the arrangements for her son's journey and through the medium of an emigrant broker all details were fixed. The necessities required for such an adventure in 1634 make interesting reading: 'Your sonne shoold have with him iij seruants at least', including, 'if it were possible, a cooper out of the country, which wee cannot get soe redily heare.' These would cost him £12 each for 'passage and apparel'. For his own accommodation '. . . hee maye bring vp with him a fether bed, bolster, pillow, blanketts, rugg, and 3 payre of sheets'. Corn was sometimes in short supply through the 'covetiousnes of the planters', who preferred to plant the more lucrative tobacco, and Tom is advised to bring some with him 'least there shoold happen to be a scarsety in the cuntry'. The 'flower, the fowlinge peeces, the stronge waters, and the grosery wares', have already been bought and so, for a total fare of £56, 'littell more or less', the errant is despatched.

Lady Verney writes a kindly letter to the broker asking 'that if any acquaintance doe goe with him, that you may trust, a little to direct him in his coarses', as '. . . My sonne hath neither been bread abroad nor vsed to any bartering at home, but only bredd at schoole . . . if you would be pleased to write to some of your friends there that are of the better sorte, a little to direct him in his way of proceeding, and but acknolledg him to be the sonne of his father, you shall engage both his father and my self to acknolledg your cortesye: and shall pray to God for his prosperity, and leave the success unto his divine providence.'

On the 8th of August 1634 Tom sails on board 'the good shipp caled the marchants' hoape of London', leaving behind him an authority signed on the same day which entitles a Mr. William Webster, 'in the case of mortallity of the said Mr. Thomas Verney, to sell and dispose of his goods, provisions, and servants . . . which doe amount to 117L. 13s. 6d.', for the use of Sir Edmund Verney.

We know nothing of Tom's 'coarses' in Virginia except that in nine months he was back in England, having lost all his money and equipment, including, presumably, his servants.

He was next sent as a volunteer on board the *St. Andrew*, a King's ship, then cruising in the Channel with the rest of the fleet raised by the ship-money tax. In a letter addressed 'at the Downs' he writes to his 'loving and kind brother that we are bound to the French coast to see what they will say to us'; and again a little later: 'There is warre proclaimed with France, the King of Spaine is soe much the more joyfuller, by reason that our kinge's fleet doth assist him in it.' This letter ends with a postscript begging 'that you will speak for mee to my mother, for travellers ever want money'.

This attempt to keep the rogue occupied did not last long, for, after only a few months at sea, Tom writes that he is off to Flanders:

'I do not intend to make a long stay there, only to see what fortunes a younger brother might attain unto, and withall to see how I shall like the country. . . . I hope you will speake to my friends for a little money to carry mee over thither, ffor if they will send mee non, I am resolved to goe over with that little I have.'

Quickly tired of this, he is soon back in England, lodging with the keeper of the prison of the Marshalsea, a servant of his father. By this time Sir Edmund and even Ralph are heartily sick of Tom's escapades. Every letter from Tom contains a plea for assistance of one kind or another, each accompanied by equally fervent promises of repayment. By now, though, Ralph is too involved in his own affairs, and the troubles of one of his other brothers, to give much time to the pesterings of brother Tom.

Mun, the third son, was first educated at a school in Gloucester, and then, at the age of sixteen, transferred to Winchester. School-life in some respects seems to have altered little in the 300 years since Mun was at school. In one letter he complains that 'his schoole master being at London, the propositors begin to affront mee, which my companions are free from, I doe intende to intreate him to suffer mee to enjoy the same libertyes that they doe'. But Ralph's answer saves him from adopting this course and he soon finds that 'the propositors words are more than their deeds, and your fraternal letter has made me careless, not fearing what they can doe unto me'. On another occasion he is worried that he might not be allowed home for the Christmas holidays and writes pathetically:

'I hope to see you at Crismas, if my mother goeth not to London, as I believe she will not. If you please do you your best endeavours that I come. I shall acknowledge myself much beholden . . . our stay is but three weeks, the earnestness of my sute makes my father I feare mistruste that I neglect my time, but it is not soe.'

Mun evidently disliked writing letters as much as any school-boy, for, after a more than usually long period without news, his father reproaches his son, then aged eighteen, who makes amends in a classic letter:

Sir

Not daring to present any unpolished lines to such a judicious reader, but finding how farr greater a crime it is to neglect duty than to lay my defects to a wel wishing father, I have adventured to write to you, humbly beseeching you to pardon what I have written, by which meanes you will encourage me to make a second adventure. With my humble duty remembered unto you, I remain your most obedient sonn.

                                                    Edmund Verney

Winton Coll.
Feb; 10
1635

After two years at Winchester Mun is sent to Oxford. His finances seemed to have been bothering him at this time, as he enquires 'whether my father will pay for the carryage of my trunk and bed and my chambers rent for the Michaelmas quarter, which amount to the sum of 19*s.* 10*d.* . . . .'

Ralph had been the intermediary in the business of getting Mun to Oxford. Sir Edmund had written to him to arrange it all: 'I praye send yor Brother to Oxford assoone as you can; I will allow him forty pound a yeare, & hee shall have a cloath sute made him against easter or sooner if neede require. Advise him to Husband it well; for I knowe it may maintaine him well if hee will; & more I will not allow him,' and again later says: 'Now for Mun, I did ever intend to paye for his gowne over & above his allowance, but what the other charges will come to I know not. If he will provide his gowne himself, I will allow him for that & his entrance fee 10L besides.'

The move from school to Magdalen was evidently a success, as Mun writes shortly after his arrival:

'Oxford & my tutour I lyke very well. The Vice Chancellor spoke to me very courteously when I came to be matriculated, he could not find fault with my Haire, because I had itt cut before I went to him. I must not forget to give thanks for the loade of woode y^u gave me. Had I time I would be more large, but now I must crave pardon for my brevity. I pray command in whatsoever I am able.'

Mun's next letter concerned payment for his tutor:

'According to your desire I asked . . . what it were fit for mee to give my Tutour. He told me Mr. Jones gives him £1 5s. the quarter, and that he would advise me to give him the lyke. I must needed make me a sute of clothes presently, but as I will doe nothing without your advice, so I will entreate you to name the stufs and to speake to your man to give order to Miller [the tailor who later makes a 'sober grey sute' for Mun] for the making of it. I pray retaine so much of my quarteridge as you think will discharge this. Let me beseech you that my own ignorance may be appologie for my boldnes with you.'

It is interesting to see that it was then the custom at Oxford to wear the hair short; apparently this was a rule closely observed, for later that year the King visited the University and precautions were strict:

'There is a Proctor for every house during the king's continuance in Oxford,' writes Mun, 'the chiefest thing that they will endevour to amend is the wearing of long haire. The Principal protested that after this day he would turn out his house whomsoever he found with haire longer than the tips of his eares.'

Other regulations were as closely complied with, and Mun was unlucky enough to be caught in the act of breaking the rigid fast-day rules:

'All the newes is that Mrs. Gabriel is lyke to dress noe more meate on fasting nights. It was my fortune to be there on Friday at supper, with a Master of Arts and two Batchelors of our house, when Dr. Browne of Christchurch came in and tooke us, commanding mee to come to his chamber next morning.'

He was lucky enough to get off this time, as his captor happened to be a friend of Sir Edmund's.

Doubtless the notes Ralph had himself at Oxford came in extremely useful, but Mun also collected a number of books. In the Claydon library there is copy of *Spede's Atlas* and on the flyleaf is written in Mun's hand the inscription, 'This Booke did formerly appertaine unto . . . but now 'tis myne.'

However, Mun's promising start at Oxford does not last long, and very soon he starts keeping ill-company. His tutor is forced to write to Ralph:

'I must needes confess, tis extorted from me, that your brother
Edmund doth not carry himself so ingeniously as he ought in every
respect. He hath in a strange manner (for what reason I know not)
absented himself from my lectures, and likewise from prayer in the
Hall. I would say more, but I desire to speake with y^r selfe. I will
meete you any day . . . that you appoint this week.'

Ralph intervenes and manages to smoothe things over this time,
but it does not last and soon Mun is once again in serious trouble.

This time, not only is he up to his old tricks, but has also
borrowed money from those who could ill-afford to lend it. Ralph
offers to pay his debts, but evidently attaches impossible conditions
to the loan, as Mun, while acknowledging his 'respect and thankful-
ness for your greate love', still refuses the gesture as 'to yield to your
demand would have made me the laughing stock of the whole
university'. But the position is no better and Mun seems unable to
help himself. In one letter he declares he is 'utterly undone' and
another time that his 'misery is unsupportable.' His father seems completely shattered that his favourite son is caught in a net of disgrace:

'Sonne, And now I have said that, my griefes grow high upon
mee, for you were a sonne in whom I tooke delight, that I had a
p'ticular affection for, above some others, and above most of my
children. But God has in you punisht mee for that partiality. For
your former offenses, though they were great and of a base nature,
yet when I had your many faithful promises for a reformation,
my love to you was such that I was not only content but desirous
to remitt them . . . that indulgence has wrought no other effects
than to encourage you to bee more wicked; you are now grown so
lewd and false that I blush to think you mine. . . . As you have been
so unnaturally base as to follow your drunken, lyinge, false humor,
and as you have left yourself and mee for your meane company . . .
will take no further care . . . but that by being my unworthy sonne
I am made your unhappy father.'

At last Mun writes beseeching his eldest brother's help, saying
that unless he leaves Oxford he cannot leave the 'ill coarces' he has
taken, and imputing it to 'noe other cases than my own ambition
in perpetuall desiring of greate company'. The letter ends with a
touching confession that it was his own 'facile nature, soe apt to be
drawne the worst way' that was to blame.

Good Brother

There is a proctor for every
house during the Kings continuance in Ox=
ford, and the cheifest thing that they
wil endeavour to amend is the wearing of
long haire, The Principle protested that
after this day he would turn out his house
whomesoever he found with haire longer
then the tips of his eares, I beleeue this
severity wil last but a weeke, therefore
I pray if you can conveniently send for
me towards Satterday. Beggers must be
whipt, I pray execute this law upon Ses-
sions who is resolved to beg a peece of
Venison of you. My Tutour wil be there
who wil better deserue it, that Miser,
who (in my conscience) if not boyle it,
yet wil put it forth he finding Venison,
and the other finding trust. An hast
I rest
                              Yours ever to Command
                                  Edmund Verney

Mag: Hall.
August 25:th
1636

Letter from Mun at Oxford to his brother Ralph

Raphe:

yor sweete chielD is goving apace to a better woarld; shee has but a short time to stay with ves: I hope you have such a sence of gods blessings to you; as you will not repi: att his decrees; make all convenien. haste to yor good wife who wants yo comfort, ~~strikeout~~

~~strikeout~~

not to faste for that maye heate yo bludd; and that maye give an inD to all our comforts; as deere I shall intreat mey thing from you take car of yor selfe for this is a dangerous yeare for heats and coldes; the gud o Heaven Bless you;

this satturday morning   yor loving father
about one of the clock   Ed: virney

Letter from Sir Edmund to Ralph on the death of his grandchild

In this extremity they seek Crowther's assistance. Ralph's former tutor is now married and has settled down in a living procured for him on his retirement by Ralph's father. The old man is delighted to take on the task and Sir Edmund himself writes to thank him for the 'curteous offer of receiving my ill-disposed sonne; truly I was never in more paine for anything than now I might dispose of him where I might have hope to reclaime him'.

Crowther's task is a hard one, for he finds Mun 'by his owne confession hath wholy lost all his time at Oxford, and understands not the very first grounds of logicke or other university learning, and hath no bookes to initiate him in it'. So, once more, the notes collected for Ralph 'to go on with for the present' come into use. But only for a short time, for within a month the old man is 'taken extreame ill' and soon afterwards dies.

This is the turning point in Mun's life. Given a little responsibility looking after the affairs of the widow, he becomes a changed person, showing consideration and kindness to all he meets. There was a suggestion that Mun should go abroad and he writes to Ralph:

'When my father was here he made a proposition to me by my uncle Dr. [Denton] and Mr. Aris [the rector] of my going my Ld Warwick's voyage; he prayed them to propose it, and to learne whither I were really addicted to such an undertaking, and would not motion it himself first, least I should accept it however. Truely, Sr in my opinion it was a most noble and free way of propounding it. Who can sufficiently honour such a father? I have undertaken it, and writt him my answer since. . . .'

Only eighteen months younger than Mun, Henry, the fourth and last surviving son, showed little aptitude for anything but sport. Intended for a soldier by his father, at an early age he was sent to Paris to pick up French and learn his trade at the hands of the then acknowledged masters of the art of war. He appears to have absorbed neither of these, but on the other hand did acquire an overweaning interest in horse-racing and dogs. His letters home are an amusing mixture of apology for being a bad scholar, and enthusiasm for anything to do with his own pleasure.

'Pleade for me', he writes to Ralph, 'in my behalfe to my father if I have not write in french so well as he expects, but howsoever I presume a line to testifie some little knowledge in the same, and

F

hope in time to expresse myselfe more radier, as the old proverbe is
. . . *il fault du temps pour appendre* . . . please to send the doggs by
the frenchman that is lately gone over for doggs for my lord . . . I
hope my father will not fail to send them for my lord expects them,
with theare names, theare ages, and coulers and markes.'

At the age of twenty-one he takes part in the wars in the Low
Countries in company with the son of his father's friend, Sir Edward
Sydenham, and other contemporaries. But this is not the life for
him, as he graphically describes to his brother:

'I tell you truly I doe not like of it. I wod have you think it is
not the firing of the boullots that fears mee at all, but the true reson
is that I have alwayes given myselfe so fer to the sports and plesurs
of the wourld that I cannot give my mind to this course of life—but
to give my father content and the rest of my frinds, I will tarry this
sommer in the contry, for to learne the use of my armes and to
knowe the duty of a soger, that when I comeof it, shall bee for my
credit and honnor. It shall not be mee that will be judg of it, but
my Captaine. If hee say noe, belevet I will not come of. For I had
rather louse my life then to come of to bee laught at, or bee slighted
by my frindes which I doe think dous love mee. If my father is
angry, I knowe hee will spake with you of it, let me intreate you to
passify him as well as you can.'

And later:

'It is not out of feare which makes mee dislike it. . . . I know not
whether I dare fight or noe for maybe the multitude of people and
boulets flying soe thicke the very noise of them will make me a maised
being soe strange a sport and not being ues to it for ceartainely I am
not of soe milde a sperit but when I see others fight I can fight for
companies sake to.'

Horse-racing is his particular pleasure and the unfortunate
Ralph is forever being besieged by requests for a saddle, or a bit,
or a bridle, and even on one occasion for a horse which 'will be
very wilcom, for sommer drawes on apace, and if I am unmounted I
know but wan way I must trust to, which is to march afout. and I
am an ill foutman.' This particular demand can have met with little
response, as Henry has to try another approach, and says that if he
has a horse 'twill be to ease' his 'weary limes not to try his speede

for the cup', as Ralph had assumed to be the case, doubtless quite rightly.

Henry wasn't entirely unsuccessful in his chosen career, and his letters are full of his past and projected triumphs. 'I can right you noe nuse,' he says, 'but of a horsmache, as is to be run yearely at the Hagge for a cupe of 50 pounds, as every offecer gives yearly 20 shillings towards the bying of it. I hope to winit afore I die myselfe. I have rod but to maches cince I saw you, and have won them both, I hope likewise to win the cup for the third.'

This last elicits the cynical retort from Mun, who was wryly watching the proceedings from Hillesden: 'I doe not at all wonder at Brother Henry lyking a souldier's life, senc he can follow that and horse maches too.'

V

The Court and London

'. . . at this very hour
Do forge a lifelong trouble. . . .'

TENNYSON

THE INFORMALITY and unlicensed chaos of Court life under James I were not at all to the liking of his son. Impressed with the order and elegance of the Spanish and French Courts he had visited on his abortive quest to Spain, no sooner was Charles on the throne than strict etiquette and disciplined silence replaced the barbarities of his father's regime.

The Stuart Court was in three principal divisions. 'Above Stairs', and closest to the King, were the officers of the Chamber—these were presided over by the Lord Chamberlain. 'Below Stairs' was what was commonly known as the 'Household'—this was under the authority of the Lord Steward. Outdoors, in charge of the stables, the falconers, the buck and otterhounds, was the third great officer —the Master of Horse. In all there were nearly 1,500 Court attendants, and this excludes the households of the Queen and royal children—probably a further 400.

It can have been no easy task to keep order in this vast Court. To do so, however, was the responsibility of the Knight-Marshal— and it was to this position that Charles appointed Sir Edmund shortly after his accession.

84

Court wages and expenses were a perennial drain on the Exchequer. For years old retainers and dependants had been getting free meals in the kitchens; also the wives of courtiers had been living in considerable comfort with their husbands off the King's bounty—in an effort to institute some measure of economy both practices were stopped. Nevertheless, each year the personal charges of the King and his Court absorbed nearly two-fifths of the total revenue of the State.

A list of some of the functionaries at Court gives an idea of the extraordinarily numerous and diverse requirements of the King: Within the Chamber were the officers of the wardrobe; the Treasurer of the Chamber, the Master of the Robes, the twelve Grooms of the Bedchamber, the six Pages of the Bedchamber, the four Gentlemen Ushers of the Privy Chamber, the forty-eight Gentlemen of the Privy Chamber, the six Grooms of the Privy Chamber, the Library Keeper, Black Rod, the eight Gentlemen Ushers of the Presence Chamber, the fourteen Grooms of the Great Chamber, six gentlemen waiters, four cup-bearers, four carvers, four servers, four esquires of the Body, the eight Servers of the Chamber, the Groom Porter, sixteen Serjeants at Arms. Besides these and also of the Chamber were the officers of the revels, of the music, of the plays, of the hunt; the messengers, trumpeters, heralds, pursuivants, apothecaries, surgeons, barbers, chaplains. There were four Physicians in Ordinary, a Master and Treasurer of the Jewel House, a Geographer, a Histriographer, a Hydrographer, a Cosmographer, a Poet Laureate, a Notary and several Apothecaries of Odiferous Services who managed the very necessary King's perfumery.

There was too a Master of Ordnance with a Lieutenant, a Master Armourer and seventeen under-officers. There were two Embroiderers, one Serjeant Skinner, one Cross-bow maker, one Cormorant Keeper, one Hand-gunmaker, one Master and Marker of Tennis, one Mistress Sempstress and one Laundress; one Perspective-maker, one Master-Fencer, one Haberdasher of Hats, one Combmaker, one Serjeant Painter, one Limner, one Silver-Smith, one Peruque-maker, one Keeper of Pheasants and Turkeys—and many others covering all aspects of Court life from a Spurrier to a Cleaner of Picturers.

Besides those who were permitted to be within the precincts of the Court itself, clustered round the gates was a vast concourse of petitioners and beggars of all sorts striving to gain admittance.

There was also a kind of rough market where were sold some of the 'Beefs and veales' for the monarch's table.

This 'multitude of idle and masterless persons' about the Court had long been a source of annoyance to King James and in 1619 he had issued an edict expressing 'our highe displeasure and offence at the bolde and barbarous insolency of multitudes of vulgar people'. King Charles, too, had found himself continually plagued by the same trouble and had decided to limit 'the great and excessive number of landers and landresses that follow our court'. So he appointed only a few 'of good reputation, not to over burden our court with vagabonds'.

Sir Edmund and his officers are bidden to:

'give their due attendance in the Court, for execution of all such things as shall concern the office of the Marshalsea, within the precinct of the verge. And among others, the same Knight Marshal shall have special respect to the exclusion of boys and vile persons, and punishment of vagabonds and mighty beggars, not permitting any of them to remain in, about, or near unto the Court . . . he shall take good regard that all such unthrifty and common women, as follow the Court, may be likewise, from time to time, openly punished, banished, and excluded, and none of them to be suffered near thereunto. . . .'

And these orders were 'to be put in effectual execution, as he will answer unto the King's Highness at his peril'. To help him he was allowed a Deputy with a number of Provost Marshals or Vergers.

He acted under the orders of the Earl Marshal and on State Occasions carried a white rod as symbol of his office. In Procession he walked behind the Gentlemen of the Privy Chamber, while his men under the Deputy went at the front to clear the way. Remuneration was reasonable, too, for with his new appointment the King granted Sir Edmund a pension of £200, and at the same time his previous pension for the same amount was extended from 'during pleasure' to the duration of his life.

The Marshalsea Court, which sat on Fridays, came under the direct jurisdiction of the Knight-Marshal. This, and the concomitant Court of the Verge, dealt with all cases concerning any member of the Court or which arose within a radius of twelve miles about. The jurisdiction of the two courts was confused, so in 1630 they were merged into the new Palace Court, the King's Court of the Palace of Westminster, where the Knight-Marshal, the Lord Steward and the Steward of the Court presided as chief judges. The Courts of the Verge and Marshalsea had been originally set up to administer direct and swift justice to any of the monarch's domestic servants, to avoid their being drawn into the protracted procedure of the normal courts of law. Their jurisdiction in the Verge arose from the ancient 'Privilege of the King's Palace' which extended from the palace gate 'three miles, three furlongs, three acres, nine feet, nine palms, and nine barleycorns'. Within this area any offender was privileged from arrest by ordinary officers of the law. So it indeed remained until the privilege of sanctuary was abolished for ever in the eighteenth century. However, neither the Courts of the Verge nor the Marshalsea, nor even the Palace Court, were subject to the Chief Justiciary, and the Londoner considered them as on a par with the iniquitous and notorious Star Chamber, which in their eyes was designed 'to discountenance and suppress all bold inquirers and opposers'.

When the Privy Council was in session the Knight-Marshal's men attended outside the door ready to remove anyone sentenced to imprisonment in the Marshalsea. The prison itself was situated on the south bank of the river in Southwark High Street, next to the King's Bench. Here were confined those junior courtiers and others who had committed an offence within the Verge. Here, too, were sent other State prisoners and evidently Admiralty prisoners, for the seven captains held partly responsible for the La Rochelle fiasco in 1627 were duly confined in the Marshalsea; as indeed was Sir John Eliot after his release from the Tower in 1629. Thus it appears that the Marshalsea was often used for those not worthy to be accommodated in the Tower, yet too important for incarceration elsewhere. Within the gaol wealthy prisoners could buy privilege, have their meals sent from outside and have private rooms. The poorer prisoners, on the other hand, were given comforts from the compulsory contributions levied on the villages and hundreds throughout the country.

On progress, but not on chase, the Knight-Marshal continued to execute his authority within the statutory twelve miles of the King's person. Preceding the Court was the Knight-Harbinger to prepare the way and arrange rooms for the arrival of the sovereign; with him went the Removing Wardrobe which was carried about with the King whenever he moved. And these moves were frequent; for every year Charles set forth on Progress to some part of his domain.

No hasty affair were these Progresses—usually taking place in the summer months when road conditions were good and when it was, anyway, advisable to quit London to avoid the plague—they lasted for anything up to three or four months. Making his orderly, unhurried journeys across his kingdom, Charles crossed the same country, stayed with the same people, hunted the same forests. He knew well certain counties or tracts of counties, but he knew nothing of many others and he had never in his life been to Wales or Ireland. By nature shy and aloof, and hampered by a slight impediment of speech, he was never really known or understood by his own countrymen and remained a remote figure except to those nearest him. His courtiers regarded their King and master with a touching devotion, his other subjects accorded him respect, often fear, but not until the end did he win their love, even then it stemmed from pity and sense of duty rather than genuine affection.

Within the Court existed an iron authority. Every servant knew his job to the last detail and woe betide any that made the smallest mistake. In fact, life at Court would have been deadly dull, with this cold unsympathetic monarch, were it not for the gaiety of the sumptuous masques and pageants organized and enjoyed by the King's Catholic Queen, Henrietta Maria.

Brought up as she had been in the light-hearted but polished atmosphere of a French Court, Henrietta Maria was not willing to accept the sober authority imposed by her reticent, studious-minded husband. Masques, often written by Ben Jonson with scenery devised by Inigo Jones, succeeded one another with bewildering rapidity, each outdoing its predecessors in the magnificence of décor or costumes and the morality of the pious platitude which was the customary theme.

This was in striking contrast with the masque in the days of King James, which had often ended in bacchanalian revels with even the actors too drunk to perform. There is an account of just such a one in celebration of the visit of the King of Denmark to Theobalds, the King's country-palace near Royston.

The arrival of the two Kings was sumptuous enough, with the roads bestrewn with artificial oak leaves emblazoned with the words 'Welcome, Welcome' in gold, and the Poet Laureate declaiming a suitable ode which began 'Enter, O long'd for Princes, blesse these bowers'. Thereafter the days were spent in continuous hunting or feasting while great crowds came from London to witness the event.

The celebrations seem to have been generous, for a courtier, Sir John Harrington, writes:

'We had women, and indeed wine too, of such plenty, as would have astonished each beholder. Our feasts were magnificent, and the two royal guests did most lovingly embrace each other at the table. I think the Dane hath strangely wrought on our good English Nobles; for those whom I could never get to taste good English liquor, now follow the fashion, and wallow in beastly delights. The ladies abandon their sobriety, and are seen to roll about in intoxication. . . .'

However, the climax of the visit was to come and Harrington continues:

'One day a great feast was held; and after dinner the representation of Solomon's temple, and the coming of the Queen of Sheba was made, or (as I may better say) was meant to have been made, before their Majesties. . . . The lady who did play the Queen's part did carry most precious gifts to both their Majesties; but, forgetting the steps arising to the canopy, overset her caskets into his Danish Majesty's lap, and fell at his feet, though I rather think it was in his face. Much was the hurry and confusion; . . . Now did appear in rich dress, Hope, Faith and Charity; Hope did assay to speak, but wine rendered her endeavours so feeble that she withdrew, and hoped the King would excuse her levity. Faith was then all alone; for I am certain she was not joined to good works, and left the court in a staggering: Charity came to the King's feet, and seemed to cover the multitude of sins her sister had committed; in some sort she made obeisance, and brought gifts, but said she would return home again, as there was no gift which Heaven had not already given His Majesty. She then returned to Faith and Hope, who were both sick in the lower hall. . . . Victory did not triumph for long; for after much lamentable utterance, she was led away by a silly captive, and laid to sleep in the outer steps of the chamber.' 'Peace' reached the throne only by clearing the way before with her olive branch.

Such scenes were unthinkable under the new King; however,

what offended the Puritans more than the masques themselves was the Queen's habit of permitting ladies to come on the stage, instead of allowing boys to be dressed as women, as hitherto—even sometimes coming on herself.

When Henrietta Maria originally came from France she brought with her many attendants, and as time passed these grew more numerous still. By treaty she was allowed three score servants, but by 1626 the total was nearer 460—and these were costing the State £240 a day.

There were serving-men and maids, sempstresses, washerwomen, even 'kitchen scourers', but, above all, priests, 'the most superstitious, turbulent and jesuitical that could be found in all France'. These exiles, loathing the English as much as they were themselves disliked, proved a constant aggravation to Charles. Not content with worshipping in private, they brandished their religion abroad, interfered at grace and even interrupted the King's own devotions by their chatter. At length, exasperated beyond control, he banished the lot—firstly to Somerset House and thence, with the help of the Yeomen of the Guard, to Dover—thirty coaches and fifty carts full of them. Most of London turned out to see them go, and amid derision and cat-calls they departed. They seem to have had the last word, however, for it was later discovered that all the Queen's dresses had departed with them and she was left with only the gown she was wearing and two smocks.

As part of her jointure the Queen was given Somerset House, then known as Denmark House; and later Charles settled on her Greenwich Palace, Queen Elizabeth's favourite residence. The Palace had been originally settled on the wife of James I, Queen Anne of Denmark as she was known, and under her instructions Inigo Jones started building her 'House of Delight' near the Palace itself. It was ten years, however, before this masterpiece was completed, and even then Henrietta Maria had little time to enjoy it before the ultimate catastrophe broke upon the nation.

Most of the King's attendants were housed in or near the Palace of Whitehall, which was the King's principal residence in London. Here every Christmas the Court revels continued for days on end. Here it was, too, that Charles housed much of his fabulous collection of pictures, 400 in all, including twenty-eight Titians, eleven Correggios, nineteen Veroneses and seventeen by Tintoretto, acquired from all over Europe by the faithful Endymion Porter or Nicholas Lanière, Master of the King's Music. With many by the Court Painters, Van Dyck, Mytens, Gentileschi and others.

But Charles's interest in the arts was not solely that of rich collector and benefactor. His magnificent collection of paintings passed on to him by his brother Prince Henry, himself a knowledgable art critic, were a continual source of pleasure; and the King himself is said to have touched up his own paintings, and was skilled in 'limning and pictures'.

Whitehall was a small city in itself; rambling from Charing Cross to Westminster, its twenty-odd acres covered all the ground between St. James's Park and the river. Of this vast conglomeration of buildings only the magnificent Banqueting House remains, designed by Inigo Jones and completed in three years, with a ceiling painted by Rubens depicting the glories of King James's reign. Here were performed many of the masques on which so much care—and money—was lavished by Henrietta Maria, although some were considered as likely to damage the valuable pictures and were staged in a wooden pavilion built especially for the purpose.

St. James's Palace, the King's other London residence, benefited, too, from the artistic taste of Charles and his consort. Soon after Henrietta Maria's many attendants had been banished—much to the satisfaction of the housekeeper at St. James's, who complained that the French had 'so defiled the house as a week's work would not make it clean'—extensive redecorating was carried out and the Palace was completely refurnished. A few years later it was described by a French courtier as 'very magnificent and extremely convenient . . . the whole were furnished by the particular commands of the Queen of Great Britain'.

Apart from paintings and tapestries, Charles accumulated a staggering collection of bronzes, marbles and other works of art. Knowledgeable and with an excellent taste, the King set a fashion which was followed by many in the land. In common with other cultural activities the passion for music was in spate. The development of the country-house existence, the rising standard of living, and the political and religious unity experienced in the previous century had created conditions in which the arts thrived. The newly rich merchants and landowners were the driving force behind this search for culture. As the tempo of their lives quickened in the competitive, commercial world of the sixteenth century, so the need for relaxation became greater.

The popularity of instrumental music increased at the expense of the purely church music. In the hands of the growing breed of musical amateurs drawing-room music prospered. Proficiency at the virginal, or the guitar, or 'the softly-singing lute', was considered part of the education of the day, and 'private musicke', performed by from two to six players, took place in many country-houses.

This interest in music was not limited to the rich. The common people also loved their tavern and dance tunes, so that there was a general appreciation of music and musicians in town and country alike. By 1620, however, a distinction began to appear between the 'music of the many' and the 'music of the few'. As the years passed musical splendour became to be associated more and more with the Court and its followers, while simple music belonged to the people—and the Puritans. In church, too, there was a revival of rich, extravagant music and this seemed to point to a return to the old style indelibly blackened with the stain of Catholicism.

Under the influence of the King, however, music societies and concerts flourished. A musical education was considered essential for any woman, and doubtless the 'yonge girles' at Claydon were taught how to play an instrument—although the family do not seem to have been very musical then. There is reference, however, to a 'gittarre' which had been bought in Paris which 'is spoild which I am very sory for, it was thought heere a very good one . . . it was the most beautifull that I could find for it was of Ebony enlayed with Mother Pearle'. This instrument accompanies Mary on exile to France with her husband and it is hoped she may find 'something of plesuer wher you are, the gittir i hope will take you up much, strive for cherfullnes with it'. It may, indeed, have been a solace to the exiles, for many bits of verses and songs for the guitar came back with Ralph's letters from France. Mary evidently took the 'gittir' back with her to England when she returned to arrange for the desequestration of Claydon, since Ralph cheerfully writes to her: 'But for your Gittarr, if you have forgot any one lesson, nay if you have not gotten many more then you had, truly I shall breake your Fiddle about your pate, therefore looke to your selfe, and follow it hard, and expect noe mercy in this point.' Apart from these references, the letters are free of any mention of music or concerts—even at the Court.

The tradition of 'Royal Musicke' was a long one. Charles

himself had '64 musicians in ordinary, fifteen trumpeters and kettle drummers, seven drummers and fifes', and 'musitions for windy instruments' attached to the Court—this besides the King's own small private orchestra that played to him during dinner. His example and interest did much to encourage musical popularity.

Royal patronage also extended beyond the arts; inventors and scientists were welcome visitors at Court and many a project owed its existence to the King's purse. Mathematicians, engineers, physicians, were all encouraged in various ways—and anything with a scientific bent interested the King. Dr. William Harvey, discoverer of the circulation of the blood, was one who received the King's bounty in this way. He was appointed tutor to the little Princes as an appreciation of his work, and allowed to use the royal deer for his experiments.

Few but the professional courtier and the place-seeker frequented Whitehall—many people, frightened off by the Catholic atmosphere surrounding the Queen, looked upon the Court as the seat of iniquity, and the growing list of converts won by the priests gave them ample cause for reflection. Somerset House, where a large chapel had been built, was the gathering place of the fashionable. But to the Puritan Londoner it was the gateway to Hell, and there is no mention of any of the ladies of Claydon ever attending at Court, where the Catholic prominence must have been anathema to them.

The gaiety surrounding the Queen was the only light-hearted amusement to be found in Whitehall. Generally a sober-sided gloom pervaded the place and it was to escape this restraint that the younger courtiers looked elsewhere for their pleasures.

Seventeenth-century London had an unenviable reputation for vice—the low haunts along the south bank of the river, the disreputable Paris Gardens at Bankside, described as 'a foul den rather than a fair garden', were a terrible lure for the unwary.

Several attempts had been made to clean up the city, but all in vain. In 1614 even the Lord Mayor 'had informed himself by means of spies, of many lewd houses, and had gone himself disguised to divers of them, and finding these nurseries of villany, had punished them according to their deserts, some by carting and whipping, and many by banishment'.

The ale-houses of the day often had a plot of land attached to them for playing bowls, or, as in the case of the famous Bear Inn at the foot of London Bridge, there was an archery green ready for practice. The Bear was one of the best-known inns in London, renowned for its fare—'I stuffed myself with food and tipple till the hoops were ready to burst', described one. Here, too, was the landing-stage for the boat-trip to Greenwich and Gravesend—and for this reason the Bear had the envied and unique authority to leave open their back door for travellers to use.

For the rich and fashionable there was the newly opened Hyde Park, where horse-racing was the popular sport. St. James's Park, with its mulberry trees and pleasant walks, was also a haunt of the better-off until Charles, disgusted by the licence that was displayed there by day and by night, closed the place.

At Piccadilly flourished what Clarendon called 'a fair house for entertainment and gaming, with handsome gravel walks with Shade, and where were an upper and lower bowling-green, whither very many of the nobility and gentry of the best quality resorted both for exercise and conversation'. Amongst the Claydon letters is a small playing card on which is written, in Ralph's hand: 'Measurements of the Billiard Board at Pickadillie', which then gives details of the dimensions of the table, which were very much the same as today, adding: 'There are noe Boxes on the Edges or at the Corners, but the Edges are 2 inches and a halfe deepe within. . . . The Bottom of the Board is layed cross and there are 6 legges to it.' There were other similar resorts, and many fine mansions had been converted to become bowling-alleys and gaming-houses.

Besides these gentlemanly recreations there were the more vulgar and incredibly cruel public spectacles of bull- and bear-baiting. Southwark seems to have been a centre for this kind of sport; here were 'two Beare gardens . . . wherein he kept Beares, Buls and other beastes to be bayted. As also Mastives in severall kennels, nourished to baite them.' Supported too were the by now well-established theatres and playhouses.

King James and his Queen had given royal patronage to the players who performed before them, ensuring they were well clothed and taking an interest in the tours they made outside London. These provincial tours were frequent in summer, for, by law, no gathering was allowed in the capital when the plague was rife and deaths in each week exceeded forty. The principle of royal licences was continued under Charles. Two companies, called the King's Men and Her Majesty's Servants, after their respective patrons, performed before the Court, and when not acting there they played at one of the six theatres in London.

The theatres were the object of much Puritan antagonism. Royal patronage of these 'ancient Devil's Chapels', as Prynne put it, was the theme of his pamphlet *Historio Mastrix*, published in 1632, which cost the author the loss of his ears and a very heavy fine. Particularly virulent was Prynne's attack on the temerity of a French company brazen enough to introduce a woman on to the stage; an incident described by another authority as 'giving just offence to al virtuous and well-disposed persons in this town. . . . Glad I am to say they were hissed, hooted and pippin-pelted from the stage.'

In a straggling city of close on a quarter of a million inhabitants, with narrow alleys and poorly lit streets, crime was inevitable, and crime there was in plenty. Law-keeping was not helped by the continuance of the ancient privilege of sanctuary; this had originally applied only to refuge of the criminal in a church, but usage had altered it to include certain areas of the City as well. Only debtors could claim the immunity of sanctuary, felons and traitors could still be taken in these districts, and it was under guise of this pretence that many a bailiff's man forced entry only to provoke cries of 'Arrest, Arrest' when he was discovered. In the event only a hurried exit could save him from the loss of his ears, or worse.

The narrow streets in the worst quarters of the town were hotbeds of crime of all sorts. The watchmen armed with bells rang them as they made their rounds and so announced their coming to every criminal in the path. Few were captured, but those that were suffered terrible punishment—the felon was hanged, those who refused to plead were pressed to death.

In general the streets were cobbled, though some of the main thoroughfares were paved with flat stones, and the meaner alleys were of bare mud. There were no pavements and no semblance of drainage; refuse was cast out into the streets, where the kites and crows scavenged as they liked. Masterless dogs roamed the streets by the hundred, and filthy urchins romped in the muck. By Act of Parliament, however, no stable nor dove-cot could be paved—this so that the saltpetre-men could collect the dropping-impregnated earth, which was used for gunpowder for the royal ordnance.

London was the largest port in the kingdom—ocean-going ships could berth as far upstream as London Bridge. Through the hands of the merchants flowed goods from all points of the known world; from the Mediterranean came silks and indigo, from the West Indies tobacco, from the East Indies and China spices and chintz. This was in addition to the internal traffic from the country: coals from Newcastle, corn and meat from the Thames Valley, fruit and wool from Sussex, silver from Wales. Away from London sailed the emigrants—the colonists to New England, or Virginia, or Barbados. In 1635 alone over 100 ships left the port of London for the New World—sixty-nine of them to New England. London was indeed the capital and hub of the kingdom.

But of even more importance to the Londoner than this commerce was the plague, which annually swept his city. It usually started in the suburbs and East End, where the insanitary conditions provided an ideally favourable breeding ground for all infection. The mean, overhanging wooden houses and the airless alleys were a constant source of epidemic; the unrestricted travel to and from foreign countries, the total absence of any sanitation, and the popular ignorance of the most elementary aspects of hygiene, made London a city to be dreaded during the warmer parts of the year. Each summer the poorer classes were left to their fate, while those richer citizens who had anywhere else to go deserted the city. Many of these, who had not made prior arrangements, found themselves caught by the watch and refused entry to villages, and in the worst plague years it was not unusual to see wealthy citizens who had died on the road, their pockets stuffed with money.

Ralph and Sir Edmund seem habitually to have gone to Hampstead, or to Gorhambury, where their great friend Lady Sussex kept open house through the summer. Their letters are full of references to the plague—hardly a year is free of an outbreak, although the four great plagues of the seventeenth century were unquestionably the worst. In 1625, the year of King Charles's accession, there was enormous toll and even the coronation had to be postponed.

That year the plague started in April, but, despite a very cold May, by the end of June thirty-two parishes were affected and over 250 deaths recorded each week. Parliament sittings were completely disorganized. One Member excused his absence from an important debate because his shoemaker had fallen dead while putting on his boots. So severe was the epidemic that in July the House was forced to sit at Oxford, where the students were dismissed to make room. By the end of the outbreak over 35,000 persons had died in London alone.

Elaborate precautions to prevent the disease spreading were put in hand once the plague had struck. Though probably of little real value, they at least hampered the spread of panic and enabled some sort of discipline to be maintained. The most important task was that of the examiners, who were appointed in every parish—it was their duty to report any case of sickness. As soon as the report came in, two watchmen were posted to prevent access to the infected house. Anyone in contact with the sick or the dead had to carry a red staff —to warn passers-by to give them a wide berth. Infected houses were marked with a large red cross, streets were cleaned, the dogs killed, bonfires lit at street corners, anyone handling the dead did so under a smoke-screen of tobacco—the only fumigant known—and the clothing and bedding of the deceased was thoroughly 'aired with Fire' before being used again.

The City Government was kept active as long as possible, and the orphans or homeless properly cared for. But it was a shameful fact that in all the great plagues many of the aldermen, the common councilmen, the clergy and, above all, the physicians ran away at the first outbreak; the clergy to look after their flock and the doctors to care for their patients who had already fled—or so they said.

Constables were provided to enforce the decrees, and rakers of filth instructed daily to take away the muck from each house—they gave notice of their approach by blowing a horn. All public places were closed down, the beggars dispersed and every ale-house and inn ordered to be shut at nine o'clock.

These precautions were very necessary, for there was no cure. 'Remedies' were of all sorts, some considered 'Infallible' including purges, clysters, poultices and blisters, and the drugs recommended vary from Venice treacle and angelica root to dragon water and the seeds of burr. In face of the unknown fear of the plague, superstition, never far from the surface, flourished, and quacks drove a booming trade in 'plague water' and amulets.

During plague time all work ceased; ships lay still loaded in the port, goods remained unsold in the shops. Only the most generous gifts from the City and the King kept the people from starving. Each week Charles gave £1,000, the City a further £600 and lesser gifts from the Archbishop of Canterbury and others helped fill the coffers—this kept London above starvation level, but only just.

G

London was ruled by the immensely powerful and rich City Companies, and no scheme needing financial support could prosper without their backing. They had a hand, direct or indirect, in many ventures; some were successful, some were partly so and some were downright disastrous. One of the latter was the fenland project.

There had been several previous attempts to drain the fens. For the most part these were undertaken by 'mountebank engineers, idle practitioners, and slothful impatient slubberers'. But this time the effort was better organized and a company was floated in the name of the Earl of Bedford.

In common with several other gentlemen out for a quick profit, Sir Edmund had invested in the scheme. He had even persuaded the cautious Ralph to contribute. 'I have sent down £600 to stoare the fenns, in hopes of a good return', he writes. 'I will provide to make good your part of the bargaine in your absence. I am confident you will have a good bargaine of it, but it will cost you more than I believe you expected.'

Under Vermuyden's guidance the work started. At first all went well, but the task proved more difficult than they had anticipated. The fenmen, traditional anglers and fowlers, and described as an 'almost barbarous sort of lazy and beggarly people', objected strongly to the invasion of their privacy and the loss of their livelihood. The works were broken, the workmen stoned and generally life made miserable for the unfortunate engineers. Flooding took place and much of the hard-won land was once more under water. At the end of three years over £100,000 had been spent and there was nothing to show for it. Complaints rose on all sides, and the King was forced to set up a Board of Commissioners to investigate —they imposed on all shareholders a tax to levy money to complete the scheme. Before their efforts could be concluded, the King himself stepped in and took over the whole project, but even this intervention had no effect, and gradually the work dwindled until the whole matter fell into abeyance.

Sir Edmund and Ralph had gone into the scheme in partnership with Nat Hobart, 'Sweet Nat', as he is often called in the letters, a close friend and at that time a hardworking and impecunious young lawyer in London. When the tax was imposed on the shareholders both Sir Edmund and his son managed to find the money somehow, but the unfortunate Nat could not pay and, closely pursued by the tax-collectors, he fled into hiding, sometimes in the study under the Knight-Marshal's roof. Sir Edmund's help was sought by the young man's father-in-law, Sir John Leeke, who was desperately worried about his son-in-law and his young wife and explained that young Nat was 'loath to be in durance ... the fenns have nere drowned him: give yor ayd, yor cowncell to that Honest sweet man that he may looke uppon poore Nann and his pretty Babes. you have bine a father to all mine. be so still.' All eventually ended well and, apart from losing the money he had originally invested, Nat was none the worse and was able to pursue his legal career safe from 'the fowlers that lay lime for him', as his father-in-law put it.

Tobacco was another product in which Sir Edmund had an interest. By this time it was in common use both for pleasure and, more important, as a fumigant. They had great respect for it in those days if the following can be believed:

'If moderately and seasonably taken 'tis good for many Things; it helps Digestion, taken a-while after Meat; a leaf or two being steeped o'er Night in a little white-wine is a Vomit that never fails in its Operations; ... The smoke of it is one of the wholesomest scents that is, against all contagious Airs, for it o'ermasters all other smells. ... It cannot endure a Spider or a Flea, with such like Vermin, and if your Hawk be troubled with any such being blown into his feathers, it frees him; it is good to fortify and to preserve the sight, the smoke being let in round about the Balls of the Eyes once a week; ... being taken backward 'tis excellent good against the Cholic, and taken into the stomach it will heat and cleanse it.'

Sir Edmund's patent was for 'garblinge' [inspecting] tobacco 'within the realmes of England and Wales, and the towne of Berwicke with an allowance of fower pence in the pound'. He had gone into this venture with Lord Goring, and it was really beginning to look promising when the Lord Treasurer found it expedient to place a tax upon it. Sir Edmund was forced to sell out his portion—and, of course, managed to secure only a purely nominal price. This was typical of the experience of many who went into financial ventures of a similar sort.

Opposition to the King was building up. The petty, vexatious monopolies Charles imposed affected everyone in the land—and in many ways the poorer classes were hardest hit. The impositions were described as being like the frogs of Egypt, and restrictions covered such minute and diverse practices as the gauging of red herrings, the sealing of linen cloths and the collecting of rags, while the vintners were even prohibited from dressing meat in their own houses without licence. One authority said: 'they have gotten possession of our dwellings, and we have scarce a room free from them. They sup in our cup. They dip in our dish. They sit by our fire. We find them in the dye-vat, wash-bowl, and powdering tub. They share with the butler in his box. They have marked and sealed us from head to foot. They will not bate us a pin. We may not buy our own clothes without brokage'—there were few in the country who could find fault with this.

The unruliest section of the community was the apprentices. Always ready to revolt to defend their real or supposed rights, for 300 years they were a constant threat to law and order in the City. In James's time the worst commotion occurred when an apprentice espied the hated Gondomar, the Spanish ambassador, being borne down Fleet Street in his chair. 'There goes the devil in his dung-cart,' he shouted—the Spaniards replied and a fight ensued, one of them being knocked down. The King could not allow this affront to the Spaniard, so he ordered the offenders to be punished. This was too much, and the apprentices rose, 300 of them—only after much difficulty was the revolt put down.

With dissension, religious and secular, the years of Charles I's reign were the heyday of 'prentice revolts. Ready either to march on Lambeth Palace and the abhorrent Laud, or to picket Parliament, the young trouble-makers were of great value to the King's opponents. However, in 1642, when chaos and rumour reigned in London as Charles was hourly expected, they supported the Royalists —such was their fickle loyalty.

Another source of ready manpower was the Trained Bands. This citizen's army, composed of shopkeepers, tapsters and the like, was a handy reserve in case of trouble. With their arms held centrally in magazines, they exercised on the squares and open spaces on the outskirts of the city. Their value was limited outside their own boundaries, but, when thoroughly drilled by Swedish officers as they were in the Civil War, they became a force to be reckoned with—nearly 8,000 strong. In peace-time the mere threat of calling out the Trained Bands was usually enough to get a crowd to disperse, but as the crisis grew they found their sympathies lay all too often with those they were to disperse—usually their own neighbours. When politics assumed a growing importance, in the years immediately before the Civil War, Parliament was fortunate in being able to rely on the support of the Trained Bands. However, Charles had at his command the Westminister contingent, drawn largely from his own vast staff at Whitehall whose loyalty was unquestioned, and, situated as they were, on several occasions they were called out to quell a riot of the 'prentices, or the mariners, another umbrageous lot.

Within the City itself all the shops of one kind were obliged to be in the same quarter—all the goldsmiths in Cheapside, etc. As time passed, however, more and more traders came to ignore the order, and during the scare resulting from the loss of the Queen's jewellery in 1631 it was discovered how wholesale had been the neglect of this command. Decree followed decree ordering them back, but nobody paid any attention. By now it was too late to return without hardship and the King's attempts achieved nothing but unpopularity. The final break with the old order was made after the Great Fire when shopkeepers put up temporary stalls elsewhere, found them profitable and stayed.

Other attempts by the King to meddle in City affairs were as unpopular. He forbade the Weavers' Company to admit any but members of the Church of England; and he threatened to debase the coinage when the City did not produce their share of ship-money.

In the early days of his reign Charles could count on the support of the City Companies and the goodwill of the City as a whole. By tradition the Crown put forward selected nominees for many of the principal positions in internal City affairs, and it was the custom for the Recorder of the City of London to be appointed Speaker of the House of Commons. This privileged hold over the City Government was studiously maintained by the King, long after the true feeling in the City had turned against him.

Charles placed complete trust in the City and, faced with an increasingly intransigent Parliament, he became accustomed to rely on the loans they reluctantly provided. Even later, with sublime self-confidence, he continued to depend on the goodwill of the City towards him—ignoring the fact that his own policy of petty impositions and taxes was exasperating the merchants almost beyond control. Further, he had the temerity and foolhardiness to attempt to tax the age-old charters and privileges of the City Companies themselves.

Political alienation was slow to build up. Only towards the end did the City Government come out in blatant opposition to their King. But even when it became apparent that Charles was turning the merchants against him, he made no attempt to mollify those he had offended, and more outrageous than ever were the demands made on the now not so willing City.

Another cause of grievance was the privilege enjoyed by certain classes of not paying taxes or their City charges—this particularly applied to the barristers who lived in the Inns of Court and the residents in the precincts of Blackfriars and Whitefriars. One complaint, at least, Charles could in no way be blamed for: the chimney-sweeps claimed that householders were neglecting to have their chimneys swept regularly, with the resulting 'great danger of fire, and the starvation of our kind'—200 in number.

Rents were of the order of £30 a year—more, of course, in the better quarters of the capital, such as Cheapside and Ludgate Hill. The fashionable part of the town was now where Westminister linked with the City north of the Strand—at Drury Lane, Lincoln's Inn Fields and Covent Garden. It was at Covent Garden that Sir Edmund rented two houses, with coach-house and stable attached, in Great Russell Street on the south side of the newly built Piazza, and here the rent was £160 a year.

The state of Covent Garden had evidently changed little since the turn of the century, for the new owner stipulated that he re-served the right to give up his lease with six months' notice if he were not able to live there 'with any convenyency'. There was a form of open drain or gutter which ran from the market through the Strand right against Durham House, once the residence of Sir Walter Raleigh, but otherwise there was no method of clearing rubbish and the refuse continued to accumulate in the streets in ever-larger and more evil-smelling heaps.

Water was fetched from the Walbrook, the Fleet and the many springs and wells along the Strand and elsewhere; also from the New River, which was over thirty-eight miles long and had been completed in King James's reign. The Thames, however, dominated the life of the capital. In its tidal waters could be caught 'fat and sweet salmons' as well as many other fish. The river was always liable to flood during high spring tides and on several occasions the kitchens of Whitehall Palace had to be abandoned in a hurry.

River transport was widely used, but the litter was the customary mode of getting about, and the rivalry between the watermen and their competitors was bitter. Rudimentary coaches or waggons soon after made their appearance—they had no springs and 'men and women are so tossed, tumbled, jumbled, and rumbled', complained one victim. The hackney was there too, as indeed was the sedan-chair—introduced in 1634. Innovation was as fiercely contested then as ever, and one of the chief arguments against the growing use of the coaches for long journeys was that so many 'cloth-workers, drapers, tailors, saddlers, tanners, carriers, shoe-makers, spurriers, lorimers, and felt-makers' were thrown out of employ. Formerly they were 'full of work, got money, lived handsomely, and helped, with their families, to consume the provisions and manufactures of the kingdom: but by means of these coaches these trades, besides many others depending upon them are become almost useless'—such was the cry.

So great was the number of carts in the City that strict regulations were laid down limiting their standings, their number and even the traffic instructions as to where in the narrow streets two carts could pass.

Public hackneys made their first appearance in London in 1625, when a stand was established at the Maypole in the Strand—prior to this they could be hired only privately. In 1636, however, under the pretence that 'the King and his dearest consort the Queen, the nobility, and others of place and degree were disturbed in their passage, that the pavement was destroyed, and the streets pestered by the number of coaches for hire', the King allowed hackneys to take only those wanting to go three miles out of town. At the same time he also declared that every proprietor should always have ready four able horses for the Royal service if required. Later, by way of further limiting their number, the King allowed licences to only fifty persons, each for twelve horses, and over this scheme he placed the Master of the Horse, then the Marquis of Hamilton.

This was another unsuccessful venture Sir Edmund dabbled in. His share of the patent was a constant source of annoyance and aggravation to him, for the coachmen, not unnaturally disgusted with the King's restriction, did their best to make difficulties at every turn.

After over four years of feuding and unsatisfactory service it was decided that a Royal Proclamation was the only thing that would bring the hackney-men to their senses. They were prepared to accept this, but by then any proclamation from the throne was inadvisable, and this, like so many of Sir Edmund's projects and schemes, came to nothing.

Though gullible and ignorant, the Londoner was better in this respect than his fellow countryman. The busy merchant and shop-keeper had no time for the myriad superstitions that bewitched the country-dweller. Nevertheless, portents and omens were of impor-tance, everyone had their own lucky and unlucky days, and it was astonishing what dreadful forebodings could be read into the light of a candle or the flicker of the fire.

Witches and second-sight were widely believed in, and one Ellen Evans had the power to summon the Queen of the Pygmies at will; while Sir Robert Holborn was unlucky in that he 'formerly had the sight and conference with Uriel and Raphael, but lost them both by carelessness'.

But, powerful though this kind of superstition was, religious prejudice was the most omnipresent emotion. The Elizabethan had a wholesome fear of Roman Catholicism, but that was as nothing to what was felt by the majority of Londoners in Stuart times; their hatred of all things Papist was fed by the all too common spectacle of impoverished refugees from the Continent—Huguenots and those from the Palatinate driven out by the Inquisition wolves.

Extremists went too far the other way as well: sports were denounced as irreverent, the study of Latin and Greek was objected to as 'encouraging idolatry and Pagan superstition'—one critic dis-approved of Christmas festivities and changed the name of Christmas pie to mince pie. Even accidents were used as proof of heavenly intervention against the Papists, and the disaster known as the 'Fatal Vespers' was pointed out for the next forty years as an undoubted sign of disapproval from above. In this calamity an impromptu chamber used as a chapel next door to the French ambassador's house suddenly gave way, precipitating into the room below most of the congregation of 300. Of these some ninety-five died and many more were badly injured; but the chronicler with great glee points out that there was no explanation for the sudden collapse of the floor, that the beams were all sound and that only Divine providence could be responsible.

Such was the religious feeling in the London of the first half of the seventeenth century. Prejudiced, ignorant and superstitious, his town a warren of narrow streets begrimed with filth, the Londoner watched the crisis grow around him. Although proud of his connection with Court and King, and proud too of the central place his city held in the government and commerce of the kingdom, as soon as he felt his own liberties oppressed in any way no silly sentiment affected his judgements. Soon the loyalty of London was the loyalty of a tradition and a heritage, not the loyalty of affection. And, when the King consorted with the dreaded Spaniard and tolerated Catholics in his immediate circle, even this loyalty faded and died. It was the knowledge of certain support from this quarter that did so much to encourage Charles's enemies.

VI

Friends and the Family

'Friends, kindred, days,
Estate, good fame,'
EMERSON

S IR EDMUND'S Irish friends were great correspondents. Of
these, Lady Barrymore, daughter of the 'Greate Earl of Corke',
and her husband were quite frequent visitors to England—the
former making an annual pilgrimage to take the waters at Bath.
The Leekes were another family with close connections to the
Verneys. Sir John Leeke had married Sir Edmund's half-sister, and
rented a house on the Barrymore estate where he farmed the park.
Doll Leeke, the youngest of his several daughters, helped Lady
Verney to run the house and family at Claydon.

These connections were a considerable help over the projected
purchase of lands in Ireland—yet another of Sir Edmund's financial
schemes.

The practice of laying illegal claim to land had been common in
Ireland before Wentworth started his career of 'Thorough'. As
soon as he came to power, however, all that stopped. The vast
underdeveloped tracts of land that had been granted to various
nobles were now taken back by the King, and settlers brought over
to manage them properly. It was some of this newly released land

that Sir Edmund was interested in, chiefly in Connaught. Many of
his friends in Ireland advised him to buy, Sir John Leeke amongst
them: 'Now that the Deputie hath browght into the King's power
3 Counties and they have submitted themselves to the King's
mercy', he writes, 'it is conceyved the Kinge will take the fowerth
of each countie. . . . A great plantation wilbe and excelent lande. . . .
Be quicke for many gape after this plantation', and he adds as a
postscript: 'If you may w^(th)out hurte to y^rselfe speake a good worde
for me, I shall bless god and you for itt. I have littell hope of the
sowre Deputie'—such was the unpopularity the dour Yorkshire-
man had earned for himself by his iron rule.

On another occasion some land came up for sale 100 miles
north of Dublin, but at a considerable price, and Sir Edmund is
advised:

'By taking upp moneyes, . . . and laying them out on purchases
here, you might with advantage discharge interest, and after 20
years clearly gaine the lands purchased . . . other hazards in regarde
of payments from tenants, there is not in purchasing there, rather
in other parts of the kingdom; but in troublous tymes whither they
be occasioned by intestine rebellion or forreyne invasion, this parte
of the kingdome lyes farther from being sheltered by the wings of
the State then peradventure some others doe.'

However, these schemes came to nothing—which was perhaps
as well in view of the catastrophe which later struck that country.

Sir Edmund, and later Ralph, are for ever being asked to do small
things for their Irish friends—to put in a good word for some
relation at Court, to help over a knighthood for a future son-in-law
of the Leekes' and even to assist Lady Barrymore find a 'mounsher'
as tutor for her son. This last commission must have been particularly difficult, as it appears her Ladyship's standards were
high:

'Noble Sarvant', she begins, and then goes on to say she has had
a 'distillation out of my head, which is fallen into my jaws and teeth',
which has prevented her from writing before, 'to aske the favour to
finde a good tuttor for my young master. I would have him a
mounsher, one that might teach him to right and good garbe, and
that might still be with him when I send him to scoule. I would not
have him too ould nor too young, but one of a verey temprate
carrege. For his wages I refer it holey to him for what he agrees to I

will God willing see payed. I like him so well for a governer for myselfe that I humbly desier hee may chuse one for my mad boy; and
that he may com over with as much speede as may bee, for hee be
spoyld for want of one.'

Just in case Sir Edmund might forget this particular duty Sir
John Leeke backs it with a letter: 'Lady Barrymore hopes you will
favour her so much as to send her a cyvill monsiere to breed her
son.' Unfortunately, nothing more is heard of the 'mounsher', nor
if he was 'cyvill' enough.

Sir John Leeke had a large family, and the marrying off of his
many daughters seems to have been a bit of a problem. Of the five,
in the end only Doll remained single. The youngest of all, Bidde,
appears to have been very happily married, initially, at any rate, if
one can tell from her father's effusive letter: 'God all powefull hath
effected this match, and I dowght not but that arme will still and
ever cover and bless them, for never man I beleeve cann more truly
love then he.' Unhappily, Bidde's husband died soon after, and
swiftly the father is once again negotiating for a suitable marriage
for his daughter. One possible candidate seemed admirable in
every way, except that he was not nobly born, and Sir John considered it essential that before the marriage he should be knighted
—another task for the long-suffering Knight-Marshal:

'Truly I finde Bidde's affection well enowgh to the mann were
itt nott that hir place must be in the fase of all the country and I
beleeve if any thinge hinder itt that wilbe the rubbe, for wee stand
heere more uppon place then in England heere are mayny startupps
that wealth doth advance from baseness to prferrment.'

One of Sir John's daughters, however, does not seem to have
been so lucky in her choice of husbands and is married to a drunken
sot; bewailing her fate, he says: 'My pretious Katherine is somewhat
decayed from the sweetest face I ever saw (and surely I have seene
good ones). She is keapte and longe hath bine by the foulest Churle
in the world; he hath only one vertu that he seldom cometh sober
to bedd.'

Even when Ralph has come out against the King the correspondence never flags, although Lady Barrymore now addresses
him as 'Noble Enemy'.

There is a curious letter written in December 1640 from Sir

John Leeke to Sir Edmund when Wentworth was about to depart
for good as Lord Deputy. In this he suggests that Sir Edmund should
be the latter's successor:

'I writ this purposely to give you to understand of the petition
and remonstances our Lower House of Parliament submitted to
the new Deputie, and that they might be suffered to go into England
a selected committee to make good the grievances for we groan
insufferably under them. . . . We hear from good mouths that our
Lord President must be removed, for which I am sorry heartily,
for he is and always hath been my good and noble friend, yet if it
please his Majesty to think him fitt for other employment, I then
wish with all my hart I had as good a friend in his place. It is worth
£1,000 per annum from the King, a troop of 50 horse and a company
of foot, with some other duties and perquisites it may be worth
£2,500 per annum. I could wish you had it, if you would be content
to part from the eyes of your master, or think this a better place
than the marshal's; it is a thriving place, for our noble president doth
thrive exceeding much. But if you shall not hold this a place for your
content, then put to all your friends and power for honest Barrymore. Lastly from myself I have so much ambition that I do desire
you were the Deputy. Examples have been that in Queen Elizabeth's time some of your rank and some of meaner condition as
Sydney, Fitzwilliam, Parrott, Chichester, after a lord, and this
Wandesford lately dead. Let Sir Ed. Verney have some ambition to
be our governour or our kingdom's governour. I pray take this
close to you as things not impossible.'

Nothing ever came of this, and no more is ever heard about the
proposal from any other source. It is probable that the imaginings
of Sir John got the better of him, and perhaps hopes of his own
advancement were not all that far from his thoughts.

But the best-liked and most frequent Irish visitor to Claydon was
young James Dillon, eldest son of Lord Roscommon, and Ralph's
contemporary at Oxford. This brilliant young man was early picked
out as exceptional, and no less a person than Archbishop Ussher
recommended him as a 'jewel of price' to the Master of Essex, who
himself referred to Dillon as a 'young man of pregnant parts'.

An amusing person and full of fun, James was continually with
the Verneys while still at Oxford and after. He was always a welcome
visitor at Claydon, not the least to young Doll Leeke, with whom

he seems to have kept up a running flirtation for many years, often accompanying his letters with little gifts to his 'brother Doll'.

Apart from Doll Leeke, the Irishman had a sincere affection for Ralph's wife, Mary; then only seventeen, although mother of a baby born in 1634, to whom James was godfather. Most of his letters at some stage refer to 'the tow sweet soules'. On one occasion Mary and her young cousin sent a folded sheet of blank paper enclosed in one of Ralph's letters, writing on it: 'Open not this letter till you all meet' and 'Doe us the favor not to censur our lines.' James, however, was well able to counter this, and replying to Ralph he says:

'I have here enclosed the letter from the tow soules that give life to the company wherein they are. Reade it and see what it was they were haching when you writt your last to me, but for the world betray not any secret in it. Upon Wednesday next with God's leave you shall have me there, till then farewell . . . tell the tow faire ones from me that I am ashamed to see a letter from them tow wherein there is not one modest word.'

James's letters are full of gallantries. One summer he sends 'five little combes . . . whereof there are three intended for my Lady Mother, tow for my daughter Verney, and my neice Leeke. For these tow there are tow thimbles that the one should not hurt a fine finger by the making of my handkerchiefs, nor the other receive a prick in working of my Lady's buttons.' When Ralph's mother produces another child in 1633 James sends his congratulations and asks to be remembered to 'the Ladie Verney the Elder, the yonger, the Lady Mairasse of Abingdon [Mary, Ralph's wife], and to the prettie plumpe rogue, my brother.' He signs himself 'Gillian Bogland' on this occasion. Faced with his irrespressible gaiety, even the serious and rather sober-sided Ralph entered into the general spirit of light-heartedness.

In Ireland, evidently, James Dillon's 'pregnant parts' found favour in high quarters, for in the latter half of 1633 he is attached to the Lord Deptuy's staff and accompanied his master wherever he went.

A year later there is an interchange of portraits between the two. Ralph had his own picture by Jansen copied to send to his friend. 'I have now sat three times for my picture,' he writes in February, 'as soon as it is finished I would willingly send it to you, but I must first be informed by what way, for such a rare jewell deserves to be carried with much care; my hart, farewell.' In return Dillon sent his own, also by Jansen, but now missing.

The tenderness of James's messages to Doll Leeke continued unabated through the years; therefore, Ralph was rather taken aback to hear rumours of his friend's marriage and writes to ask if they are true. In reply Dillon hotly denies any such idea:

'I was towards noe marriadge nor crossed in any, nor by any bodie that came out of England. My Lord Deputie goes shortly into England & it may be then a good time for my grandfather then to order things concerning his business. I presume I shall over with him, & give you an account of all that may be looked for from hence. I am full of many things.'

Ralph is obviously relieved for he writes:

'I am glad to heare that those reports concerninge your marrage are untrue. I hope the first inventors of them will suffer by the ill tongues of others, as you did by thers. If my Lord Deputies cominge into England may bee a cause to draw you hither, the sooner hee comes the welcomer hee shall bee to mee, though I confesse I know but few that are fond of his presence. . . . I am now going to meete some of my neighbours a Duck Huntinge, I am told they have exelent Doggs. therefore excuse my haste.'

But Dillon had been deceiving Ralph, and soon after he is married to Lord Wentworth's sister. It is an embarrassing position, but after an initial asperity between the two the situation clarifies and they are friends as before, except that now poor Doll gets but a passing mention as 'my gossip'. Only a few more, rather awkward, visits to Claydon took place.

James's wedding was one of the last occasions on which the two friends met. Inevitably their ways drifted apart as Dillon became more and more preoccupied with the affairs of his master—and soon after the correspondence ceases altogether. The next time we meet the dashing Irishman is in 1642 when Mun runs into him in Dublin, and he asks to be remembered to Ralph. Later that year Dillon's father died and he became Earl of Roscommon. With that, all reference to James vanishes from the letters until, in 1647, both he and Ralph found themselves fugitives in France together; even then they do not meet, but in a letter it says: 'Sir, if you have not hard itt, the Earle of Roscommon is dead, whoe visitinge some of his frends in a compliment avoyded the light of a candell, ran hastily to the chamber door, and fell downe a greate paire of staires, which caused his death.'

The major doubt in his life began now to press upon Ralph. Brought up as he had been in an almost Puritan atmosphere, both at Oxford and at home, it was not unnatural that his leanings should be towards that growing circle of men who began to question the wisdom of the King's policy. Although not yet a Member of Parliament, his day-to-day contact through county affairs with the great men of the shire, so many of whom had the same political feeling as he, set him to wonder on his own place in the Constitutional struggle which was so clearly drawing near. Ralph was rarely in London, but he had many friends near the heart of affairs and was able to keep in touch with feeling in the capital. Sir Edmund at this time was occasionally at Claydon and his concern communicated itself to his son. But, unfettered by the bonds of loyalty engendered by nearly twenty-five years' personal service to his King, Ralph could do as he chose, and joined the ever-growing opposition—although not until 1640 did he actually take his seat in the Commons.

His wife had produced two fine children for Ralph. Two years after their marriage they had lost a child and the following year another; however, in 1634 Mary was safely delivered of a baby, a daughter, despite old Crowther's prayers for a 'lusty heyre'—she was called Anna Maria, and James Dillon was godfather. Immediately Dame Margaret, her grandmother, took her under her loving care and 'Mrs. Anna Maria', as James referred to her, soon became a great favourite.

Tragedy struck when the little girl was only four, and in a pathetic letter written at one o'clock in the morning by Sir Edmund to his son, away in London at the time, he says:

'Raphe, yor sweete child is goeing apace to a better woarld; shee has but a short time to staye with uss. I hope you have such a sence of god's blessings to you; as you will not repine att his decrees; make all convenient haste to yor good wife who wants yor comfort; yet come not too faste for that maye heate your bludd; and that maye give an end to all our comforts; as ever I shall intreat any thing from you take care of yor selfe for this is a dangerous yeare for Heats and coalds; the god of Heaven Bless you.'

Lady Sussex, after Van Dyck
This is believed to be a copy of the portrait mentioned in the text,
and now in the possession of the Marquis of Exeter.
Reproduced by courtesy of the Marquis of Exeter

Lady Margaret Verney, the wife of the Standard Bearer
ARTIST UNKNOWN

She was buried three days later. Even the normally callous and indifferent Henry had a soft spot in his heart for little Anna Maria, and Ralph writes to him: 'You shall herewithal receive a ringe filled with my gerle's haire; she was fond of you, and you loved her therefore I now send you this to keepe for her sake.'

Dame Margaret was a stern task-master, but her children and grandchildren were devoted to her and she lived to see little Edmund, Ralph's son, growing up. This little boy had been left in the care of old Lady Denton at Hillesden. He was a great favourite, and she evidently had high hopes of him, for she had previously written to Sir Edmund that his 'grandson is very wel, and I will pray that he maye prove as onest and true harted a man to his frends as you have byne to your frendss'. In 1639 the child was sent to join his parents in London, but his behaviour there was not all that was expected, for he was found 'shy and rustic'. The old lady comes quickly to his defence:

'I heare he is disliked, he is so strange. Sonn, you did see he was not soe, nor is not soe, I pray let time be given him until he be a quanted, and he must be woone with fair menes. Let me begge of you and his mothar that nobody whip him but Mr. Parrye; yf you doe goe a violent waye with him, you will be the furst that will rue it, for i veryly beleve he will reseve ingery by it, and I pray bare with him the rather.'

Then she goes on:

'Indede, Raphe, he is to younge to be strudgeled in any forsing waye. i had intelygence your father was trobled to see him soe strange. i pray tel frome me, I thought he had had more witt then to thinck a childe of his adge would be a quanted presently. He knowes the childe was feloe good a nofe in my house. i praye shewe him what I have written abought him, and be shore he is not frited by no menes: he is of a gentel swet nature, sone corrected'—the little boy was only three years old at the time.

Mun was evidently on the side of his small namesake and in typical fashion enthuses over the boy's virtue, 'that sweete promising countenance of you pretty sonn is able to inspire even the ignorant with such a prophesying spirit, there's not that lineament either in his face or body, but prognosticates more for itself than we cann doe for it'.

H

The nursery at Claydon was the province of old Nan Fudd. She must have been a formidable old body, highly respected, even feared, by the closer relations, most of whom she had known for as long as they could remember. She was the mainstay of the family and many of their friends while Ralph was in exile, and nearly every relative near and far seems to have passed through old Fudd's hands at some time during those troubled years.

Nursery life of those days seems unbelievably cruel by modern standards. Purgings, sweating-pills and other horrible remedies were constantly being used. There is even a letter from Mun, when he was sojourning at Claydon after leaving Oxford, referring to some medicine for Ralph's eldest child: 'I have carryed his nurse the Rhubarb, and shee promiseth he shall constantly drinke it.'

In the Parliament of 1628 Sir Edmund was returned as one of the two Members for Aylesbury Borough. This meant that he was away from Claydon more frequently and for longer periods, thus the management of the estate almost completely devolved upon the ever-willing Ralph. Rents, greyhounds, the stock, all came his way—as indeed did the affairs of the brothers. The rents are particularly interesting, for many of the fields at Claydon bear the same names to this day. Sir Edmund writes: 'Send to goodman Grace and if hee will give 20 shillings the acre for little Napson, or £5 in grass, let him have it', and again:

'I would take 19 shillings the acre for little Napson, but I think you may gett more for it, nor under 20 shillings for great Napson I will not take. Bid Roades have a care for the timber of the ould barn att the Inn and lett him laye the ould thatch where itt may make muck or els uppon great Napson meadow, if he thinck itt fitt.'

Not even the smallest detail of farm management escapes the distantly vigilant Knight-Marshal:

'I praye call upon Raphele to sell the sheep, he is mad to keepe them soe long. If Lea will deale for the cloase for twelve yeares, I will ditch and quick sett it, and mownd it well, but then hee shall be tied to mayntane itt, soe that his cattle maye not spoyle the quick, or els hee will every yeare carry awaye my hedges and make mee bring new.'

Later:

'Your coach gelding does very well and soe is babington and your little nagge, but your coach mare hath a ring bone on the same legge whereon her spavin is which Nick Aris [a neighbour and knowledgeable horse doctor] thinks to be her greatest greife, he will doe his best to take of both and beginns with her tomorrow morning.'

However, he takes a cynical view of Ralph's competence in handling his precious hounds:

'I am glad you are soe merry with my Hounds, I am contented to reprive them, but it were Alms to hang you, for I knowe you can accuse them only by hearesaye, for you will not take the paines to informe yourself by taking a view of them.'

At another time Ralph is given further instructions:

'I desire my bitch may doe if shee has not already taken the Dogg. that shee should bee sent to Clarendon parke neare Salsbury by some carefull messenger . . . it is for a spectiall Hound that my Lord Chamberlain [Lord Pembroke] has ther to ward her. but lett the messenger bee very carefull that noe dogg kisses her by the waye.'

Only occasionally were father and son together, sometimes in London, sometimes at Bath. There is a rather charming letter from the latter place from Sir Edmund addressed to his 'good daughter Mary', the date is August 1635:

'I cannott prevaile with y^r Husband to leave mee without a quarrell, therefore good heart forgive us boath, since his absence is against boath our wills, hee is every day in the bathe, I praye God it may doe him goode; for my parte, I am suer I find none in it, but since I am come heere, I will try the uttermost of it, that I may not be reproacht att my returne for doeing things by halves; att our first coming the towne was empty, butt now itt is full of very good company, and we pass our time awaye as merrily as paine will give us leave . . . and soe deare heart, fearwell, yor lovinge father and faithfull frend.'

Lady Sussex's innumerable affairs kept Ralph more than busy. She was a prodigious correspondent, and Ralph was far too good-natured not to reply to her almost illegible letters, seeking advice on every conceivable subject. Either Ralph or his father is consulted on anything she did—from arranging her business affairs to ordering curtains, carpets and even gowns; on one occasion Ralph is even asked for his advice about the 'coles' she should get. Attached to one such note is a piece of magnificent sky-blue figured satin, destined as a 'cote to my godsone this Easter'. This is in perfect condition and has lost little of its colour.

Most of her letters start and finish with fulsome praise of Ralph's goodness to her; the spelling is often very original, to say the least, and she has a tiresome habit of writing 'the' for 'they'—but often her gushing letters throw interesting light on the business of the day.

Eleanor Wortley, as she then was, first married Sir Harry Lee, also a close friend of Sir Edmund and living near Claydon. Sir Harry died in 1631 and two years later the widow married the Earl of Sussex, many years older than herself and already somewhat infirm.

'My olde Lorde', as she refers to her husband, led a cloistered existence at his house at Gorhambury, near St. Albans, a 'sade retired life' not at all to his wife's liking. She was godmother to Ralph's son, for whom she is always tendering advice and forecasting the most rosy future. Her chief interest was in politics and after the death of old Sussex she married in quick succession two of the principal figures on the Parliament side.

Lady Sussex had an unmarried daughter, Anne, who was a frequent visitor to Claydon. She had the endearing habit of giving nicknames to her acquaintances, one of whom she unflatteringly calls 'Boutared Eggs'. Suitable 'maches' for the high-spirited Anne were constantly being urged on Ralph and his father: of these 'on of the best maches in inglande that is to be hade', as her mother puts it: 'The estate lies on the edge of Wales, the grandfather was a merchant, and the grandmother a Dutchwoman; they bred the young man up at home, his mother being very tinder of him; his father seems to be a good solede man, very harty for the Parliament. The sone is littell, hath wite enofe, I belife, a littell refining woulde make him very pasable'—but nothing came of this project and Anne did not marry until several years after this.

Her Ladyship's home must have been almost entirely furnished by the products of Ralph's labours on her behalf. 'My thinkes to you for my sattine,' she writes, 'it cam very will; some of it i employ for the backs of chers; the rest i entende for cortines; when the chinse stofes come in, if you see any prity ons remember me i pray you for to or three peses', and again some time later: 'I am very sory i dide not consider of the figerde sattine when i was at chelsey for truly though the prise be unresonable i hade rather give it then by any of the figerde sattines that are to be hade hear; thorty shillinge the yarde the axe, and the color lokes lyke dort to that i have.'

Commissions of all sorts crop up in her letters, and in time the long-suffering Ralph must have become a very proficient buyer. There are a few complaints, however: 'the damaske i have loked on and truly it tis very good and well worth the mony, but the couler i confes doth not ples me for wher i would imploy it for is to made cortines for the rome i entende my crimson fagude [figured] sattin for. and that is so puer a couler that it makes this damaske loke very dede and dole therfor i becech you get the man to take it agane.'

In November 1639 she is persuaded to sit for her portrait—to be painted by Van Dyck. She was unconscionably hard to please, however, and Sir Edmund must have many times regretted asking her. Initially she is very reluctant to have it done at all: 'Your father sended me worde Sr Vandyke will do my pictuer now—i am loth to deny him, but truly it is money ill bestowde'; but later she seems to enjoy making everyone's life a misery over the details of the portrait. Again to Ralph she writes: 'Put Sr Vandyke in remembrance to do my pictuer well. I have some sables with the clasp of them set with dimons—if thos that i am pictuerde in wher don so i think it would look very wel in the pictuer', and later: 'i am glade you have prefalede with Sr Vandike to make my pictuer lener, for truly it was to fat, if he made it farer, it will bee for my credit—i see you will make him trimme it for my advantige every way.' At last the masterpiece is completed, but even when it is too late to have it altered she pesters poor Ralph:

'I am glade you have got hom my pictuer, but i doubt he hath nether made it lener nor farer, but to rich in ihuels [jewels] i am suer, but it tis no great mater for another age to thinke me richer then i was. i see you have imployde on to coppe it, which if you have, i must have that your father hade before, which i wish coulde be mendede in the fase, for it tis very ugly. i becech you see whether that man that copes out Vandicks coulde not mende the fase of that—if he can any way do it, i pray get him and i will pay him for it. it cannot bee worse then it tis—and sende me worde what the man must have for copinge the pictuer, if he do it will, you shall get him to doo another for me. let me know i becech you how much i am your debtor, and whether Vandicke was contente with the fifty ponde.'

The biggest job of all is conveying the precious portrait to Gorhambury. Many methods are proposed. Lady Sussex even suggested using 'the cole wagon' which 'will bee in london this weke', but wisely adds: 'but i doubt he cannot carry the pictuer with the glase', and later: 'I am very glad if a coppell of porters would undertake to bring it done carefully for any reasonable matter, suer that is the sanest way. But if the will not I will send a hors for it with paniers.' When at last it arrives the finished product hardly meets with her approval at all:

'Swite Mr. Verney, the pictuer cam very will, many harty thinkes to you for it. the fram is a littell hurt, the gilt being robbede off. the picture is very ill favourede, makes me quite out of love with myselfe, the face is so bige and so fate that it pleses me not att all. It lokes lyke on of the windes poffinge—but truly I thinke it tis lyke the originale. If ever i com to London before Sr Vandicke goo, i will get him to mende my pictuer, for thow I bee ill favourede i think that makes wors than I am.'

Lady Sussex's affairs, however multitudinous, were considerably more pleasant to deal with than those of Brother Tom. Age seems to have had no mellowing effect on the scapegrace, whose doings were a constant source of concern to Sir Edmund, and to Ralph who was more intimately connected with them.

After his abortive efforts on the Continent, Tom returns to England, only to find that his father has given 'express command' that no one is to lend him money nor to buy anything for him without leave. He is rather hurt and writes his customary letter asking for forgiveness, and 'doth desier', his father when he has read his captain's report out of his 'noble mind will remitt and forgive all my former offenses, and those faults which I have formerly and in such base manner committed against so good a father as you are'. His intentions for the future are 'to beare a noble mind in all my actions, as where before I was ignoble. . . . Let these lines stirr you to have pitty upon mee, that I may receive one smiling and merry countenance from you, which I have formerly seen angry and frowning.'

He signs himself 'your true penitent and obedient sonn till death'.

Evidently Sir Edmund relented, for there is a letter from Tom thanking him and promising his father that he shall never regret this kind act:

'Understand that I am leading a new life, which shall not only yield great comfort to yourself, but be a comfort to all my friendes. Therefore deare father, let mee again upon my bended knees crave att your mercyfull hands pardon and forgiveness for that ill-spent life which I have formerly lead. I doe the rather crave pardon to you in writing, becaus I cannot by word of mouth so freely utter it.'

After this he joins the army of France and soon he is in trouble again. In a short time he is sent back to England on business, but not unnaturally, knowing nothing of the business concerned, Ralph and his father misconstrue this sudden reappearance and a very angry Tom writes:

'I understand that my father and you doe mistrust that I am run away from my Colonel, which is noe small grief to me; becaus I have brought soe many letters from my Collonell to his ffrinds in London, and I hope in God to carry him as good news back. This is the last you shall receive from mee as long as I have being, sinc you have so ill opinion of me. If you are troubled at this letter, I will meete you at another hous to speak with you, becaus I will not come where yu and my father have a being.'

He relents in a few days' time, however, and warns he will 'be with them, by the grace of God, with my best love within a fort-night'.

After another spell in France, during which he incurred more debts, he suddenly writes he is on his way to 'Stockhollam', in Sweden.

Within a month or two he is back in England—fluctuating between London, where he fights a duel, and Claydon, where, if we are to believe him, he leads a miserable existence, 'living like a hermitt or a country fellow'. His suggestions for his own employment follow with bewildering rapidity; one day it is the Palatinate, the next it is New England, or the West Indies or 'some unknown place in the world'. His letters vary between constant assurances of the new life he has now decided to follow and pleas for clothing of all sorts:

'Ther is a sute of cloths come to me, but never a coat with it, it will be very unseemlie for mee to wear my sute, and never a coat but one sorey thing which I bought about two months agoe, att a broker's, and some say as it is your old coat that you gave to your man, and I confess that it is very like yours, and as farr as I know it was yours; therefore I pray doe but judg of the goodness of it.'

Exasperated by the supposedly callous lack of response to his many requests shown by Ralph and his father, who refused to see him, Tom threatens suicide: 'Rather than lead this hellish life, I will take a rope and make an end of myself, and then neither father, mother, brother, nor sister, nor any friends els shall take any more care of me.' Everyone in the area had been warned of Tom's ways and would lend him nothing, not even a horse which he was quite capable of selling. This 'is extremity itself and this is not the way to make mee lead a reformed life', he bursts out; and again after more 'aggravations': 'Idleness puts many wicked thoughts in one's head. But perhaps you may object that I may read, or walk up to Mr. Aris [the Rector] sometimes and conferre with him, or walk in att one doore and out att the other.'

As the errant had such a healthy fear of his father, it is poor Ralph that receives the brunt of these explosions, and Tom seems to expect his brother to devote much of his time to his well-being: 'There is no excuse for you not doing as I ask; my father is busy, but for you, you should send every day unto the docks enquiring after a shipp for me.' He does, however, have the good grace to apologize for this and other ingratitudes.

Complaints of Tom's behaviour were not confined to those at Claydon. Even Lady Denton, a very forbearing old lady, writes to Ralph: 'Your Brother Tom . . . the delaye of the jurny hathe bred such a dele of reportes that hath come to his years i, not daringe to crose him that is gron a most unsofferable creture.' Tom's final departure for the 'Barbathos' must have been accompanied by great relief all round, though he evidently did not leave without another brief reversion to his normal ways. Ralph writes to his brother Henry telling him of Tom's having left 'not at all amended, for about three days before hee went, hee played mee a slippery tricke, though I had many deepe protestations to the contrary. It was not discovered till he was goan.'

While Tom was enjoying his 'hellish Life' at Claydon, young Edmund was there also, but instead of bemoaning his fate, as did his brother, Mun went out of his way to be helpful to any he could. His letters of this period are full of the little kindnesses he performed, and also include bulletins on Tom's behaviour:

'He carryeth himself without all exception . . . he is not so ill as his own indiscrete discourse argues him. It is really thought that it is his facile nature that hath ever wronged him; As you have done many good offices for him, soe truly he doth often acknowledge them by protesting that he thinks there's not a more kind and loving brother in the world.'

But the scene has changed somewhat a few weeks later and he reports:

'I know I am noe judge to pass my censure on him; I must rather admire your continual love towards him, for truely it doth exceede the possibility of my commendation. I believe my brother Tom will continue well so long as he is heare, but rather feare now 'twill be when he goes hence.'

On one occasion 'Lady Verney the Elder', Mun's grandmother, asks him to go to Albury to inspect the vault where old Sir Edmund was buried. He cannot go himself but sends a servant, who returns with the parson, 'one Gilpin, a Maudlen Hall man in my time, and I think in yours too'. The vault was in 'as good repaire as it was when my grandfather was buryed there he proffered one complement, which I durst not acquaint my grandmother with, that upon a weeke's warning he would be provided of an excellent funerall sermon for her'.

At another time Mun intercedes on his sister Susan's behalf. She was only seventeen and not always 'amenable', but was often left in charge of the children when her mother was away in London. Evidently she had got into some kind of trouble, for her brother writes that 'shame and a kind of amazed fear hath deterred her from pleading an opening'.

Ralph's son, Edmund, aged two, was at Hillesden for his health and Mun often visits his namesake, disjointedly passing back any news of the child he may have:

'His teeth have not yet cut flesh, which makes him a little froward but he is very well with them . . . hee is very like his mother . . . he imparts his affection to me, which I am not a little ambitious of. Were I as skillful as Œdipus I should be puzzled to say whether I love him or his father best. His gummes are so sore that he will suffer none to look into his mouth, but he presented this morning his duty to you as well as hee could doe it.'

The months pass pleasantly enough, but at last the long expected opportunity of military service arrives and Mun hurries off.

The other soldier in the family, Henry, was still in the Low Countries and in October 1637 he takes part in the recapture of Breda. The original taking of the town twelve years before had been the aftermath of the ill-fated Walcheren expedition, and so it was a matter of considerable prestige as well as strategic wisdom to recapture it. After a long siege the Prince of Orange at last made an entry against the Spaniards, who stoutly defended the place. Writing of the glorious exploit, Henry says:

'In our a proches there has bine nothing done cence the taking in of the hornworke, but in count William's a proches, wee lost some to hundred men of the choitches, and diverse offesers besids, in faling in of the hornworke. After, as thay had sprung there mine and where in the worke thay weere beate out of it for want of there seconds comming up which were the Dutches. This was all the servise that was seene afore the towne that is wourth speking of, but wee lost great store of men that weere shot in our a proches by misfourtune. The towne is now ours and it was given up the six of October, nue style, and the 10 of the same mounth they marcht out of it with wan and fifty flying coulers, and there was not at all gest to be above sixteene hundred men, straglers and all. This is all the nues that I can wright you word of.'

This great deed seems to have temporarily fired his martial ardour, for shortly after he declares he is 'not yett so absolute a soldiur though I love my profession to dispise and contemne these sports so farr forth as they tende to pleasure and recreation, but to settle my whole intencions that way as formerly I have absolutely left'.

However, he did not entirely 'contemne' his sports, for he writes: 'I rod a mach of six mile with a Dutchman for 50 pounds and won it, but it was not for myself but for a friend.' Ralph feeds him with any news there may be of his favourite pursuit, and writes of the matches at Brackley:

'My Lord Carlile's white nagg hath beaten Dandy, and Sprat woone the cup, and Cricket the plate; and which you will most woonder at the Weavor hath beaten the Sheepheard shamfully, and offerrs to run the same number of miles for £500 with the Sheepheard, and bee tied to hopp the last 12 score yds. My Lord of Salisburies horse Cricket was matched with Banister's bauld horse for £1,000 a horse and £200 forfeiture—they are to run the four miles at Newmarket—they would never run for so much money unless they certaynly know Banister's horse to be sound.'

Henry is very anxious to have a horse, 'not such a one as my kind aunt Poutne sent me', he says ungratefully, and points out that should he not get one he must 'make use of a Dutch Dogg'. On another occasion he tries to take advantage of a recruiting agent, who is in England collecting volunteers for his regiment, and suggests that a horse should be sent back with him; 'the nag's meate by the waye is to be provided for', he mentions as an afterthought. In the same letter he tells of his latest moves and appraises Ralph of the agent:

'If you can help him to a man or to I pray doe. Bridwell is seldome so empty but they may spare some, and, for his honesty, I'le promise you not to enquier after it, for let him be neer so bigg a rouge the beter. I can no wayes requite you with newse, but I am now in the Hauge and if you have any sute to the Queene of Bohemia you need not doubt to prevayle in it, if you please to command her greatest favourite.'

Elizabeth, King Charles's sister, exiled in Holland from her Bohemian kingdom, gathered around her a glittering array of courtiers. The 'Queen of Hearts', as she was called, was more than a mere lodestone to gallantry, for in her was embodied all the Protestant aspirations of the English people, and nothing did more damage to the King's popularity than his obvious reluctance to go to the aid of his poor sister. She seems to have been very kind to both Mun and Henry when they were at The Hague, and her charm and beauty completely won over the two young soldiers, as indeed it had many great gentlemen.

So by 1639, with the family grown up, Sir Edmund should have been able to settle down to the peaceful existence he so wanted. But it was not to be, and the trouble which had been smouldering north of the border could be suppressed no longer.

VII

The 'Scotch War'

'It lies not in our power to love or hate
For will in us is overrul'd by fate.'

MARLOWE

THE CORONATION at Holyrood in 1633 was Charles's first
venture into Scotland. Even then the ritualistic form of ceremony
chosen for the occasion was taken as a deliberate affront by many.
The King and Laud never tried to understand their northern
brethren, whose form of religion was so at variance with their own,
and the sovereign's remoteness, both spiritual and physical, helped
little to bridge the gulf of mistrust that separated the two countries.
Using the Marquis of Hamilton and a few advisers as intermediaries
in conducting government business, Charles had little dealings with
or personal feelings for his Scottish subjects; they, for their part,
although loyal to the King's person, disliked his policy and dis-
trusted his counsellors; above all, his religious ones.

King James had preached caution to Laud in his proselytizing
campaign against the Scots; but Charles had no such discretion in his
make-up and saw only a subject people practising a religion odious
to him with 'no liturgy, nor the least appearance of any beauty of
holiness'. It was the King's peremptory order to the Scottish bishops
to draw up and introduce a prayer book on English lines that sparked
off real opposition.

To Laud this was the first step in a religious movement aimed at reducing the Scottish Church to the position of 'a particle of the diocese of York'. And, not content with bringing Scottish worship to a level with that in England, the Archbishop even introduced into the new book extreme features which it was intended would eventually find their way into the English service; so the unfortunate Scots found themselves not only faced with a prayer book basically repugnant to them, but they were also to have inflicted upon them a form of service that no one yet had dared to present to the English people.

Despite forebodings of what would happen were it to be introduced, the new book appeared in July 1637. In St. Giles's Cathedral a near-riot broke out; people 'began to clap their hands, uttered the most discordant notes, and soon fairly overwhelmed the voice of the minister'. Some cried: 'Woe, woe! for this doleful day, that they are bringing in Popery among us!', and one more forthright than her companions threw a stool at the Dean's head, this was followed by a shower of 'whole pockfulls' of clasp bibles. The Bishop, a stout man, courageously mounted the pulpit to call the mob to their senses, but was greeted with cries of 'Crafty Fox', 'False anti-Christ Wolf' and 'Beastly Bellygod'. Eventually it was necessary to call the magistrates to clear the church, and this was done only with difficulty.

Similar protests occurred in other churches in the city, and crowds flocked into Edinburgh proclaiming their antagonism. It was clear the attempted introduction of the service book was a complete failure. By the end of the year Charles had no alternative but to withdraw the offending document or resort to force—the King's pride and stubbornness made it impossible for him to concede the former, so he had no recourse but to turn to war. But with what? For there was no standing army.

There was also no money to pay for an army, and without an army the English taxpayers could never be persuaded to provide funds enough to pay for a war against the Scots, a war in which, if anything, their leanings were towards the King's enemies. Such was Charles's dilemma. By hand of the many beggars who traversed the country, the Scots were able to appeal to the people of England, and this helped to dampen the already lukewarm enthusiasm for the King's cause. So it was against a backcloth of growing pessimism that Charles set about raising his army.

He could count on the material and financial support of only his nobles and courtiers; gifts of money came from a few, and a rich London merchant advanced the sum of £100,000, but otherwise there was little co-operation, and many took the opportunity of showing their opposition by withholding support under various pretexts. Apart from the motley, ill-conceived body of men his followers raised from their estates, the King had promise of an auxiliary army to be raised in the North of Scotland by the Catholic Marquis of Huntly, as well as an Irish contingent being collected by his faithful Lord Deputy, 'Black Tom' Wentworth. There had been mention also of a sizable Spanish contingent, but this came to nothing, perhaps fortunately.

Besides the difficulty of raising forces for his war, the King did his best to render them ineffective by his choice of commanders. Court intrigues and jealousies made a generally popular choice almost impossible, but Charles's final decision was indefensible on any grounds. Titular Commander-in-Chief was Arundel, hereditary Earl-Marshal of the Kingdom, who had recently been responsible for rearming the borderers on the English side against the marauding Scots—with bows and arrows. His lieutenant was the Earl of Essex, an experienced and competent professional soldier as well as an ardent Protestant respected by the Puritans; this would have been an admirable choice had not the King been persuaded by Henrietta Maria to appoint Lord Holland general of cavalry, thus splitting Essex's command and utterly nullifying his authority. Finally, Charles placed Hamilton in command of the Fleet; unfortunately, though, Hamilton knew nothing about the management of ships; and the Earl of Northumberland, Lord High Admiral of the Fleet, who had been so cavalierly set aside, was bitterly offended and not one jot consoled by being given the high honour of looking after the Queen, left behind in London! Such was the confusion and mismanagement that lay behind the King's preparations for the First 'Scotch War'.

No such confusion bedevilled the Scots. Fortified by a religious and righteous fervour, volunteers flocked to defend the Covenant. Command was vested in Alexander Leslie, an 'old little crooked soldier', veteran campaigner and talented general. Under his leadership the 'stout young ploughmen' who rallied to the cause grew into the semblance of a formidable army lacking only experience. As leaven to this mass of ignorant soldiery came the hardened veterans of the Scots brigades, then fighting under Gustavus Adolphus in Germany. These officers and men, blooded by many a campaign, and with a reputation second to none on the Continent, flocked back in their thousands, rallying in their country's need and providing an experienced nucleus for Leslie's army. The whole, roused by the twice-daily exhortations of their preachers, became a force inspired with a fanatical, burning, religious passion; a force of 22,000 foot and over 500 cavalry well disciplined and well trained pitted against the gaudy, half-hearted rabble ill-led and ill-provisioned which was all the King could muster.

In common with the King's other courtiers, Sir Edmund was summoned to attend His Majesty. The command arrived on the 7th February 1639, addressed to 'my very loveinge freind Sir Edmund Verney, knight, one of the gentlemen of his majesty's most honorable privy chamber in ordinary. . .' It bade him, having 'all occasions sett apart,' to be . . .

'in rediness in your owne person by the first of Aprill next, att the citty of Yorke, as a curassier in russett armes, with guilded studds or nayles, and befittingly horsed, and your servant or servants which shall wayt upon you horst in white armes, after the manner of a harqobusier, in good equipage, there to act and doe such dutyes and services as may be expected from or shalbe required of you, which yf your necessary occasions . . . will not permitt, you are then to send for you and in your stead, as a gentleman of his majesty's most honorable privy chamber, some gentleman of quallity, in all poynts provided according to the directions above given, to wayt for you.'

The summons came at a difficult time for Sir Edmund. He had lately been racked by sciatica and was in no fit state to undergo such an ordeal as the forthcoming campaign. Old Lady Sussex saw more in his ills, though, than mere physical discomfort and voiced her fears to Ralph:

'Your good father, mythought, lokede very sade this crismas: i fearede he hade bene discontentide some way; but he tolde me it was not so, but that he was often in a great dele of pane. i praye God he may get some helpe, or else it will shorten his time, i doubt.'

Sciatica, indeed, was the least of Sir Edmund's cares—a more spiritual ill was troubling him, as it was so many other gentlemen at

Tom Verney
BY EGMONT

Charles I, by Van Dyck
Portrait presented by King Charles to Sir Edmund in part payment of a debt

the time. The King's folly was becoming all too apparent, and, though Clarendon might call the Scots 'vermin', the majority of Englishmen had no quarrel with their northern neighbours, least of all over their religion.

The difficulty of his position was now becoming clear to Sir Edmund. A fervent Protestant all his life, and sufficiently close to affairs to appreciate what was happening in the kingdom, he was by nature inclined to agree with those who felt that 'Their own great sufferings, made them easily believed that the Scots were innocent and wronged by the same hand by which themselves had been oppressed.'

For twenty-five years Sir Edmund had served his King. He respected his master not for his policies, but as a man, as a sovereign and as a friend. Charles for his part seems to have trusted the old courtier utterly, never doubting his loyalty and complete integrity. As well as holding the post of Knight-Marshal, Sir Edmund was still a Gentleman of the Privy Chamber in Ordinary, and was, in effect, more a trusted confidant to the King.

Ralph had by now made his own position clear; many of Sir Edmund's great personal friends in Parliament and the county were supporters of the opposition; Lady Sussex was adamantly against the King's policy, although she steadfastly refused to influence Sir Edmund in any way.

Sir Edmund's decision must, therefore, be a purely personal one, no one could help him in his dilemma. He would never sway with the wind of popular opinion, yet he knew that if he joined the King now he must be divided from his beloved eldest son and many friends—perhaps for ever. The decision was no easy one, and he knew that once made he could never go back on it. Conviction and sentiment led one way, conscience the other—he was torn with uncertainty. It was probably the reliance that Charles placed in his trusted servant that decided him. Sir Edmund knew his master too well to believe he could ever persuade the King from a course the latter felt right, but if the King needed him—then he must go. The old knight was too kind and conscious of his duty ever to desert a master whom he had served for so long. So, sick in mind and body, he took his irrevocable decision to go to his King.

Before departing Sir Edmund makes his will, 'considering the frailty of mankind, ye certainty of death, and the uncertainty of ye time of death', as he puts it. He appoints Ralph his sole executor, 'having had experience of his fidelitie unto me and of his love for

I

his brothers and sisters', and instructs that his body 'shall be interred
in ye chancel of the Parish church of Middle Claydon, with as little
pomp and charges as my executor conveniently may' . . . 'Such estate
of goods and chatels as it has pleased the Almighty to bless me with
in this transitory life' is distributed amongst his relations and
faithful retainers—to Tom and Henry he gives an annuity of £40,
to Edmund and his sisters one of £5 and the same to Will Roades
'my faithful servant and bailiff at Claydon'. Ralph's wife, of whom he
was especially fond, is given £40 for a ring 'which I desire her to
wear for my sake'. To his 'dear and beloved wife' are given 'all
such moneys as are in her custody at the date of this my will' and
the 'fuell of wood, furze and cole at Claydon, the coach and four of
the coach horses with their harness and furniture', also half the
linen and use of half the plate and household stuff—to be shared with
Ralph. To his men legatees he leaves cloth 'for a mourning sute
and cloak', and the same for a 'mourning gown' for the women. So,
having tidied his affairs and leaving copious instructions to Ralph
on the management of the estate, the next day Sir Edmund made
haste to join his King, who was preparing to leave London for the
north.

Young Mun, too, had volunteered and was bound for the same
destination as his father. He passed through Buckinghamshire on his
way northward, but just missed Ralph, who was away from Claydon
at the time. Writing from Hillesden, he bids farewell and in typi-
cally optimistic vein forecasts the campaign ahead:

'Sweete brother,—I came away in that unexpected sodaynes that
I had scarce time to give farewell to those friendes that were then
within, and beleeve me I was much greevd that you were not of that
number . . . for my part, I thinke the journey will prove but an
ordinary progresse, and then I shall have the happines of seeing you
againe next winter, if not the latter end of the summer; but if it should
come to blowes, yet why should not I thinke of escaping as well as
any other? All though I'll speake it, and yet forget vaine glory, that
I'le endevour to attempt as much as any in a brave way, and yet my
ambition in this is not comparable to that which I receive by my
constant remaining your most affectionate servant. . . .'

At the end of March the King set out from London 'with a
glorious attendance of nobility and gentry, that looked more like
the pomp and parade of an Eastern Prince, than the expedition of an

English Monarch'. Few viewed the forthcoming campaign with any anxiety. Confident reports from the north signified that all was not well in the Scots camp, and Charles rode on not doubting that a show of force and his own presence were all that were needed to send the Covenanters packing. His own preparations were well advanced: an army gathering in Yorkshire, Hamilton and his seaborne force making ready for a landing at Aberdeen, and the Irish but waiting for the word to assault the western coast of Scotland.

On the 30th March the King rode into York—to be greeted with disillusionment; for, far from the highly organized, well-disciplined fighting force he had been led to expect, he found an ill-organized rabble, and no money to pay for it. On top of this, reports filtered in of a series of Scots' successes, and it became clear that by these quick, concerted actions, abetted by incredible ineptitude and ill-preparedness, the King had lost nearly every foothold he possessed in Scotland.

The Court was cast in gloom. None more so than the Knight-Marshal, who was grief-stricken at leaving his son and Claydon. He writes:

'Good Ralphe, since prince Henrys death I never knew soe much greefe as to part from you; and trewly, because I saw you equally afflicted with it, my sorrow was the greater. But Raph, wee cannot live always togeather. It cannot bee longe ere by cource of nature wee must bee severd, and if that time bee prevented by accident, yet wee must resolve to beare it with that patience and courage as becomes men and cristians; and soe the great God of heaven send uss well to meete againe, eyther in this woarld or in the next.'

There was talk, too, of treachery in the royal camp . . .

'The King has been basly betrayd', writes Sir Edmund. 'All the party that hee hoped uppon all this while has basly left him. As wee are this day informed, the two cassels of Edenbrough and Dunbarton are yeelded upp without one blowe, and yett they were boath provided soe well as they were impregnable soe long as they had vittle, which they wanted not. Dekeeth, a place of greate strength, wher the crowne septer laye, is yeelded to, and the covenanters has taken awaye the crowne and septer, and a greate deale of armes and munition too; yett my lor tresorer of Scotland [Traquair] undertooke to the king to keepe all that safe; and all thes are given upp without one blowe. Aberdine wee heare (but I must confess that news is not soe certayne that I can say it for a trewth) is yeelded upp to, and noe blowe given; the king sent 4000 of the choysest armes hee had theather; soe that now I am confident the shew of making a party ther for the kinge has been only to gett arms for uss, and to feede uss with hopes till they were fully provided. My Lord Clifford sent woard this morning to the king that the inhabitants of Carlile had left the towne, uppon a fright they tooke of the high-landers coming suddenly uppon them, but hee has put 300 men into the towne, and they saye they are resolved to fight it out. The hilan-ders are in number 2500, and six cannon, as they heare. Our army is but weak, our purse is weaker, and if we fight with these forces and early in the year we shall have our throats cut, and to delay fighting wee cannot for lack of money to keep our army together. . . . Saye little of this to the woemen, least it fright them. . . . Yorke, this Monday, 3 of the clock after noone [1st April, 1639].'

With all this talk of warlike preparations even the pacific Ralph is stirred into action.

'I have been a little too negligent of getting my armes, but now I will hasten them' . . . , he writes, 'I praye send mee your opinion whither I had not best bespeake a Waggon presently and what other provisions I had best make. I should be loath to bee utterly un-provided . . . I hope if need bee you can furnish mee with an horse, that will be readier than any that can be brought by mee.'

This elicits the response from his father:

'I will inquire for a nagg for you, but charity beginns at home, and I will first provide for myself if I can . . . I pray goe to Nedd Herbert from mee, and tell him I will not wright to him till I can send him an inventory of the Skotts I have kild.'

News at home was sparse and bedevilled by rumour. Ralph's wife, who was still in London, writes in extreme anxiety to her mother at Hillesden:

'I should be glad that yr newes of the Scotish business were true, for heare is none good. Wee heare that they have turned all that are on the King's side into England, and that they have stopped all passages soe that the king send no certain intelligence of their proceedings; all our frindes are gone out of towne and when my sister is gon to I know not what to doe.'

Her fears can have hardly been set at rest, for Mun, now serving with his regiment at Selby, writes: 'What with exercising and divers other petty employments . . . we are kept in that perpetual action that I have yet but small time to present my service to any of my friends.'

But entertainment was good at York, and gradually spirits were restored. On Wednesday in Easter week Charles held a fine parade of his troops at Selby—amongst them Mun—and this display of martial magnificence did much to persuade him of the renewed certainty of his success. However, in the midst of the gaiety came the disastrous news that Aberdeen had surrendered—'a resonable defencive towne, well vittled . . . delivered upp too, without soe much as a bluddy nose', as Sir Edmund put it.

The Knight-Marshal had more personal ills to trouble him, too. 'I am infinitely afraide of the goute', he writes, 'for I feel crewell twinges, but I hope to starve it awaye, for, God willing, I will drinck but once a day.' This was bad enough, but a shattering family blow now smote the unhappy man.

Sir Edmund's wife had several sisters. One of them, another Margaret, was married to a certain John Pulteney. She seems to have been a good wife and 'deserved his estate for she saved his soul', or so says the record. She was also an excellent housewife and was known as Madame Spye-Fault by the family. However, in 1637 Pulteney died, leaving his wife a fine fortune. Besieged by several noble suitors, the rich 'wido' played one off against another with considerable skill, sending the various love letters she received to Ralph, who gave his advice on each claimant, discussing their means and morals in the most intimate terms. One 'hath 2500 in demeanes & 1800 was parsonage land', subject to only £300 rent, but as he did not live in Bucks was not considered suitable by old Lady Denton. This brought the reaction from the widow herself that 'it was knowne before ever he came to the howes where his estate laye'. Of another she says: 'i am soe much against it that I will for no conditiones in the world here of it', but her mother in this case is strongly in favour, 'for she heeres he hath a greater estate than this'. She is in a dither of indecision and by the end of 1638 was considered 'mached' to two gentlemen at the same time.

The suit of Lord Howard was strongly favoured by some: 'honor-
ablye descendede, & upon report is onest & worthye', he was a
widower with five children, who were, however, considered 'such
an obstackle'. The other contender was a certain Lord Charles,
and he was backed by the Lord Chamberlain. Mrs. Pulteney
had given some kind of promise not to make her choice for a
little time, and this left her in bad odour with the supporters
of either side, who each considered she was pledged to their
favourite.

Matters were left thus when Sir Edmund departed for Scotland,
but no sooner was he gone than she imparted the news to Ralph that
she had been privately married some time before, and to a third party
one William Eure, who by this time was well on his way to join the
royal army in Scotland. Ralph was thunderstruck at this ingratitude
and disrespect, not only to the two suitors but to the Lord Chamberlain as well. 'I fiend from boath the Lords that shee assured them shee
was yett a free woeman, and that shee would keepe herself soe till
Michellmas, without ingaging herself to any boddy: soe that if it
shall be discovered that shee is marrid, shee will appeare a foolish
and a falce woeman.' But he was more than thunderstruck when he
heard that his aunt's choice was a Roman Catholic. Such infidelity
was a terrible disaster to the whole family, brought up as they had
been to associate the Other Religion with a kind of horror and
loathing incomprehensible now. To Sir Edmund it was a bitter blow,
nor does Ralph's letter acquainting him with the marriage leave
any doubt as to how the latter felt about it all:

'Oh Sr shee is married, shee is married! and therefore now tis
past recall. this unlucky deed was done before I mistrusted ever twas
... I find her hart hardened against any things the world or her
other friends can say. I have advised her to goe downe and conceall
this, at least untell his returne from the North ... this I conceive
will bee the best course to blind the world and protect her credit
from perpetuall shame.'

Sir Edmund's reaction was violent: 'I protest to God, when I
redd your letter, a palsye tooke my hands, soe that in five houers
I could hold noething steddyly', and in another letter: 'my soule is
greeved for her misfortune. . . . I praye deale cleerely with her, and
lett her preserve as much of her discretion as shee can; for, beleeve
mee, shee has made a large forfeit of them boath.' The final out-

burst of feeling comes when he hears about his future brother-in-law: 'I heare he is a vast spender, and has a father and a Brother to releeve that has not bredd to eate; he sould his land for six thousand pownds. all this layd togeather, God help some boddy.'

Old Lady Denton's views were much the same, only coupled with a fierce anger, particularly against the unfortunate Ralph on whom she lays most of the blame:

'Your mother writes me word about a samite gowne, i remember i did here tofore of such a thinge, but now i pray tel her if she would provide me sack cloth and line yt with asshis, then i mought morne for the folie of my wise disobedient children. i hear he is with out exception, only his religione—but that is such a cut to me that yt hath a most killed me. . . . Your house is ye common scare of towne and cuntry howe he and shee hath foled you all, but I know some of you knue of this, when ther was helpe of yt.'

Happily, the marriage was a success, and even old Lady Denton softened somewhat so that in May the 'wido' was able to write: 'my mo is in betir temper than shee was and is willing as we should live here'. Unfortunately, Eure eventually persuaded his wife to change her religion and so cast her in the eyes of most of the family to perpetual damnation. He died in the autumn of 1644 and is referred to as truly 'a gallant man, the whole nasion has a lose in him; he had but one fault'—that of his religion.

Meanwhile events had gone from bad to near disastrous for the King. Hearing that Lord Huntly in the north had not only ceded Aberdeen to the rebels but had even signed the Covenant himself, Charles determined to ensure the loyalty of his followers by getting them to declare a new oath of allegiance to himself and his cause. To his utter dismay, two dissented—Lords Brook and Saye—the latter marching off with his own troops, a more serious loss than the damage occasioned to the King's pride. Further unrest in the King's camp was caused when Essex, despatched to forestall the Scots in Berwick, handed over a letter, delivered to him by the Covenanters, but which was addressed to the King. This action, although scrupulously correct, gave rise to rumours of Essex's treachery, and partisan elements soon formed within the army determined to prove or disprove these claims.

The letter itself was phrased civilly enough and protested no thought of injury to the kingdom, but, as Sir Edmund feared, 'it will rather exasperatt then mollify, and add fewell to that fyer that raged inoughe before', and he goes on to say:

'Trewly I thinck it will come to blowes, but you must not saye soe to your mother. The king increases his army, and makes all the haste hee can theather, but I hope it is but to see what party will come to him, for our men will bee long ere they learn theyr lesson.'

The King remained at York until the 29th of April. Then, moving north, on the next day he reached Durham. But the army was in sorry plight. The elaborate arrangements made in London to keep them supplied broke down at the start, and now the unfortunate soldiery found themselves with no tents and ill-provided with food or drink. With no material comforts, and even less spiritual inducement, little the wonder that they showed such reluctance in this unwilling war.

The condition of the army was obvious to all. Yet the King's advisers still urged him on. As Sir Edmund put it:

'My lord marshall putts on the king to fight by all wayes and means he can possibly devise, dayly urging the king how nearly it concerns him in honner to punish the rebells. . . . Then the king is perswaded to it, too, from Whithall, with all the industry that can be imagined. The catholiks makes a large contribution, as they pretend, and indeed use all the means and wayse they can to sett uss by the ears, and I thinck they will not faile of theyr plott. I dare saye ther was never soe raw, soe unskillfull, and soe unwilling an army brought to fight.'

Then, in another letter:

'My lord marshal himselfe will, I dare saye, bee safe, & then he cares not what becomes of the rest; trewly here are manny brave Gentlemen that for poynt of honor must runn such a hazard as trewly would greeve any heart but his that does it purposely to ruin them. for my owne parte I have lived till paine and trouble has made mee weary to doe soe; and the woarst that can come shall not bee unwellcome to mee; but it is a pitty to see what men are like to bee slaughterd heere unless it shall pleas god to putt it in the kings Hearte to increase his Army or staye till thes may knowe what they doe; for as yett they are as like to kill theyr fellows as the enemye . . .

it is 3 of the clock in the morning, att which time I am very sleepy.'

This is followed by news that the Scots are within ten miles of Berwick: 'Wee shall soone have blowes now, but I beleeeve it will bee skirmises with the hors, and noe battle till towards the end of summer. It is folly to thinck any longer of a peace.' Mun, now encamped five miles from Newcastle, echoes his father: 'we dayly expect orders to march away . . . I verily beleeve that within one month or sixe weekes wee shall see what businesses will come to. Wee that either are or would be souldgers feare the best and hope the worst.'

On Ascension Day the King left Newcastle. A day or two later the army marched. But so ill-provided were they that to prevent a mutiny the soldiers were allowed to pillage for themselves—and this can have done little towards furthering the King's cause in the Border country.

All these 'warlike propensities' alarmed Ralph, miles away at Claydon. Nor were his anxieties allayed when he received a letter from his uncle, Dr. Denton, who was serving as the Court physician. This hinted that Sir Edmund was going to the Borders and was needlessly exposing himself to danger.

'Oh Doctor,' Ralph distractedly replies, 'if my father goes to the borders hee is lost. I know his corrage will bee his distruction. Noe man did ever soe wilfully ruine himselfe and his posterity; god forgive him and grant me patience; certainly his hart is more than stone, or else hee could not soe soone forget both freinds & Wife and children, and all to get (that which he can never lose) honour, should hee spend all his time contrivinge which way hee might make us most miserable, hee could not invent a readdier cource than this. Did he beget us to noe other end but to make us the sad spectacles of the world? Will noething moove him? Deare Dr: try, & try againe & set all his friends uppon him . . . give him noe rest till hee hath yeelded to stay.'

By the same messenger he writes to his father:

'I find . . . that you meane (voluntarily) to attend my Lord Holland to the Borders (though many others stay with the Kinge, that have farr lesse reason) for Sr you know your yeares, your charge, your distracted fortune, your former life, were priviledge enough to keepe you Back, without the least staine to your reputation; . . . hath the vaine hope of a little fadinge Honour swallowed up all your good nature? are your compassions quite shut up? wil neither the numberlesse sights of your dearest freinds, nor the uncessant cries of your forlorne widdow, nor the mournfull groanes of your fatherlesse Brood prevaile to stay you? are you absolutely resolved by this on act, to blot all your former? and (by needlesse hazardinge your selfe) expose your wife, and children to perpetual misery, and intaile afflictions uppon your whole posterity. I beseech you consider it and bee not soe egere to make your selfe & us (your unhappy children) the very objects of pitty it selfe, pardon my boldnesse, it concerne mee neerly; should I now bee silent, perhaps heerafter 'twould bee too late to speake, therefore let mee once mor beseech you to consider this seriously, and give not the world soe just cause to account me your most unfortunate sonne.'

Sir Edmund's reply was comforting, and Dr. Denton assures Ralph: 'Be confident that I will leave noe stone unmoved that I can leave maye knocke your father's fightinge designes on the head, and preserve him.'

News from Scotland is as uncertain as ever. Dr. Denton in the same letter tells that the 'kinge goeth towards Barwicke . . . and intends to intrenche himselfe within 5 or 6 miles of it, but on this side of the Tweede. . . . I hope that the kinge doth not intend to fight this summer, but thinkes, by drawinge his forces soe neere them to tempt them to bringe out theire forces in a body, and by that meanes to exhaust them; but I feare he will be cozened, for I beleeve that they be as cunninge as they be wicked.'

Each hour produced either 'something that is new, or some alteration of our former resolutions', as Sir Edmund writes, and Mun, now preparing for the march to the Borders, complains of frequent 'contradictions'.

Every few days Sir Edmund writes with the latest news:

'Lastly threatens to fight uss, but if hee comes not quickly hee slips a fair occation. . . . Wee have had two of the coaldest dayes heere that ever I felt, and I feare it if continues it will kill our men, that must lodg uppon the ground without anything over them . . . part of our army is marcht awaye . . . to within fower mile of Barwick. Tomorrow the king removes. . . . I am instantly goeing to view the grownd, and place his tent reddy against hee comes. . . . Within tenn or twelve days we expect a great supply to our army, and if they lett uss aloane till they come to uss and that wee are intrencht, wee thinck they will not bee able to hurt uss, and yet wee shall always vex them. . . . Wee are now incampt within two mile of Barwick, and by to morrow wee shall bee intrencht. Wee have seene noe enimy as yett.'

This last from a camp called 'Lasly's pride'.

Sir Edmund was concerned about his 'armes', for after six weeks they still had not arrived:

'I beleeve ther is never a long Gauntlett sent,' he says, 'lett Hill [the armourer] make one with all speede he can possibly; for it will kill a man to serve in a whole Curass. I am resolved to use nothing but back, brest and gauntlet; if I had a Pott for the Head that were Pistoll proofe it maye bee I would use it if it were light. . . . Say noething of this Gauntlett to yor mother; it may give her causeless fears.' Most of his equipment arrives soon after this, but the 'pott' in particular causes a lot of trouble. 'I have receaved all my armes that you sent,' he states a little later, 'pray hast awaye my pott, and take care it bee wide inoughe, for this is soe much too little that noe boddy but a madd man could have been soe madd as to mistake soe grosly. . . . This will come uppon noe part of my head, it is soe very little.'

He becomes even more worried when fighting seems imminent and still no 'pott' has come: 'when my pott is done', he writes, 'let it bee quillted and lyned, and sent to mee, for heere is noe hope att all of peace, and wee are like to have the woarst of the warr'. Hill seems to have hurried things after this, for evidently he sent a 'pott' to Claydon, but unfortunately Ralph tried it on and, as it was far too small, sent it back. Sir Edmund is very upset: 'Ralphe, as it falls out I am verry sorry you were soe curious to try the Pott, for an ill one had been better than none. I doubt it maye come to late now.' Happily, he never had to use this piece of his equipage and rumours of a treaty sounded so promising that he can gleefully write at the end of May: 'I heare noething of my pott from Hill. I will now keepe it to boyle my porrage in.'

Delivery of mails was uncertain and very risky. Letters of this period are full of adjurations to 'keepe this to your self' and 'burne this letter'. The ones that were delivered covered the distance from the North of England to Buckinghamshire remarkably quickly —four days on the average—but many must have gone astray, for Sir Edmund and Ralph are often complaining of not receiving the expected replies.

The King was not entirely without support in the Border country and it is probable that the hardy northerners relished this opportunity of renewing hostilities with their traditional enemies—even with the bows and arrows so thoughtfully provided by the Earl of Arundel. In another letter Sir Edmund sums up the position:

'We fiend all the meaner sort of men uppon the Scotch border well inclyned to the king, and I beleeve when time serves they will express it well; but the gentlemen are all covenanters, and I beleeve most men are weary of the government ther now, for they lay heavy burdens uppon the people.'

Despite this oppression, however, few men of note came over to the royal army, and with this lack of success the King's followers became more discouraged than ever.

'The trewth is wee are betrayed in all our intelligence,' writes Sir Edmund in early June, 'and the king is still made beleeve in a party that will come to him, but I am confident hee is mightily abused in it, for they are a people strangly united.'

Conditions in the royal camp were nearing the critical. Provisioning of the army was haphazard in the extreme, and irregular supplies, with mouldy biscuits and no water, did little to raise the waning morale. On top of this came an epidemic of smallpox which laid low many of the ill-disciplined, dispirited rabble.

No success of even the most trivial nature had occurred, and in fact the only brush with the enemy had ended with ignominious withdrawal or, as Sir Edmund puts it, the Scots 'in spight of our teeths made uss soe discreete as to make our retrait'. This failure was the direct result of the King's pathetically inadequate Intelligence. Time and again information came to his ear which was either far too late or hopelessly inaccurate—this, coupled with commanders unable to act with speed and for ever feuding amongst themselves, produced an army which could in truth be described as 'never soe weak'.

The want of information in the royal camp was forcibly brought home to the King when, on the evening of 6th of June, the Scottish army suddenly advanced within sight of the English encampment at Yearford Moor not far from Berwick. Charles was ready to go to supper when the news was brought and, so we are told, was able with his 'perspective glass' to count the enemy's tents. Happily, the Scots were content with this show of force and came no nearer, but the obvious inefficiency of the King's Intelligence did little to encourage his own troops. It was, therefore, fortunate that the Covenanters chose this time to seek a settlement.

'I knowe you long to heare what wee are doing heere, and I have as great a desire still to inform you', writes Sir Edmund on the 9th of June. 'Wee are still att great quiett. The Scottish army, which is verry strong, lies now within six miles of ours. The lords of the covenant have petitioned the king that they maye represent theyr complaints and greevances by some of the Inglish nobillity for they saye theyr owne country men has beene falce to them, and has misreported them and theyr actions to the king. His majesty has assented to theyr petition, and has assigned six of our lords to meete with as manny of theyrs att our lord general's tent in our campe. They have petitioned for an assurance under the king's hand for theyr safe returne; but hee refuses it, and sayes they shall trust to his woard. . . . I doubt but not wee shall have a treaty; what effect it will produce I cannot judg; but I hope it will be a good one.'

Then he goes on to say:

'Uppon theyr petition to the kinge I was sent by his majesty with a message to them, wherein thoughe I had a hard parte to playe, yett I dare bouldly saye I handled the business soe that I begatt this treaty, otherwise wee had, I doubt, beene at blowes by this time; but I praye take noe noetice of this unless you heare it from others.'

The message that Sir Edmund took to the Scottish camp was none other than the Proclamation that the King had bade the Marquis of Hamilton read to the citizens of Edinburgh and which had sparked off the Covenant. Little wonder, therefore, that they refused to have the document read publicly to their army, and only after lengthy argument agreed even to hear it read to the principal commanders. Sir Edmund was described by a Scot as a man 'known to be a lover of our nation and acceptable to the Scottish people and therefore a good ambassador on this occasion. . . .', though whether any of this is true or how he came to be known to the Scottish people remains a mystery.

Nevertheless, the Scots were eager for a settlement of this sense-less struggle and, with Charles for once acting with sense rather than priggish pride, an amicable arrangement was quickly reached. Sir Edmund writes two days after his meeting with the Scots:

'This daye the lords on boath sides have had a meeting. The king, contrary to expectation, went into the tent to them as they begann to enter into theyr business, but I thinck it will not hurt the business. The king heard them with patience, and answered with great moderation. This meeting does not give uss inoughe wherby to judg wheather warr or peace shall follow. Thursday next is appoynted for a second meeting, and then it may bee wee maye give a better guess att it.'

Four days later all is nearly concluded and after witnessing the announcement of the King's declaration Sir Edmund writes:

'I beleeve there is noe more doubt now that wee shall have peace. Everything is agreed on, and Monday appoynted for a full conclusion. The king has promist them a new assembly, and to rattifye in parliament any thing that shall be agreed on in theyr assembly. . . . More particulars I have not time to send you, nor doe I thinck your curiosity is soe greate that news of peace will sattisfye it . . . '

So was signed the Pacification of Berwick; an agreement in which, according to Clarendon, 'nobody mean what others be-lieved he did'. On this note of uncertainty ended what was known as the First Bishops' War.

While such momentous things had been happening in Scotland, young Tom, now far away in the West Indies, had not let himself be forgotten by the family. He had been sent to Barbados on the recommendation of the Earl of Warwick, Lady Sussex's third husband to be and a great Puritan. Despatched on a sound ship with a quantity of provisions of all kinds, there was reason to hope that he would be out of mind for some time at least. But his first letter soon dispelled these dreams—the only difference now was that his demands covered a wider and more expensive field.

His wants varied from 'twenty able men, whereof two to be carpenters', to swords and '30,000 nayles of divers sorts', not forgetting six cases of strong waters for the men to drink a dram every morning, 'to keepe them in health (for my part I drink non)' —he adds as an afterthought. However, his letters give a fascinating insight into the ways of the seventeenth-century colonist.

He starts off in an encouraging fashion:

'I have obtained 100 acres of land, but not knowing how to dispose of it unless I can have such a supply as the invoise makes mention of, which, if I can have a supply according to my expectation, I make noe question but by the grace of God to rais my fortunes in a few years, nay, I shall be able in one yeare, to return back the principall, which is a great incouragement to you that doe disburs the money, and a greater to have mee continue here, which could never yett stay anywhere.'

He then goes on:

'This country is the best and healthfullest in all the westerne islands; thanks be to God here is want of nothing nourishing, both for soul and body. . . . Now another thing is the fruits that this land doth beare every month in the year, which is a great comfort to us. Oranges, lemons, limes, plantines, potatoes, pine-apples, guaves, and many more I will tell you the nature of in my next letter, pepper, cinamon, ginger. . . . As to your potatoes which is very nourishing and comfortable it is the best provision we have in the island, both for ourselves and servants—they will not desire after one month or two no other provision but potatoes boyled, and nobby to drink with them, which is only potatoes boyled and press'd as hard as they can, till the jouice is gon into fayre water, and after three hours this is good drink.

'Now the last and best fruit is your pine-apple, and there are two sorts—a Queen pine, and another, which I cannot well call to mind, therefor I will omit it. Now the Queen pine, when it is in your mouth, do but imagin a tast and that relisheth of it, soe it bee luscious. It is held such a dainty fruit, that King James swore it was the apple that Eve cosned Adam with. I might speak more of this pine, but the description makes mee long after it, and I beeleeve you will long till you taste of it, which I heartily wish you had one; but I feare it will not be till such time as I come myself, because they must have a great care in the carriage of it, or it will be labour in vain. And to proceed to my last thing: the evils that doth most annoy us, and that is partly and chiefly drunkenes, your land crabs & etc. First drunkeness, Were it not for that great thing, this would be one of the bravest islands I ever heard of: but it doth soe much increas, that I have seen upon a Sabbath-day as I have been walking to church first one, presently after another, lye in the highway soe drunk that here be land crabs in the land that have bitt of some of their fingers, some of their toes, and have killed some before they wakened, yett this doth not att all affright them. More I could say, but as they are beasts, soe lett mee leave them like beasts, and proceede to a word or two of your land crabs. Thees land crabs are innumerable, that you shall have them certayne months in the yeare be soe thick in the highwayes, that, doe what we can, we shall have them bite through our shoes, that we are not able to undoe them till we break their clawes; they are very like our sea crabs, but not att all soe good, becaus most of them are poysonous:' and he continues in this vein about 'cabiges, that grow on trees', etc.

At the same time he writes to his mother—pointing out that he is in dire need of all sorts of household goods:

'For my owne part, I take no glory in boasting of mine actions, bee they good or bad, and soe I turn upon some better thing which doth more befitt the time and my occasions, and that is concerning housekeeping. I am now building a sorry cottage to harbour men when I have them', and he asked for 'household stuff, plate, spoones, and the like, then pewter and brass of all sorts, and linnen of all sorts, both for mee and my servants.'

Shortly after this comes another long letter of demands, and forwarding a sort of testimonial which certifies that Tom is 'an extraordinary good husband and careful'—which must have caused a lot of amusement to his family.

Answering this, Sir Edmund tells his son:

'Tom, I am newly come out of Scottland, wheather I am instantly returning again, soe that by reason of my short stay heere I cannot for the present answer your letter so fully as I would doe, but I have left order with your brother to doe what can be done, but this ship makes such hast away that I believe hee will hardly gett any servants for you to send by this passage, nor doe I think fitt to send manny now, for I am informed for certaine that my Lord of Warwicke has bought a greate iland neare the place where you are, and that he intends to plant it presently. I conceive you maye have better conditions much then wher you now are, and I am sure you shall ever fiend my Lord noble and favourable to you. My Lord intends in Feb. next to goe for this iland in person, and I thinke it will bee much for your advantage to transplant yourself theather. Assoone as I return and that I know more of the businesse, I will informe you particularly of it. My Lord of Warwicke intends to fortify his iland presently, and then to plant wher hee is safe from being beaten out of it, which is a course I like best. Inable yourself to knowe what is fitt for plantations and lett me alone to assist you if you proove industrious and careful of my directions, soe that I may putt a trust and confidence in you which as yet I dar not doe, because I have found you false to your woard, and careless of all I have sayed to you. I doubt not but with your own helpe to make you a fortune, but if you continue in your old cources I will certainly forsake you. I pray God direct your heart so that I may have cause to wright myself your loving father.'

Lord Warwick's plans came to nothing, and signs of more stirring things put even worries of Tom into the background, for it very soon became apparent that the King was looking upon the Pacification of Berwick only as a means to gain time to muster his forces. The Covenanters themselves, suspicious of the King and outraged at what they considered the betrayal of their cause, were frightened by the disbandment of their army and the surrender of the royal fortresses captured in the lightning foreword to the past war. So, when the Scottish Parliament was assembled at Edinburgh in obedience to the King's promise, it was far from the subservient assembly he intended. In effect, a Scottish Government had been founded, acknowledging the jurisdiction of the King's counsellors only when it suited them.

A further and equally unpopular war became inevitable. Mun expressed the general feeling: 'I vow to you it is far from my desire. ... I heare that the King hath vast summes of money given him by his subjects, and that these forces are lyke to goe against Scotland; the former part I wish to be true, but shall ever pray against the latter.'

In the meantime, Sir Edmund had been to Bath to help ease his
K

sciatica. Before leaving Scotland he had evidently acquired a number of horses from the disbanding armies, for he writes to Ralph to 'inquier out some grass for geldings, for I have bought fifty Horses and Geldings out of one troope, and they will be at Claydon about Tenn dayes hence; the Horses I will keep at Howse till I can sell them'.

VIII

The Fateful Months

'There was in truth a strange absence of understanding
in most, and a strange perverseness of understanding in
the rest; the Court full of excess, idleness, and luxury;
the Country full of pride, mutiny and discontent; every
man more troubled and perplexed at that they called the
violation of one law, than delighted or pleased with the
observation of the rest of the Charter; never imputing
the increase of their receipts, revenue, and plenty, to the
wisdom, virtue, and merit of the Crown, but objecting
every small imposition to the exorbitancy and tyranny
of the Government; the growth of knowledge and
learning being disrelished, for the infirmities of some
learned men, and the increase of grace and favour upon
the Church more repined and murmured at, than the
increase of piety and devotion in it, which was as visible,
acknowledged, or taken notice of; whilst the indis-
cretion and folly of one sermon at Whitehall was more
bruited abroad, and commented upon, than the wisdom,
sobriety and devotion of a hundred.'

CLARENDON

Mun's fear that the King was raising another army to fight
the Scots was all too well-founded. Charles, who had indeed
all along considered the Pacification of Berwick as purely a respite,
was raising money for the purpose of crushing the Scots; but
shortage of funds also forced the King to summon a Parliament,
and so in April 1640 the Short Parliament assembled.

For the first time the father and son sat together in the Commons: Sir Edmund as member for Chipping Wycombe and Ralph for Aylesbury. Throughout this period they lived together with their wives at Covent Garden so there are no letters between them, even the rough copies of the letters Ralph religiously sent to Lady Sussex every week are missing, probably as too dangerous to keep. Only the scrawls the old lady sent in reply have survived, but from these one can sense the tension and heightening drama of those fateful months.

To the Scots, the motives behind the King's offer of peace were highly suspect. By the terms of the treaty Charles had agreed to journey in person to Scotland for the forthcoming meetings of the Parliament and Assembly of the Kirk. It was bad enough that the proclamation that called for these gatherings was offensively worded, but when it was discovered that the hateful bishops, who were the cause of all the trouble in the first place, were summoned to attend the new Assembly chaos broke out and in Edinburgh the King's Agent narrowly escaped with his life.

Their suspicions were justified. No sooner had Charles signed at Berwick than he resolved to open hostilities again. Using the so-called intransigence and distrust of the Scots as an expedient, he excused himself from attending the Assembly and Parliament, and at the same time wrote to Wentworth in Ireland: 'Come when you will, you shall be welcome.'

'Black Tom' Wentworth, the iron ruler of Ireland and the most cordially disliked of all the King's councillors, had been watching Charles's ignominious showing in subduing the Scots with mounting exasperation and growing apprehension. A dedicated disciplinarian, he was appalled at the muddle and inefficiency that ruled in the King's army. Not the least cause of his anguish was the half-hearted support given the King by his followers. Untroubled by the subtleties of personal loyalty, Wentworth was quite unable to see how anything religious or political could affect that 'stout band of allegiance' to the sovereign which had been his ruling principle all his life. He had done his best to urge postponement of the First Bishops' War, but, when Charles proved adamant, tendered excellent and timely advice; more materially, he had sent 500 men to garrison Carlisle for the King and had tried to foster the madcap schemes of the Earl of Antrim. Now, at last, he was asked to come in person to subdue the Scots, and of his ability to do so he had not the slightest doubt. After a brief interlude settling his affairs he left for England.

The membership and mood of the Parliament now assembled was not outwardly hostile to the King. Clarendon's verdict was: 'It could never be hoped that more sober and dispassionate men would ever meet again in that place, or fewer who brought ill purposes with them', and the majority, although determined to have their grievances redressed, could be truthfully described as being 'Favourably disposed towards the King's service'.

From the first, Charles's arrogant and unconciliatory attitude hardened the opposition against him. He demanded subsidies in exchange for the abolition of ship-money, but the Commons declared that 'the redress of grievances must precede supply'. Pym, in a magnificent speech, summed up the outstanding arguments—religious and political—and he returned to his seat amidst cries of 'a good oration'. The Commons was determined not to yield to the King, but Wentworth, newly created Earl of Strafford, saw in their obduracy an opportunity to bring them to heel by invoking the support of the Lords—but even this expedient failed and Charles had no recourse but to dissolve Parliament.

The general feeling in the country was one of disappointment, and not a little exasperation. Clarendon afterwards wrote that 'there could not a greater damp have seized upon the spirit of the whole nation than this dissolution caused'; and Northumberland accurately forecast that 'it is impossible that things can long continue in this condition; so great a defection in the kingdom hath not been known in the memory of man'.

The opposition's carefully laid plans were now ripening. For several years support for the Parliament party had been increasing in the capital. Working diligently on every grievance and restriction, spokesmen gradually spread an insidious unrest, while preachers added 'fire from the Pulpit'. Groups gathered at the houses of well-known Puritan leaders. Holborn was one centre, Hackney another. Lord Holland held meetings in Kensington. Lord Mandeville, and later Pym, held some in Chelsea. In Covent Garden itself lived another great Puritan, the Earl of Bedford, whilst in the country Lord Warwick held 'court' in Essex, and Hampden and Lords Saye and Brooke held similar meetings at their own houses or at the home of Richard Knightley at Fawsley in nearby Northamptonshire.

Within the City itself a sizable opposition to the King was

growing; for the hitherto loyal merchants were now feeling the effects not only of the King's avaricous claims on themselves but also the effect of his fifteen years' reign on the economy of the country as a whole.

London was expanding fast. This in itself placed a grave burden on the authorities, and incidentally weakened the central machinery of City Government. New industries, an exploding population and economic uncertainty made the capital a city of flux—ripe for exploitation by those purporting to oppose an oppressive Government.

But another event was temporarily to take attention from the impending catastrophe. On August the 20th the Scots crossed the Tweed and in orderly fashion advanced towards Newcastle—war was now inevitable.

The First Scots War had been unpopular enough to the ordinary Englishman, but many things had happened that made the King's new war more insupportable still. It was common knowledge that Spanish troops en route to Holland were landing in the South of England, traversing the country and re-embarking at East Coast ports for the short trip across the Channel. But when a Spanish fleet loaded with troops took shelter from the Dutch in British coastal waters, while our own navy looked on and did nothing, rumours of a Popish plot grew apace, and many believed that the army so opportunely stranded on our shores was intended not to fight the Dutch but to suppress the King's enemies in his own country. More reliably, it was mooted that a formidable force was gathering in Ireland ready to impose their rule on the English, and this traditional shadow did more than anything to increase distrust of the King's policy.

Supported by these and other rumours, feeling against the Catholic officers in the King's army reached unpleasant extremes. Several who refused to accompany their men to church were murdered out of hand; and other innocents who professed no Catholic leanings at all were in deadly peril if they showed any laxity in their own worship. Mun, despite his almost extreme Protestant upbringing, seems to have suffered similar experiences. In July 1640 he writes:

'My souldyers and I are now att one and indeede never had any greate difference above twice, the chiefe of which I writt at large

to my father the last weeke. For my goeing to church three times
in a day it was true, but it was rather my own doings to give them
satisfaction that I was noe papist then any compulsion of theires,
but once that day I a little nodded at church and had it been a
minute longer truely I doe thinke I had been pulled by the nose,
for souldyers pointed extreamely at me, and the same day pulled
up a captaine of my lord Newport's regiment to the byshop's altar,
but theire communion table and made him receive, when scarce
any of them would receive with him.'

The King's army was in a poor way. Money came only from the
Roman Catholics or the clergy. In the north the troops, unpaid and
ill-disciplined, were sullen and mutinous. Of the raw levies which
Sir Jacob Astley was to train he found 'that those expected had not
come, and those that are come have neither colours nor halbertes
and want drums', and he went on to complain that he was 'to
receive all the arch knaves of the kingdom and to arm them at
Selby'. When Strafford arrived later his opinion was little better:
the soldiers 'altogether necessitous. That part which I bring now
with me from Durham the worst I ever saw. Our horses all cowardly
. . . an universal affright in all.'

While indecision and ill-discipline reigned in the English camp,
the Scots continued their advance to the Tyne and Newcastle. The
first brush of the campaign occurred at Newburn, a ford a few miles
upstream of Newcastle itself. Here the superior discipline of the
Scots prevailed and only the personal bravery of a few cavalry
officers redeemed anything from the 'infamous, irreparable rout of
Newburn'. Writing of this reverse Mun comments:

'That we were beaten you have heard, and for the circumstances
they are reported soe various that I know not which to write to you
for a trueth; this is certaine, that if Lasley had pursued his victory
he had cutt us all of; buisnessnes were very ill managed by some,
for we had neither cannon nor ammunition by us, but went on lyke
sheepe to the slaughter. I believe we shall have peace, but if we have
not I hope wee shall have better doings, or else we are surely beaten
againe, and then I know not what part of the kingdome can or at
least will hinder theire march whither they please.'

With the resulting, inevitable fall of Newcastle, active campaign-
ing finished, and lengthy negotiations with the Scots commenced

at Ripon. As a last resort, Charles summoned a Great Council of
Peers to assemble at York and deliberate on the question of the
Scots War and other pressing matters. Mun writes on September 21st:
'whether it is peace or warr it is yet uncertaine, but I believe it will
be knowne within this 8 or 10 dayes, for all depends on the Lords
engaging themselves for money', and four days later he adds: 'the
King doth soe much sympathize with the Lords that he tells them
if they will have him disband his army tomorrow he will doe it.'
Finally, on October the 9th he writes:

'For newes, all that is now is of warr, for the Scotts contrary to
your opinion (I am sure) are very unreasonable they ask no lesse
than 40,000L for a month's longer treaty, but we have a company
of noble lords that vow to pay them in leaden coyne, but next week
I shall be able to give you a more certain information, for the Scotch
lords come to treat with the King and ours on Monday next at
Yorke.'

Despite Mun's forebodings, at Ripon on October 26th, a form
of armistice was agreed with the Scots. It cost the King £860 a day
and the occupation of the counties of Northumberland and Durham.
More important, it meant that a Parliament had to be called to ratify
the treaty. Accordingly, elections for what was to be known as the
Long Parliament went forward in an atmosphere charged with
excitement and mounting apprehension.

The Long Parliament met on the 3rd of November 1640. Both
Sir Edmund and Ralph, who was shortly afterwards knighted,
had been returned as Members for Buckinghamshire for their old
boroughs, and their compatriots as representatives for that county
included such well-known names as Bulstrode Whitelocke and John
Hampden, the latter to become one of the outstanding figures on the
Parliament side.

The number of Members who were neighbours, or relatives,
or close friends of Sir Edmund in this momentous Parliament is
remarkable. The brother of the Speaker, Lenthall, had married a
cousin of Margaret Verney's. Hampden had married another and
lived less than twenty miles away from Claydon. Sir Peter Temple,
another opponent of ship-money and who lived at Stowe, was her
uncle and M.P. for Buckingham. Sir Edward Coke, who lived at
Stoke Poges and had been Member for Buckinghamshire. Sir
William Uvedale, lately the King's Treasurer at War, a close

friend and M.P. for Petersfield. John Ashburnham, who had been a Groom of the Bedchamber and was now Member for Hastings. Sir Roger Burgoyne, M.P. for Bedford, and a very close friend of the family. Sir Alexander Denton, Sir Edmund's brother-in-law. Sir Edward Herbert, the future Attorney General, whom Sir Edmund had known since he had become the first steward of the recently formed Palace Court, which was the Knight-Marshal's concern.

In the other House Sir Edmund's connections at Court gave him many friends: Lords Saye and Brooke, who also lived near Claydon—the former had married an aunt of Sir Edmund's wife. Lord Pembroke, the Lord Chamberlain. Lord Warwick, who was to become Lady Sussex's third husband. Lord Mandeville, who as the Earl of Manchester was to be her fourth. Lord Carnarvon, later killed at Newbury, and whose wife's picture still hangs at Claydon. Lord Arundel, the Earl-Marshal, who was Sir Edmund's immediate superior at Court. Lord Goring, business and army associate. The Earl of Bedford, whose scheme to drain the fens Sir Edmund had supported and who was his landlord at Covent Garden. Falkland, who lived at Great Tew beyond Oxford, and many others who knew Sir Edmund and respected the Knight-Marshal for his unswerving integrity and high-mindedness.

The House of Commons of the day included only 460 Members, and Mun writes from the north: 'I commend my humble sute to you and the rest of the 460 Kings who sit at Westminster to have regard to the honour of us souldyers'—evidently Ralph and his friends failed to do this in his opinion, for the irate Mun refers at a later date to 'the 460 tyrants who rule over us'.

The daily Parliamentary business began normally at eight o'clock in the morning, but ended proportionately early. Once Lord Warwick asks Ralph to attend a Committee on the Posts, in which he was concerned, at seven o'clock and apologizes for disturbing him at this 'unseasonable hour'. As things grew more anxious, the House, according to Clarendon, started 'keeping these disorderly hours and seldom rising till after four of the clock in the afternoon'. Apparently there was also a break for the midday meal, and there is an appeal from the then Speaker 'against the rush of members betwixt twelve and one midday, such that he was feigne to tell them they were unworthy to sit in this great and wise assembly that would so rush forth to their dinners'.

Sittings were confined to the daylight hours. On one occasion in 1641, when events were moving rapidly to a climax and tempers were rising, we read: 'it being dark some members called for candles; the majority opposed the proposal, it being so very late'. Unfortunately, the candles arrived by mistake, and the resulting shindy ended with two Members being confined to the Tower for a number of days.

No record of the debates was officially allowed, and Ralph must have experienced great difficulty in writing without being detected. His notes are written in pencil on small sheets of paper which he carried in his pocket and held on his knee. One can sense the rising excitement from the writing, and when debates became heated, or the speaker incoherent in the uproar, this becomes almost illegible. Often there are great jogs across the paper where a neighbour knocked his elbow, but these notes provide a verbatim record of the memorable events of the time and as such are invaluable.

There are very few twinges of humour amongst the notes. On the whole the tone is one of unrelieved severity. However, Ralph does allow himself slight levity when writing of a certain T.T. who, 'contrary to the custom of this House, doth seate and place himselfe neare the Speaker's chaire, where non but Privy Councillours and men of distinction are wont to sit, to the great scandall of the House. The said T.T., in a loud and violent manner, and contrary to the custom & usage of Parliament, in the Speaker's (ear), at the putting of a question about the militia, on 3rd Jan. '41, standing neare the Speaker's chaire, cried "Baw!" to the great terror and affrightment of the Speaker and of the members of the House of Comons, and contrary to his duty and the trust reposed in him by his country.'

Old Lady Sussex kept in close touch. She seems to have wielded considerable political power even in those days. Later she was popularly known as the 'Peeress of the Protectorate', for her third husband, the Earl of Warwick, was an outstanding Puritan figure, and her fourth, the Earl of Manchester, commanded the Parliamentary forces for much of the Civil War.

At the start of the session she writes to Ralph giving her advice and more substantial assistance:

'Now you will be taken up for your great affars. i pray God it may be a happy Parlyment to us all. When you have any idell time i pray let me have sometimes a lyne or to from you—and i will send you some bisket to put in your pokete and jhelly to comfort you up, as sone as my woman is in tune to make it.'

On another occasion she sends a 'gely of pippins' and some 'perly-cakes', and she goes on: '... you hade nede to ete good brekefast for your parlyment i believ keeps you in hy times longer than you expect'. These provisions were doubtless very welcome, but it cannot have been easy for Ralph to 'let them be tosted before you ete them', as she suggests.

From the outset Parliament was in no mood to compromise. Many of the King's supporters had failed to gain re-election, and when there was any disputed ballot the Parliament Party candidate was invariably chosen. Pursuing an independent course, item by item, the Commons remedied their grievances against the King: ship-money, the monopolies, tunnage and poundage—all the oppressive measures that had crushed the English people beneath their unyielding weight for so long were abolished for ever. But beneath it all the real business ahead lay undiscovered.

On the 9th of November Strafford arrived in London. Writing to him prior to this when the Earl was still in Yorkshire, Charles had assured him that 'he should not suffer in his person honour and fortune'. So, reluctantly, and fully alive to the peril that lay before him, Black Tom did his duty towards his sovereign as he had done it throughout his life.

Timing his stroke to perfection, Pym in the Commons raised a general accusation against the 'Tyrant'. Passed with enthusiasm there, it was sent to the Lords when Strafford was opportunely away, and when he returned it was to arrest on a charge of high treason.

While Strafford was preparing his defence, the Commons moved from strength to strength in their reforming zeal. Bastwicke, Prynne and Burton, imprisoned in 1637—the 'great incendiaries in the State', as Laud described them—were released amidst joyous uproar. Their tormentor, Archbishop Laud, himself was imprisoned. Charles's own revenue was curtailed—the King being powerless to prevent it; and his secretary, Windebanke, guilty of issuing Letters of Grace to Catholics and being lax in collecting recusants' fees, fled to the Continent when faced with imprisonment, closely followed by Finch, the Lord Keeper—who thus publicly confessed his guilt.

While these stirring events were happening in the capital, discontent in the army in the north was growing. Mun, writing to his brother from Ripon in January 1641, complains of their condition:

'Next Tuesday we have 6 weekes due to us and unlesse ther bee some speedy course taken for the payments you may well expecte to heare that all our souldyers are in a mutiny to the ruine of the country, for they are notable sheepe stealers allready. . . . This I will say to you of the parlyament, you are the worst paymasters I know.'

And later he bursts out:

'I beleeve you are busyed in the parlyment and yet neglect the mayne business of supplying the army, the effect of which with the terrible threatening musters may very well produce strange things, even not to be named. The horse have sent theire peremptory answere that they will not muster till they are payde; if the foote doe the lyke, beleeve me it can tend to noe lesse than a generall mutiny. A worme will turne agayne if it be trod on. Souldiers are now used ass though it were sure there should never be farther use of them. Apes have bits and bobs, but we have bobs without bits [i.e. blows without bites—of food]. If it hold thus but a fortnight longer, you will have a letter in way of petition to redresse our greevances or to cashiere us. There are divers officers that owe ass much ass their pay comes to, and are put to such shifts, that it is hard to say whether it goes hardest with them or the common souldyer. What foul dishonour is this to uss in our owne nation.'

On March the 22nd Strafford's trial began, and on the following day Ralph began his notes. They continue until the end of the trial, but with one break, for in April Margaret Verney died. Sir Edmund hadn't been well for some time now; as the situation grew graver and the tension rose, he became more and more despondent. Thus the effect of his wife's death at such a time was utterly shattering to the unhappy man and he never really fully recovered from the blow.

Margaret Verney's death was evidently quite sudden, for Lady Sussex writes to Ralph: 'The unexpected sade neuse gave me a harty soro, most for your lose of such a mother and for myselfe of soe deare a friend. . . . a bettir woman livede not then your good mother.' And later: 'I entended a cote to my godsone this Easter, and now I know he is in mourninge therefore have sent him a porringer to ete his breakfast in.' But the business of Strafford's trial was so serious that neither Sir Edmund nor his son could get away for long, and, after accompanying the body down to Claydon for the burial, both returned to London.

The mourning was a very serious affair and the 'blake bed and hanginges' once more came out of disuse. In August Sir Edmund writes to Roades:

'gett the oulde saddles at home covered with blacke, against I use them, which I thinke will be about the beginning of the next weeke. You may do them at Buckingham either with cloath or baize, and if you have no blacke bridels, sende me worde and I will buy some here.'

Margaret's will, which is addressed to Ralph, is very detailed. Her one-time good fortune seems to have been largely absorbed into the Claydon estate, for she mentions: 'All such of my goods wch y^r father hathe given me leave to dispose of . . .', nevertheless, she possessed many belongings of her own especially linen and the fine holland sheets of fourbredths 'which were never washed' are specifically named. She goes on: 'Give your wiffe, my diamonde claspes, sheepe heade and the reste of my odd diamonds and my sable muffe and six of my new great smockes.' While to Ralph's eldest son she leaves the sheets, a diamond ring and £100, which Ralph was to 'put out until he is a neare to bee married, then, bestow it in good plate as ffarr as it will in that wh^{ch} is moste yousefull for him'.

Charity and the many servants were not forgotten either, for she continues:

'Give Allcocke [the housekeeper] £40, the poore at Middle Claydon five pounds, Mr. Aris [the rector] £5; . . . Betty Coleman £10 to plase [place] her and pray take som care toe see her plased with it. . . . If cooke is with me give her sum £3 and sum of my worser gowns, and give my man accordinge as he is. . . . Give your father my guilte tankard and the case of silver-hafted knives, and dessier him to leave them to your elldist sonn. . . . Bestow sum £1 apeece of toyes or blake ringes for my mother, my brothers and sisters and their husbands and wives . . . there is monie enough in the Red Box which with the firste halfeyears intrust will pay your father and the 1 pound toys presently. . . . Pay the undermaids, and poore, and Mr. Aris next before the bigger sums.'

Other items follow:

'Take your father's tablett Picktuer yourselfe and give him Prince Henneris. They boathe lye in the Red Box. . . . Now pray lett non of my papers bee seene; but doe you burne them yrselve. All but my noats and account and medsinable and coockery Boockes, such keep. . . .'

It was probably the marks of the great burns that made her so reluctant to be seen in death by anyone outside the family, for she says:

'Let me be buried in leade att Claydon next where y^r ffather porposes to ly himselfe, and lett noe strandger winde me, nor doe nott lett me bee strippte, but put me a cleane smoke over me . . . and lett my fase be hid and doe you stay in the roome and see me wounde and layed in the firste coffin, which must be woode if I doe nott dye of anie infectious disease, ellse I am so far from desieringe it that I forbid you to come nare me. So the God of Heaven bless you all.'

But there was no room for personal grief whilst such momentous things were happening in London, for Strafford was now fighting for his life. The original case was supported by nine general and twenty-three specific charges, but by a brilliant personal defence he cleared himself of these. In this extremity Pym turned to the Bill of Attainder—an outdated expedient whereby no detailed proof was required, merely the suspicion of treason being enough to convict.

A copy of the secret minutes of the Council which took place after the dissolution of the Short Parliament was produced. This had been stolen from his father's papers by the son of the secretary, Sir Harry Vane, and was sent to the Lords, who were extremely irritated at the interruption. 'It is an unnatural motion for the head to be governed by the tail,' said one.

On the next day Sir Ralph continued his notes:

'My lord Straford did sum upp his evidence. . . . Sir H. Vaine's words swourne. Hee spake dubiously, for hee promised plainnesse, but spake but to the best of his remembrance, and afterwards swore the very words or to that effect. But hee is a single witnesse, and all the rest of the juncto remember noe such thinge.'

Popular feeling against Strafford was roused. Lady Sussex, writing to Ralph, says:

'Yon great lorde i hope will come to the honor of behedinge; if he scape he will do more ill than ever was don. Your Parlyment makes many sade harts, i hope you will make this a happy kaindom before you have don; i am very glad of your nues, for we have much but littel true here', and later: 'I pray God your hoses may agree, and that they may make an end of this greate lorde.'

The law of Strafford's treason was immaterial—the technical proofs were lacking, but the general suspicion was there. Quoting Lord Falkland, one of Parliament's chief spokesmen in the Upper House, Ralph writes:

'How many haires breadths make a tall man, & how many makes a little man, no man can well say; yet wee know a tall man when we see him from a low man, soe 'tis in this. how many illegal acts makes a treason is not certainly well known but wee well know it when we see it.'

. . . faced with this the Lords hesitated.

Now came another factor to seal Strafford's fate. For weeks past a number of amateur conspirators had been meeting, some-times in the Queen's apartments: Jermyn, the Queen's Master of Horse; Colonel George Goring, Governor of Portsmouth and son of Lord Goring, the two poets Suckling and Davenant, and one or two others. They were the backbone of a gathering militarist bloc extremist in their views and dedicated to restoring the King's prestige. As perhaps only a first step to greater things, they intended the rescue of Strafford from the Tower. Goring was elected to lead the conspiracy, but was no sooner chosen than in order to in-gratiate himself with Parliament he gave warning of the plot. Thus it came to the ears of Pym, who took note—but did nothing.

And now, when the information would do most damage, he revealed the details—the proposed rescue of Strafford, the possi-bility of a French landing at Portsmouth, the Irish implications. The conspirators fled. London, by this time seething with rumours and always ready to seize on a new one, was in uproar—a tangible Popish plot, the army undermined, foreign interference, Parliament to be restricted—the possible mixed with the fantastic, but all was believed. Amid shouts of 'Justice', Londoners besieged the Parliament building.

The Lords hesitated no longer. As they made their way to Westminster that very morning, stories of 'invasion' forces on the way were widespread; faced with the clamour, they could not refuse, and before a depleted House the Bill of Attainder was passed. Strafford's life now rested with the King.

But the King did not know. He sought guidance: one adviser bade him yield, another told him to follow the dictates of his own conscience—he was no wiser. But help from an unexpected quarter released Charles from his dilemma. Strafford wrote from the Tower:

'The minds of men are more and more incensed against me, notwithstanding your Majesty hath declared that, in your princely opinion, I am not guilty of treason, and that you are not satisfied in your conscience to pass the bill . . . I do most humbly beseech Your Majesty (for preventing of evils which may happen by your refusal) to pass this bill. . . .'

On the 10th of May Charles gave his consent to the Bill of Attainder and two days later Thomas Wentworth, Earl of Strafford, died on the scaffold. The King's conscience was ever after to trouble him for this betrayal of his faithful servant, and on his own scaffold, eight years later, he was to allude to Strafford's death: 'an unjust sentence that I suffered to take effect is now punished by an unjust sentence upon me'.

With Strafford perished the last hope Charles had of finding a leader able to impress obedience to the King's will. On the same day that he signed the Act of Attainder he consented to a Bill whereby the existing Parliament could be dissolved only at their own behest —the royal prerogative to raise and prorogue a Parliament was lost for ever. Other prerogatives were swept aside at the same time: no longer could the King make his own appointments in the navy; the notorious Star Chamber was abolished; and, as the culmination, the prerogative courts were taken from his hands. Little by little every privilege of kingship was either removed altogether or else made to pass through the net of Parliament.

At this vital stage in the conflict between King and Commons the division between the Upper and Lower Houses became acute. Critical of the wisdom of some of Pym's wilder ideas, the moderates

Mun Verney
BY EGMONT

in the House of Lords moved further towards the King; and as
Charles continued his conciliatory policy, so the rift widened.
Pym's campaign against the bishops, too, had exceeded prudence—
not daring even to attend debates, wherever the churchmen went
it was to cries of 'Popish bishops'. The association with the Scottish
Presbyterians seemingly dedicated to uproot the Established Church
was also viewed with mistrust by fair-minded churchmen and
laymen alike. The description of the church services as 'new-
vomited paganisme' or 'sensuall idolatry' was going too far and
there was much grumbling amongst responsible persons. The
common intention all along had been to remove the oppressive
measures that encumbered their daily life, not to supplant the
established order of things. As Clarendon said, 'there was not a
grievance or inconvenience, real or imaginary, to which there was
not a thorough remedy applied'; and it suddenly became apparent
that the new authority they had placed over themselves was as
grievous as the old. This was Charles's opportunity. If he could
continue in his conciliatory attitude of repentance and co-operation
he would rally more and more to his side. When Parliament adjourned in August 1641 the prospects for this were set fair.

The following month the army in the north was disbanded.
Many made their way south, if only to plead for their long-overdue
back-pay, and this influx of disgruntled soldiery did nothing to ease
the tension in the capital. Mun himself went to Claydon, where he
found his sisters and Doll Leeke, who delighted in teasing him:
'I never yet saw such double diligence used in tormenting a poore
man', he writes to Ralph. 'I cannot live long if these thunderclaps
continue.' They were all very fond of Mun, and Pen, then aged
nineteen, calls him 'My dearest combeannion the casseir [cashiered]
Captaine'.

Before Parliament adjourned Pym persuaded them to elect a
committee of fifty to guard the nation's interests during the recess.
Meanwhile, the King had decided to go to Scotland, where he was
now bestowing honours and good humour on his faithful subjects
there. Parliament, fully alive to the dangers of his presence in
Scotland, sent a party of six 'observers' to see and report all. The
initial impression he made was not to their liking. For Charles's
popularity increased visibly as the visit progressed. But on the
surface only—for beneath it all there was rumour of plot and
suspicion.

L

All came to a head when The Incident, as it was called, came to light—a scheme to kidnap Argyll and Hamilton from the very rooms of the King himself. Improbable though it was, and however much Charles denied all knowledge, it was widely believed that the King was implicated and at once all his hard-won popularity was cast to the ground.

This gave suspicion enough to the English that the King was not quite as open in his dealings as he appeared, but worse was to follow: and the revolt in Ireland broke like a thunderclap on the astonished Parliament and people, whilst their attentions were focused on the King's progress in Scotland.

The disbandment of the Irish army demanded by Parliament of the King had not in fact been enforced. Collected near the ports were small bands of soldiers, who had enlisted in foreign service but were unable to find passage to their new masters. Loyal to their officers, but acknowledging no higher allegiance, they watched disgruntled, unpaid and ready to make mischief.

The country was uncertain and apprehensive. The collapse of Strafford's iron ministry had left a dangerous vacuum. Little was needed to touch off revolt, but in Dublin the Lords Justices did nothing.

Priests were roaming the countryside fomenting rebellion and stirring discontent. They noticed with alarm the success of the Parliament faction in England and worked with renewed vigour and urgency. For, with a Puritan party in power, extreme Protestantism, with its elemental obliteration of the Catholic religion, might at any moment be imposed on Ireland. To a warlike and unrepentant people such a move was not to be tolerated; only one answer remained; and by 1641 a revolt was inevitable.

October 23rd was the day appointed. Throughout the northern part of the country, in Monaghan, eastern Ulster, around Belfast, the insurgents swept on their remorseless way, pillaging, burning, murdering as they went. The rising gathered strength. Newry was in flames. Drogheda threatened from the north. Leinster up in arms. As reports filtered in, it became clear that this was no unco-ordinated revolt.

While Dublin cried for help from Parliament, the rebels pressed on relentlessly. In England invasion was expected hourly and precautions were taken in the west. Meanwhile, the King rode leisurely south from Scotland—as yet there was no sign of his being implicated. Events were moving, however, for in Ireland Sir Phelim O'Neill was bragging of his Royal Commission to rid the King of his enemies and pointing out the Great Seal as final proof of its authenticity. Although an obvious forgery, the damage was done: the King was now associated with a Catholic cause.

Pym and his creatures need work no more. The effect of his news was cataclysmic. Memories of his father's religious vacillations and Charles's own trip to Spain came flooding back. Religious distrust was heaped on political discontent. Coupled with the many doubts of Charles's sincerity, knowledge of this involvement with the Irish rebellion was conclusive—he was branded for ever.

Meanwhile, Pym's schemings came into the open and on the 22nd of November the Grand Remonstrance was presented to Parliament. This, a conglomeration of all the grievances against the King, was passed by a majority of eleven amidst unparalleled uproar—only Hampden's calmness prevented bloodshed. All was not yet lost, however, for the narrowness of the majority revealed how deep was the rift between factions. The presence of a considerable moderate party still held out hope for the King. If these moderates remained in support his enemies would have no legal power.

Lady Sussex upheld the common interpretation of events, and writes on November 29th:

'Your glorious show we have in printe; my thinkes the kainge should love his pepell of inglande best; for suer ther bonty and obedynce is most to him; i pray God sende your parlyment agree will; . . . i becech the god of heaven to bles and keepe you all safe from any filinus parties; ther will bee much bisynes in your hose suer, now the kainge is com; god power is above all; i hope he will derect you to do for the best, every way. Thow i am ever most glade at your lettirs i forbide them but when you have lesuer, for i know you can not but bee tyerde out ever day with bisynes.'

On the 1st of December the Remonstrance was presented to Charles at Hampton Court—the deputation returned with no satisfaction.

Pym's next move was another assault on the Church. Once again the cry of 'No bishops' was heard about Whitehall, and only with the greatest difficulty could the churchmen make their way to attend debates. The militia was the next target, and a bill to place all military and naval appointments under Parliament's control passed its first reading. In Ireland, though, the situation had reached a state of chaos and uncertainty. The Government was powerless with the ineffective force at their command and the Roman Catholic gentry came out to join the large bands of rebels sweeping the country leaving ruin in their wake. Still no aid had been sent—and Parliament would send none until the question of command was settled. To save the remnants of his sovereignty and to jolt Parliament into some action to save his subjects' lives, the King now stepped in and offered to help or go in person to Ireland— but even this genuine move was instantly declared a breach of privilege.

The tempo was quickening. Riots were an everyday event in London. The pro-Parliament apprentices, with their monotonous cry of 'No bishops', 'No Popish lords', were outside Westminster on every occasion of real or expected friction to give evidence of the popular fear of a general uprising. Petitions were raised on every conceivable subject or supposed grievance. Well-organized demonstrations were held in assembly places—the Piazza or at Moorfields, or in the Artillery Gardens. The rudimentary news-sheets were exploited to the full. Even the Commons, for 'safety', moved to Guildhall and there carried on their debates in reach of help if needed. Within the City the election of the nominees of the Parliament Party went on unhindered. The King was utterly powerless and watched impotent as the last vestige of his authority was swept aside.

In the midst of this hubbub Charles received word that the impeachment of the Queen might happen at any time. Now he acted; on January 3rd, 1642, Pym, Hampden, Haslerig, Holles, Strode and Lord Mandeville, eldest son of the Earl of Manchester, were accused of high treason and their surrender demanded

The Commons immediately declared the accusation a breach of privilege and refused to yield them up. Force was imminent. That night Charles sent a message to the Lord Mayor forbidding him to send the Trained Bands to the help of the Commons, and authorizing them to fire on the crowds if the need arose. The following day he went in person to Westminster to arrest the traitors, but too late —warned of his coming they had fled. The attempt had failed, the birds had flown.

There was now no hope of averting a clash. Greeted with cries of 'Privilege' wherever he went, the King was lost. Declarations of support for Parliament were flooding in from all sides. Charles had no recourse but to leave. On the 10th of January he saw London for the last time as a free man.

IX

Separate Ways

'There is a tide in the affairs of men,
Which, taken at the flood, leads on to fortune;
Omitted, all the voyage of their life
Is bound in shallows and in miseries.
On such a full sea are we now afloat,
And we must take the current when it serves,
Or lose our venture.'

SHAKESPEARE

BY THE end of 1641 Tom has returned. His promise to behave
was too good to last and having exhausted his supplies and luck
in Barbados he is once more in England—penniless. His long-
suffering father sends him back the following year, but any illusions
the family may have still held were soon dispelled by Tom's first
letter:

'My proceedings which are (thanks be to God) indifferent well.
First for our voyage by sea praysed be God I lost not a man; but
most of them God visited with a sickness, some with the small pox,
and some with the feaver. And it pleased god to visitt mee with an
extream burning feaver which held mee soe long that I was not able
to rise without two to help mee up, and soe weak I came a shore.
... When I could hardly speak six of my men (with the conceit they
took of the island) fell very sick of the Ague, and of the feavour,

166

that it did much perplex mee becaus I was not able to look after them myself, soe heareing that they did not mend I hearkned for a chapman, and having obtained one I sold all my men and goods in a lump, and within a very short time one of them dyed. Butt all my cotton is shipped in a dutch ship and is bound for Amsterdam . . . I would beseech you to give mee notice whether it were unpossible for mee and your men, with the great helpe of bridewell and prisons to procure in two months space an hundred men or more, which if they are to be gott I shall be mighty joyfull, and most thankfull unto you and shall by that means make amends for my losses I have sustayned by reason of my sickness.'

This news must have been bad enough for his father to swallow, but worse was to come.

'The men', Tom continues, 'have bestowed many a wholesome curs uppon mee although I gave them all some small matter to eays there fortunes. One of the three brothers attempted to stab mee but that God prevented him, I beseech you and my brother to have a speciall care of their brother that liveth with Sir Edmund Pye. For the devill may Doe much with his saints. For he told mee before my departure that in case he heard I sold them that he would be the death of some of my generation at home, in case I came not my self.'

In these circumstances Tom's inevitable return must have been almost welcome. Sure enough, within eight months of leaving England the traveller is back, preceding his homecoming with a letter to his father's steward asking him also to remain silent on what had happened in the West Indies:

'If any of my men's friends doe enquire of you . . . how they are disposed of, I pray answer them with as much brevity as may be that they are all well and are upon another man's plantation till my return thither agayne. And if they should tell you that I have putt them of to other people, tell them it is not soe, and endevour to the uttmost of your power to perswade them to the contrarye.'

He had brought back with him a cargo of cotton and tobacco, shipped 'for feare of enemies abroad . . . in an Englishman and a Dutchman', but both sold at a loss and soon he is getting into debt again. When Ralph complains Tom writes back:

'Now whereas you write mee word that I will never leave borrowing of such poor creatures, let me tell you lords and knights, and gentlemen of farr better rank then myself are and will be still indebted unto Taylors, and therefore I count it noe disparagement. There was a kinsman of ours (He shall be nameless becaus he is dead) that lived after a verey high rank, and perhapps you thought that he would have scorned to have been credited by a poor taylor, yet I know he was deeply indebted to one, but the taylor is now dead and soe is he.'

The outbreak of the Civil War saved Sir Edmund from Tom's further importunities and debts, and it must have been with considerable relief that his family heard he had enlisted in the King's army.

Brother Henry, too, keeps Ralph and his father busy on his behalf. At this time he is hankering after a company, which he notes may be had for £700: 'it is not deare considdering the profett of it', he adds.

His chances, however, fade when Henrietta Maria goes over to Holland as Charles's emissary to try to buy munitions for the coming war. He dolefully reports her coming 'is expensive to all . . . here are divers gentlemen of great qualities wch are come over with our queene that stands for the first company that falles of our Platton . . . and all they can pretend to is hopping to imbrace a fortune by the queene's favour more than for their good service'.

Sir Edmund had evidently promised to do his utmost for his son, for Henry writes to Ralph thanking him for having 'moved his sute'. Another who had promised his aid was the Prince of Orange, and Henry writes:

'When I went to take my leave of his Highness a incouraged mee much in promising mee to doe for mee; wth all a has given mee an act under his owne hand voluntariley of himselfe to remaine in the Armey this sumer; it is a favour, and a great one I can assuer you; I dare sware it is the first a hath given to any of a strange nation in his life. I hope if any fortune fall sence a hath don this a will thinke of mee; in earnest it is a good signe, though a greate charge to mee and my ffather. I have sent to him for a nagg. I hope a will be plesed to send mee wan . . . for I am so lame of my leggs that I cannot march.'

All this is in vain, and shortly after he writes in wrath that
although three vacancies had fallen open he had been passed over
for all of them. He attributes this to his father and Ralph's doings in
Parliament, but more particularly to Goring's intrigues:

'Now sence this I have bine with Sir Thomas Stafford and . . .
intreated him to move the queene to recommend mee to the Prince;
a reply'd a durst not, for a sed a was sertaine her Majestie would not
be plesed to spake for mee. Wth all like a noble freind as hee con-
seved a tould mee the reson of it: thinke but of Wickcom and
Alsberie and you may both easley find the sence of it; the truth is,
I beelive as has tryed her and was deneyd . . . truley I find by him
that I am far more unlikeley of getting a companey then I was the
first day a come here; my lord Goring hath bin the occasion of this
and non else; had I deserved the lest unkindness from him it would
not have troubled mee; his being my enemie I am confident will
cast me out of my coronells good opinion, and then to get higher
it is impossible. . . . This weeke I goe to my gareson and there shall
stay this summer.'

And, later, adds:

'for Wickham and Alisbery stepping in my way, I believe that is
noe hindrance, though, indeed, I have bin tould by more than one
or teu it has. The opinion, I see, of the great ones most att the Court
is that my father and you are all for the Parleyment and not for the
King, wch here I find they take not kindly. My father's lett^r will
let you see more playneley how little I regard shuch false jelosies,
and truley as times goe now, and considdering the difficulty of
getting mee a company, a need not much regard it; for, let mee
travill where I will, soe I go not to hell, a more baser place to make
a fortune and less beelive I cannot finde;'

Lord Goring justifies his actions to his friend Sir Edmund.
Nevertheless, neither Henry nor his father are quite satisfied with
the explanation, and the latter cannot forbear to add to one of his
letters to Ralph about a troublesome horse: 'I would faine have you
ridd of that beast for all the Horses I know I doe not like him, but
hee will serve Mr. Gorings turne very well to take a view of his
Regiment.' Despite this, nothing further happens over Henry's
company and he is left as disgruntled as before.

Later Ralph suggests that his brother should join the forces of the Parliament, and Henry writes back in typical vein, concerned only with his own welfare and completely unfeeling of the higher issues behind this offer:

'I confess the imployment wth you I hold to bee much better; where the continuance of it soe certaine as thes here, and the cause soe just as that of ireland; as earnest as I am in presing to ataine to a bet^{er} fortune, yett my prayers are daley for peace in that kingdome. To speake the truth, I must needes say of late I have bine much crost in my advancement, and when I am alone and thinke of the maliciousness of that man wch did prevent mee of it makes mee madd, and in a maner weary of my profession, for if a possess my coronell once against mee, as long as a lives I shall not gett a company.'

Ralph has no illusions as to Henry's conscience in these matters and cynically observes: 'I presume the army will not entertain him, what they will do I know not but I believe they value him not, nor do I think unless he hath great hopes of a speedy settlement . . . he will easily engage for he is naturally idle enough.'

At last, on the prompting of his father, he returns to England and like his brother Tom takes service with the King's army.

Before doing so, however, he cannot resist a last grumble: 'Had I gon, Captaine, for the North att first, as I desired, when divers other offecers here did, wch had bet^{r} command then myselfe, and now for Eirland, I had had more then five hundred pound in my purse, when now I have not a grao^{t} to speake of, or else I must have spent my time ill.' Even Henry's presence—however limited its value—would have been welcome in Ireland, for by now the situation was critical, and the plight of Sir Edmund's Irish friends was terrible in the extreme.

The rebellion seems to have come as a great surprise to everyone and found them completely unprepared. Sir John Leeke writes at the end of 1641:

'The frights and terrors wee heere live in, cannot welbe expressed but by such as suffer and feele the distraction, whereof many are com for England that cann relate itt as eie witnesses, . . . I protest I am most miserable, for though I have friends, yet noe friend to lend me tenn pounds. No man will part with a peny of money, and by all that is good in heaven and earth, I nor my wife have in purse

40s.—We have 20 good cowes, wee may have none tomorrow, such is the case of many men . . . my wife is in that extremitie of feares.'

Sir Ralph tries to get them to come to England and safety, in particular Lady Barrymore, and writes to her:

'Your stay afflicts mee extreamly least you should bee suddainly surprised by thos Barbarous Rebells who (if Fame belye them not) delight in cruelty, and take pleasure in insolency, above and beyond ye worst of infidells. truly maddame though I have never been much in love with Papists, yet I beeleeved them to bee christians, but if they offer violence to you, or yours, I shall change my opinion. . . .'

The many English Protestants who had settled in Ireland within the previous half-century were in a poor way. Houses and estates abandoned, the families moved as best they could to the comparatively strong garrison towns, but even there they were scarcely safe from the depredations of the Irish. Sir John Leeke writes again in January 1642:

'Clomell, the key of Munster is taken on Saturday last; Dungarvan and the castle is taken both by the treachery of the townsmen; Kilkenny ten days since was taken by the Lord Mont Garratt and his four sons and sons-in-law. My Lady of Ormund and her children are in the castle and there imprisoned, Mountgarratt is in the castle with a face to secure the Lady, but a false heart. I am now come to Yoghall with my company, where we are as secure as in any Irish town; God knows there is no security but where a good English garrison doth secure.'

Lord Barrymore, his neighbour Lord Dungarvan (Lord Cork's son) and others rallied what forces they could, but the rebels had command of all the country except the strongest towns—communication between these was impossible and the garrisons were hard put to it to hold out themselves, quite apart from organizing any co-ordinated campaign to liberate the rest of the country. Sir John continues:

'My Lord of Broghall went before the town of Dungarvan, the next day it was surprised, with 60 horse and 50 foot, and took the praye of the town, . . . this army carryeth a brave resolution though but small in number, yet courageous and discreetly commanded; they fight for honour and their lands, all is at stake; there is not a country we can hear of but the county of Corke but are in action; Oh, we sigh and grieve for the English forces, we believe they will come, but the kingdom will be so near losing, or at least destroying, that the regaining will cost more blood and charge than the first conquest did or all the wars in Queen Elizabeth's time.'

The scarcity of food was the greatest danger. Cattle and sheep were slaughtered indiscriminately and those not eaten straight away were salted down. It was a hard winter, too, which added to their discomforts; by the time spring came the breeding stock for the year was almost entirely wiped out. Potatoes had not yet become the staple diet of the Irish as they were in the next century.

'God of his mercy', writes Sir John again, 'sent us succors and fight for us and with us to the distruction of the ungratious rebells ... I do believe that whosoever shall live to this day twelvemonth shall see such a dearth and famine as hath seldom or hardly been known in Ireland; what cattle the rebels cannot come at, we are inforced to barrell up, for if the rebels take our cattle (which they have done in infinite number, both of fair sheep and goodly cattle as in England), what they eate they kill with their skeens and let them lie and stink. ... The old Earl of Cork is full of distractions, not like the man he was; his sons are most noble, and you should hear brave things of their undertakings and performances ... I should be loath to leave Ireland until the fire burns my heels.'

As yet help from England was filtering in only very slowly. Contingents under Monk, Greville and Vavasour had indeed arrived, but they were pitifully small. Sir Edmund had at last managed to obtain a captaincy for Mun in Ormonde's own regiment bound for Ireland, but contrary winds prevented them from sailing from Chester for six tedious weeks. Finally, in January this much needed reinforcement reached Dublin—where the garrison was still just holding out.

The army was in bad shape. Starved of equipment, provision or pay from England, the near-mutinous troops had to exist on what they could pillage from a countryside already nearly swept bare.

'I'll assure you wee scarce thinke it a forfeite of our honours even att this time to quitt your service', writes Mun to Ralph, 'I admire how you thinke wee live; wee have bellyes to feeds and backs to cloath ass well ass you; wee want yet the hardynes to goe naked, neither have wee been bredd, lyke camelions, to live on ayre . . . tis not here ass it was in Yorkshire; here the inhabitants are neither willing nor able to lend, and it is sport to them to see uss undon. Our souldiers have lived upon nothing this month but salt beefe and herrings, which is soe unusual to our men that came last out of England, that of our 2,500 men, I believe we have 500 sicke.'

And he adds later:

'Had you sent 10,000 men 6 or 8 weekes since I dare say the rebells had beene neare repelled by this, and now, for ought I know, it may last you many a yeare, and the longer you stay, the more heade they will get. . . . Ireland is full of castles, and truly strong ones, and thither the rebells fly, not daring to give us a meeting, although treble our number. I will not say but that the want of armes and ammunition may be much the cause of it, but truly I doe believe them to be of a very cowardly nature.'

The country was ablaze. Only Ormonde in Dublin was able to preserve order, and it was his trained and disciplined force which raised the siege of Drogheda where Sir Henry Tichborne had held out for over four months against an enemy force superior to his in every respect but leadership. This was the first English success of the campaign.

The muddle, confusion and petty spite of the many persuasions in Ireland did little to help a co-ordinated resistance. Even in face of mortal danger the running strife and mistrust continued between the Presbyterians, the Anglicans and the Catholics. A burning hatred of the native Irish was their only bond. Atrocities of the most awful description were committed by both sides. Received gleefully by the public, and exaggerated in the London Press, the cruelty and abominations of the 'bloody Irish Butchers' became the sole topic of conversation. Only revenge and treatment in kind could heal this terrible wound, and vengeance was stored up in English hearts until Cromwell himself tilted the scales the other way.

Sir John's state was pitiful. All the hard labour he had put into his estates was wasted, and the false security they had long enjoyed was shattered for ever. 'I am most miserable', he writes. 'Money I have none, rent none to be paid, the rebells within a mile of the town the river only between, our towne supposed not to be sownd at heart.'

Only a vast sum, estimated at £1,000,000, could raise the forces to clear up the rebellion and save Ireland. But few were inclined to indulge in such a doubtful investment, for the City had no confidence and Parliament was too preoccupied with their own affairs to help their fellow countrymen in Ireland.

Sir Ralph, writing to Lady Barrymore, points this out:

'You are so hardened by this winter's sufferings, that neither fire nor sword can fright you into England; 'tis truth there's little left that may invite you hither, the unhappy distractions of this kingdom have not only reduced ourselves into a sad condition, but made Ireland, far more miserable. Till these are settled here, I shall not expect to see the rebels quiet there, especially considering these distempers have wrought so many doubtings in the minds of men, that I fear 'twill be very hard to raise a considerable sum of money, unless there do appear greater hopes of peace than yet are evident.'

But worse was to follow, and the crowning horror came when Lord Barrymore was slain. 'He left a distressed lady and four children, with an encumbered and disjointed estate, and all his country wasted', said one account.

Nevertheless, the tide was starting to turn and things were going better now. Some successes were recorded, but always accompanied by tales of the most horrible excesses. In June 1642 Trim Castle was taken after a three days' siege, and even Mun, normally the kindest-hearted of men, says: 'We had 20 men slaine and 30 hurt and 3 officers shot after we put some four score men to the sword, but like valiant knights errant, gave quarter and liberty to all the women.'

He was in command of Rathcoffy Castle, some twelve miles from Dublin, the following month. Here he was laid low by fever, but was fortunate in being able to pay for the time when he was 'given over of the phisitions for a dead man for almost a week' by pillaging to the tune of nearly £50.

Shortly after this, first the Leekes and then Lady Barrymore took refuge in England, but even here their security was as uncertain as it was short-lived.

In the midst of these doubts and disasters in England and Ireland, there was one happy event for Sir Edmund. The previous year his fourth daughter, Cary, his 'shee Darling', as Dr. Denton calls her, met a young friend of Mun's—Thomas Gardiner, eldest son of Sir

Thomas Gardiner, Recorder of London and later Solicitor General, a strong Royalist and a long-standing friend of Sir Edmund's. The Gardiners lived at Cuddesden, about twenty miles from Claydon, and shortly after their first meeting Sir Edmund promised his daughter, aged fifteen, to the young Thomas, then a captain of dragoons in the King's army.

Cary was a great favourite with the family, not least with Mun, who, when he was at Claydon at the end of 1641, tenderly passed on the news of the romance to Ralph:

'My sister Cary desiers you will excuse her not writing to you; she hath been extreame ill this day and much by fitts. Believe me, brother, shee is of ass sweet a disposition ass any creature I know living, and her affection to you is such that I thinke it expresseth what affection is or can be. In the extremitie of her fitt she will wish to me privately besides your lady for three men, my father and you are two, I thinke you may soone guesse the third, yet truly she nam'd him not. This is the first day but I thinke she hath had twenty fitts in it. I pray god they may soone cease with her. I am now in haste to goe to her therefore. . . .'

Fortunately her 'fitts' seem to have died down, for no more is heard of them. However, her prospective father-in-law soon gets himself into trouble with Parliament and it must have been very sad for Ralph to have to record the impeachment of someone so close to him. Hot-headed and intolerant, Sir Thomas quickly came to the notice of the Commons. He opposed Pym and the proposed removal of bishops and lords from Parliament, and put 'obstructions in the way of persons signing a petition'. He was reputed to have said that the petition 'tended to sedition and set men togeather by the eares', and, after being told it was for peace, ended: 'Is this your way of peace? Noe, it is for blood and cutting of throates, thanke yourselves, and your blood bee on your owne heades; I hate a papist, and I hate the petition worse.' After this it was only a matter of time before he was imprisoned. The moment came when he opposed the Militia Bill, and Sir Ralph notes down the accusations against him:

'Hee endeavored to hinder the caling of this parliament and now to destroy it. He was an abbettor of Ship-money . . . and beeing told it was against law, hee said, "Wee shall find a law for it ere long.". . . He said every man was bound by his alegence to serve the king, and noe charter could excuse them; they had already felt the waite of his little finger in Londonderry and it was a dangerous thing to anger the king.'

Despite this, the marriage goes forward and old Lady Sussex writes: 'I am very sorry for Mr. Gardiner, for I fear swete Cary will cuffer for it.' Then a little later: 'Swete Cary, i hear, is now a marrede wife; i pray god it may bee happy every way to her. Your father i presume wase far ingagede or otherways i belive he woulde not have don it att this time.'

There is a list in Sir Edmund's own hand giving his 'Shee Darling' some of the precious linen left by his wife: the 'fine-lased coyfe', and the 'seven handkerchers lased for pockets', and the 'twelve pairs of plaine bottome cuffs'.

For their honeymoon the couple went to Bedfordshire, stopping at Welwyn on the way. From their inn the bridegroom wrote back to his sister-in-law, Ralph's wife:

'After an indifferent pleasant journey, we came to our Inn at Wellen, neither came there any sorrow uppon us untill some object or other gave us an occasion to thinke on Common Garden, and truly we might well be greeved to leave such company and converse onely with hadges and ditches and durty wayes,' and then he adds: 'you shall understand likewise that I am neither Puritan nor Round-head, but am faithfully and sincerely and with all my heart, Deare madam, your truly affectionate brother.'

They returned to Cuddesden in July, where Sir Thomas and his whole family were ready to greet them. The young bride writes ecstatically to her brother:

'I must let you know how wel i lik this place. . . . Whin I came my granmother bid me very wellcom and made what entertanement shee cod, more a gret dele then I expecked, and Sir tomas and my laydy bid mee very wellcom to Coddisdon and sade they wisht it might bee my one [own] and truly uesis mee very civilly. . . . Pray when that you wright to my father present my ombel duty to him, and let him kno I am will.'

Ralph replied:

'Your letter brought mee the welcomest newes I have had a greate while; for as I must bee a sharer in all your sufferings, soe

Claydon House today—west aspect. *By courtesy of Country Life*

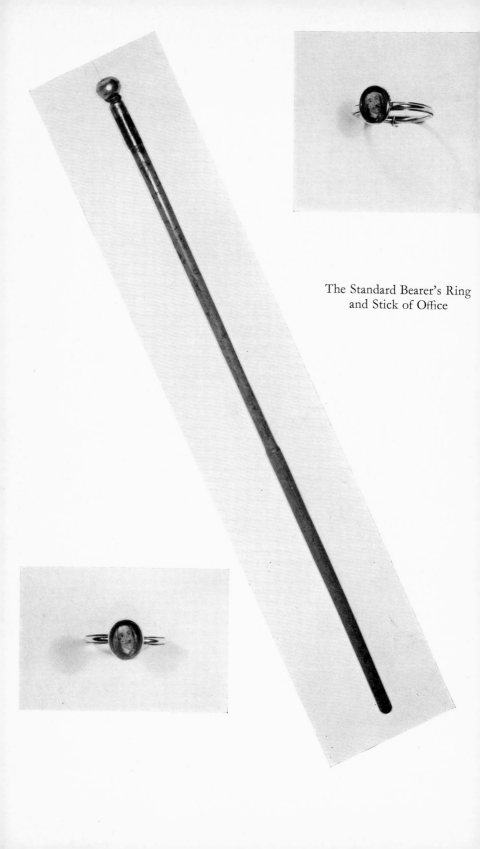

The Standard Bearer's Ring
and Stick of Office

you must give mee leave to joy in all your contentments. Those good people with whom you are now setled will still continew there love and kindnesse unlesse you faile in your due respects to them, which I am confident you will never doe . . . I longe to meete you . . . if the times prove quiet I purpose to visite Cudsden this sumer; however it will be a greate contentment to mee to heare from you often.'

But the young bride's new-found happiness did not last long, for in August her husband went off to rejoin the army in the north and she writes sadly:

'i never grouged my husband of any hapyness in my life more thin i did his seein of you and my missin of so mouch joy. i cannot say anything of him for i have not sene him almost this fore months. hee is 2 hondard mils distance from mee. think what a trobill it is to mee which has so good a husband. i du pray for a hapy meeting of us all.'

The couple were expecting a child, but in July 1645 Thomas was killed in a skirmish near Aylesbury. The young widow soon after gave birth to a 'gurl to all our griefes'. Poor Cary, left destitute by her husband's death and now completely ignored by the Gardiners, took shelter with her child at Claydon, where were gathered a small crowd of defenceless women protected only by old Roades.

M

X

———❦❦———

The Raising of the Standard

———❦❦———

'Some consequence yet hanging in the stars'

SHAKESPEARE

THE CRIES of 'Privilege' that pursued the King from the Chamber of Westminster that wintry afternoon in 1642 were the death-knell of his hopes for reconciliation. This one unconstitutional act gave the opposition the pretext they needed. Had the seizure of the five Members been successful all might have been well—but the attempt, tried and failed, irrevocably lost Charles any future chance of successful appeal to Constitutional law or practice thereafter.

With the departure of the King the Commons at once adjourned, 'With the sense that they had but just escaped a massacre.' Lady Sussex voiced the general feeling when she wrote to Ralph:

'Thes distractede times put us all in great disorder, but i hope wee shall not bee kaillede; yet i thinke you are in greatter danger than wee ar in the contry; i pray god bles you with safty; your parlyment flyes hye; truly itt is a happy thinge, i thinke, the have so much corige to stand to mentane ther right; the good tone of london it semes will do so to; truly the are to bee commendede; the

178

kainges party will bee to weke; that he must yelde to the parlyment; i pray god derect all your harts to do for the bes for the good of us all; if wee now be over cam wee are undon for ever; i hope thos gentillmen the kainge woulde have from your hose shall bee safe; the stand so much for the generall good that it was a misarable thinge if the shoulde cuffer; thes lettir will com safe, or else i shoulde not have adfentiude to have sade so much. It was a blessede thinge thos gentilmen was from the parlyment when the kinge cam, he hade ill counsill surly to com in such a way.'

The months from January to the raising of the King's Standard at Nottingham was a time of unparalleled rumour and confusion. The novelty of successful opposition to the sanctity of the hereditary monarchy seemed to take the country aback. Now that war between the two factions was a near reality, ever becoming more inevitable, the moment of truth appeared almost incomprehensible. The enormity of their past actions carried out in the heat of the moment seemed to stagger many men. A growing sense of doom and doubt pervaded the more moderate, and when it came to the point many preferred to go into exile than to oppose their King—an act they were not mentally attuned to carry out.

To Ralph, divided from his father and family by an evergrowing gulf of belief, this was a time of terrible sorrow, and immense moral courage. From his letters one can sense the conflict going on within him between loyalty to father and family, and his imposed sense of duty to the cause he espoused—a struggle that eventually led to his exile.

He received no support from his brothers. Mun himself was deeply disgusted.

'Brother,' he writes, 'what I feared is proovd too true, which is your being against the king; give me leave to tell you in my opinion tis most unhandsomely done, and it grieves my hearte to thinke that my father allready and I, who soe dearly love and esteeme you, should be bound in consequence (because in duty to our king) to be your enemy. I heare tis a greate greife to my father . . . I am soe much troubled to think of your being of the syde you are that I can write no more, only I shall pray for peace with all my hearte, but if God grant not that, yet that He will be pleased to turne your

hearte that you may soe expresse your duty to your king that my
father may still have cause to rejoice in you.'

Ralph never replied to this letter, so Mun follows it up:

'I beseeche you let not our unfortunate silence breede the least
distrust of each other's affections, although I would willingly lose
my right hand that you had gone the other way, yet I will never
consent that this dispute shall make a quarrel between us, there be
too many to fight with besides ourselves. I pray God grant a
suddaine and firme peace that we may safely meete in persone as
well as in affection. Though I am tooth and nayle for the King's
cause, and endure soe to the death, whatsoever his fortune be, yet
sweete brother, let not this my opinion (for it is guyded by my conscience), nor any report which you can heare of me, cause a diffi-
dence of my true love to you.'

Such was the chivalry and extraordinary lack of animosity
which characterized not only Mun and Ralph but also the majority
on both sides during the Civil War.

The most frequent correspondent of this period is old Lady
Sussex; hardly a week passes but she writes to Ralph to glean what
news she can—adding her own titbits of the goings-on at 'Sentor-
bones' (St. Albans). She writes in January:

'Wee have bene att our defosyons to day, and ther was some-
thinge rede from your parlyment to have all the tranede bandes
in a redines. the are all in great fear at Sentorbornes, and ever hose
[every house] the say have bought armes and gons to defend them.
i hope i shall be safe hear, though i have nether. it is ill nues to hear
ther is a pese betwixt Spane and frince, suer the will com uppon us,
and helpe eyrlande. i pray God keepe us from the misyres that
other nasyons have sufferde by ware. i am very glade to hear your
father is so will agane. i have presented him with some ihely [jelly]
and ther is eyght pots for you and your lady, how [who] i beceche
you to rember me most affecynatly to', and again writing to Ralph's
wife: 'Swite Mrs. Varny, I am hartly trubled for your good father,
for if hee shoulde goe after, sartinly it would bee very dangours
for him cominge from the hote bathes, I pray God direct him for
the best, and let me intret a lyne or to from you as sone as you know
what his resolutyons are.'

While Charles assembled his Court at York, Henrietta Maria procured munitions at The Hague. In April took place the first outright show of opposition to the King when Sir John Hotham, Governor of Hull, suspecting a ruse to capture his valuable arsenal, refused entry to his royal visitor. Charles, smarting under the affront, wrote to Parliament demanding the magazine and the punishment of Hotham, but such was the feeling in Westminster that Ralph can blandly record that 'the King's message about Hull is not worthy an answere'.

Sir Edmund had been granted leave from joining the King in the north for a few months to settle his own affairs. This in itself was enough to give his Court acquaintances to wonder at his motives. With his many Puritan and Buckinghamshire friends questioning where his loyalty now lay, and with his own beloved eldest son firmly on the Parliament side, Sir Edmund's position became more and more invidious as the days passed. 'Your father i finde is full of sade thoughts', writes Lady Sussex to Ralph, and in another letter: 'he saith littill to me of it, but sath if the kainge commands he must goo: I durst not say more to him becose i would not have him thinke you sade any thinge to me of it.' Later: 'Your father sende me worde the kainge hath given him leve to stay till he sendes for him: i am very glade of it for when he gooes i doubt the love of the parly-ment hee will lose quite, which i fear will make them do him any ill offis the can.'

Throughout the country offers of help came from all sides for the King or for Parliament; surreptitiously the gentry started to arm and drill their tenantry as best they could. Lady Sussex writes again, and even she is a little apprehensive now:

'I am sory to hear the lordes are raisnge mony and hors; truly if the sende to my lorde wee will parte with non: i hope the will not for wee are pore, and my lorde of his estate but tenent for life cannot till how to pay a debt if we rone into it: your parlymente still goo so hye that i fear all bee runede by it', and in June when Parliament had called for loans to pay for their army she says: 'I am loth to ete in puter yet, but truly i have put up most of my plat, and say it tis solde, i hope the will sende to boro no mony of my lorde; if the doo wee must denye, it tis anofe for us to pay the subsities; the talke strange thinges of my lorde of Iessex that he will seek the Kainge to London dede or alive; this is hye my thinke for pepell to talke so, i pray god keepe us in safty and pese, and that wee may be to gather on month this somer att lest.'

The Fleet had already come over whole-heartedly in favour of Parliament, so now the many recruits Charles had been receiving from the Continent had to run that gauntlet before joining their new master. Elsewhere, as the country moved towards civil war, the economic situation reached near chaos.

In London itself a scarcity of food had already been felt in the shops and markets, whilst in the rural districts hoarding was widespread. At the end of June Lady Sussex writes:

'Both sides promisis so fare that i cannot see what it tis the shoulde fight for. Thes fines and subsities on both sides will be a ruen to this kaindom and us all. if thinges should longe holde as they are, wee have nede fast and pray as much for this kaindom as for Eirlande . . . I am in such a greate rage with the parliment as nothing will passify me, for they promised as all should be well, if my Lord Straford's hed were of, and since then there is nothing beter, but I thinke we shall be undon with taxis, and if wee have no rents neither, it will be a hard cace.'

Still Sir Edmund had not gone north, but it was clear events were moving with relentless progression towards the climax, and on June 19th he writes to Roades to prepare his horse and arms for the journey to York.

'I praye take upp my mare . . . and lett her be kept att house. I shall shortly send for my coach mairs. When my mare Lea hath foaled, let the foale bee knockt on the head, and the mare taken to Howse, for I cannot spare her this summer. . . . There will be a press shortly in the country', and later: '. . . you must send mee up a paire of Pistolls with firelocks, ther is but one paire of them left at Cleydon. Send mee woard wheather Tom Isham has bought mee another gelding or noe, you shall receav a saddle from Mr. Busby, lett it bee well layed upp, bidd the groome bee careful of my Horses.'

Even the thoroughly unwarlike Ralph made his preparations, and writes from London for 'a paire of my father's Pistolls of the best sort; my father tells mee there is a paire that have White Stocks, and part of the Locks are Blew, and they are very light. Let Moses bring them upp, and bee careful to keepe them from wett, and lett the Moulds, and other implements belonging to them come upp with them.'

Lady Sussex was a rabid Protestant and held that same deep-seated traditional fear of the Papists avowed by so many of her countrymen. One of the true motives behind the rebellion was the fear of Catholic domination over the King, not necessarily the dislike of his person.

'Your father,' she writes to Ralph, 'lyke a good servant i belive is much for his master, and so i thinke wee are all; i wish he may keepe that pouer that is fit for him, but i confes i woulde not have the papests to powerfull; the most of them i belive woulde be glade to see the prodistants of inglande in as misirable a condisyon as the are in Eyrelande, if it was in ther pouer to make them so. In a fue wekes now i hope wee shall see all this is intendede; i pray daly wee may have no fitinge.'

To Lady Sussex this fear of Catholicism is embodied in the person of Henrietta Maria, whom she evidently cordially dislikes as well. When a ship bearing munitions arrives from Holland she cannot resist writing: 'The quine is ever plesede if she have so many favourites with hur; i doubt we shall all fare the worse for it; so many heds togather will bee bysie in ther plots aganst us.'

In July Sir Edmund had ridden to rejoin his master at York, and sadly sends instructions to his steward to prepare the defences at Claydon:

'I praye have the carbines att home in reddyness for the defence of the Howse if need bee,' he writes, 'and gett powder and Bulletts reddy; for I feare a time maye come when Roags maye looke for booty in such houses; therefore bee not unprovided; but saye noething of it, for that maye invite more to mischeefe that thinck not of it yett', and later: 'I praye have a care of my howse, that roages break not into it, have staore of bullett and powder, and gett some boddy to lodg in the howse that maye defend it if need bee. Have my waggon in readiness, if I should att any time send for it; gett in all such monnys as are owing you with all speede, for wee shall certainly have a great warr. Have a care of harvest, and God send uss well to receave the blessing of and retirne thancks for it. I can saye no more—Your loving master.'

Such was the curious state of affairs that Ralph then gives his approval of the precautions: 'I thinke you have lodged the people in ye house very well. I pray, bee careful of the Dores in ye Day-time. I thinke 2 men were enough to watch in ye Towne a nights, untell the times grow fuller of dainger.'

But 'dainger' was nearly upon them and Sir Edmund's daughter, Cary Gardiner, writes from near Oxford:

'Here is nothing but soulgers going up and down. The first that came, under the command of Col: Brown, a cochman, passed very quickly away, and lefte no scores. But Coll: Goodwin's soulgers, and those that came to guard Lord Saye's person has pillaged all the colleges but three already, and this day are about the rest; and say when they have don they will see what pillage the contry has, so, for aught as I see, we are lik to be undone.'

Events were moving rapidly now. The first serious clash of the war took place at Manchester on July 15th when Lord Strange with a small party of Royalists attempted to seize the arsenal— Strange was ignominiously driven out and later impeached. But, nearly two weeks before, Parliament had taken the irrevocable step of setting up a Committee of Safety to manage the conduct of the war.

On August the 22nd the King raised his Standard at Nottingham. Evidently Charles still had faith in Sir Edmund's loyalty and none of those qualms expressed by some at his Court, for he gave the signal honour of looking after the massive Standard to his faithful Knight-Marshal, who declared: 'That by the grace of God they that would wrest that standard from his hand, must first wrest his soul from his body.' It was the crowning moment of Sir Edmund's long career.

The Standard itself, according to one account, needed twenty men to support it; it was 'much of the fasion of the City Streamers used at the Lord Mayor's Show' . . . and 'on the top of it hung a Flag, the King's Arms quartered, with a hand pointing to the Crown . . . above this motto, give Cesar his due'. There were 'three Troops of Horse to wait upon the Standard to bear the same backwards and forwards with about 600 Foot Souldiers. It was conducted to the Field in great State, His Majesty, the Prince [of Wales], Prince Rupert, with divers others Lords and Gentlemen . . . besides a great company of Horse and Foot in all to the number of 2,000.' Just before the heralds were to make the proclamation, however, the King made some hasty changes to the text, handing the corrected parchment to the herald, 'who proclaimed the same to the People though with some difficulty after his Majesty's corrections . . . and the whole Multitude threw up their Hats and cried God save the King'.

The next two days saw similar scenes, but there was poor response to the call to arms. 'There appeared no Conflux of Men in obedience to the Proclamation', declared Clarendon, 'the Armes, and the Ammunition were not yet come from York, and a General Sadness cover'd the whole Town.'

To add to their discomfiture the Standard, according to one authority, 'was blown down . . . by a very strong and unruly wind, and could not be fixed again in a day or two, till the tempest was allayed'. All of which was noted with gloomy foreboding by the more superstitious.

Doll Leeke was now in attendance on Lady Sydenham with part of the royal army, and she writes to Ralph, 'the enemy are very near us; my unkell will not be amongst them for the King has given him the Standard, and he must goe no further then that; it will not remove this 3 or 4 daye and so long he will be safe'. A few days before she said in a letter to Ralph's wife: 'The King is in very good condition and increaseth in strength every day; we have nothing but good nuse to send you', and ends by trying to persuade Ralph to join them: 'I for my part wish for no more men but your husband, and I do so hartily desire him that I dreame of nothing els. I am confident that he will come. I pray tell him so and present my serves to him.'

Other friends questioned Ralph's allegiance and Lady Sydenham writes to his wife:

'My hart i ded as much long for your anser of min, becaus that you ded expres a trobell in yours to me about your hosbands reselushons. My dere hart now i hope that you ar resalefed [resolved] of what he will do, and that i finde is better to won, thin to levef [live] between hopes and fars what will happen. i kno he has chossen the strongest part, but i cannot thinke the best, but i am confedent he dus beleve tis the best, and for that he chos it. But truly my hart it stagers me that he shold not se clerly aall thar wayes, being it tis so aparant, for how tis for the lebberty of the subget to tacke all from thim which ar not of tharmind, and to puld don thar houses, and impresen thim, and levef them to the marsy of the unruly multetude—i cannot fined that this is the lebberty of the subgete. Nor do i find that it is in god's lay [law] to tacke arms aganst thar laful king to depos him, for shouer they havef not mad his parrsen knon to all thos that thay havef implyed in this war to spare him and not to kill him. But i trost god will proteckt him, and my dere if any of my frinds fall in this quarill i trost thar soles will be happy, for shuer tis laful to fitt for won's laful king.'

The King's failure to rally more men to his cause, coupled with the defeat he suffered in a skirmish at Coventry, forced him to make one more attempt to obtain peace. To this purpose he sent Lords Southampton and Dorset with a proposal to Parliament. Lady Sussex comments:

'i must thinke you for your lettir, and till you i am very glade all is will at cladon, for i hope wee shall have now the blesinge of pese, my lorde sashampton and dosete sent to boro my koch as the went by, and truly i coulde not bee so unsivill to denye itt. i hope i dide not do a mise they gooinge about so good a worke. I hear there hath bene a good younge captin of the kainges side since with Sr Tomis Mutis, and he i belive hath tolde the truth of all; wee shall have noe fitinge, for the kainge hath neither mony nor men. Ther cam in fue or non att all aftir the standarde was set up, it semes the kainge sent and gave much of his monyes to the trane bandes in yorkesher and other places, thinkainge to make them suer to him, and when he woulde have hade them they all fell of, and sade the would not fite aganst ther brethrne, and ever daye his army lesones, the fall away from him; . . . My lorde doset sent me worde hee woulde wate uppon me within fue dayes, but i presume that was but in complyment, i hope he doth not intende it; he sade he hade brought that which woulde bringe pese if the parlyment woulde harken to it; suer the may make ther one condisyons now.'

Parliament's reply was as unsatisfactory as ever, and each side continued to perfect their plans for war.

Sir Edmund was tortured by the misery of it all. The separation from his son and the general doubts of the future of the cause he so reluctantly followed weighed heavily on the Knight Marshal. Lady Sussex was the link between Ralph and his father, and to her the old courtier poured out his innermost thoughts. She writes to Ralph: 'i finde by your father's letter you sent me done, he is a most sade man. i pray God he may do well, i fear his trubles togather will make an end of him.'

In early September she received a letter from Sir Edmund and writes to Ralph:

'It was a very sade on and his worde was this of you; "madam he hath ever lane near my hart and truly he is ther still"; that he hade many affictyon uppon him, and that you hade usede him unkaindly; this was the effect of itt; The paper you sent of is [his] letter to you i bornt presently; i shall never open my lipes of that nor any thinge else you trust me with; he is passynate, and much troublede i belive that you declarede yourselfe for the parlyment: a littill time will disgest all I am confident . . . Now lett me intrete you as a frende that loves you most hartily, not to right passynatly to your father, but ovour com him with kaindnes; good man I see hee is infinetly malincoly, for many other thinges i belive besides the difference betwixt you.'

A few days later:

'I see you to much appryhende this unhapye diffirence betwixt your father and selfe; i am very confident a littill time will make all will agane and his affecyon to you ase deare and harty as ever. i pray bee not sade; that will doo you a great dell of hurt i am suer. If it ples God your father retorne, i hope one discorse or to, will make all well agane betwixt you. If Mrs Sidham [Sydenham] and the rest of your frindes with him be not harty in doinge all good offeses betwixt you, the are most file unworthy pepell. If you hade falede in any thinge of duty or love to him it hade bene some jost case of exceptyon, but in goinge the way your consince telles you to be right, i hope he hath more goodnes and religone then to continue in displesuer with you for it.'

Inexorably the two parties moved nearer and nearer to conflict. Some followed their own consciences, others did as they were told, but the clashes between King and Parliament grew in intensity as the extremists on either side won their way.

After the end of September no more letters from Sir Edmund exist, and it must be feared that the rift between father and son was complete. Events were now out of anyone's hands and the country could only watch and wait—and do nothing about the final, terrible rupture.

Edgehill

'. . . take arms against a sea of troubles,
And by opposing end them? . . .'

SHAKESPEARE

THE MONTHS following the stirring scenes at Nottingham were
spent by both sides in building their strength for the coming
struggle. In August the King had under his command 800 horse and
300 foot, but by the end of September this had swollen to 2,000 horse
and nearly 6,000 foot. Three weeks later, with the influx of a sizable
Welsh force plus other lesser contingents, the muster rolls could
total close on twice that number.

Of immediate concern was the shortage of arms and munitions
of every sort for this army. Not since the Wars of the Roses, nearly
150 years before, had a major battle been fought on English soil,
and the large armouries, maintained then as a matter of course and
common prudence, had been allowed to rust unmolested. These
were now pressed into service and weapons and armour long
hanging in disuse were taken down, cleaned and made ready;
whilst throughout the country forges rang with the clangour of
warlike preparation.

It was as well that in the intervening years the weapons of war
had changed little, so the pikes and halberds of Elizabeth's day
were now in as much demand as then. But arms rusty or not are of

small value in the hands of men inexperienced in their use; and on both sides many—reluctant volunteers or impressed tenants of great estates—knew little of the art of war. Only a few, the veterans of Continental campaigns, had ever been under fire in their lives.

Apart from the uncertainty as to how these raw troops would behave when facing a real enemy for the first time, the rival generals knew nothing of the reliability of their men. County levies had already shown marked dislike to serving outside their own regional borders, and although the mercenaries, which made up a good proportion of the king's army, were more trustworthy, their support depended on a regular supply of pay and provision. Parliament was fortunate in having the mass of unemployed from London and East Anglia from which to recruit, whereas Charles's true strength lay in the wild men of the Border country and Wales, and 'other dark corners of the land'. But the majority of the forces, and perhaps the most experienced and reliable of those on both sides, were the small, private contingents raised by rich nobles and land-owners. These were, for the most part, armed and subsidized by their masters, so had no call on the funds at the disposal of the two parties; as such, these private recruits were particularly welcome in the royal army.

The King's greatest problem was the financing of his forces. The Queen had fled to Holland at an early stage in the struggle, as has already been mentioned, and by selling her jewels, had been able to buy arms and munitions. More important, she secured the service of experienced soldiers, and large numbers who succeeded in avoiding Warwick's patrolling ships were soon on the way to join the King. Many rich nobles, like the Marquis of Newcastle, advanced what money they could and when this ran out melted down their plate. The universities followed suit, much of the Cambridge contribution unhappily falling into the hands of a certain Captain Cromwell, who, without more ado, diverted it to London. Another source of revenue was provided by one Thomas Bushell, who agreed to pay and equip three regiments of foot from the proceeds of his silver-mines. By these and similar methods the King gradually collected sufficient money to pay for his ill-assorted, ill-armed force.

Parliament was in no such straits. Rich London merchants, their loyalty to the King long since sapped by his oppressive measures, came forward with open purses, and others, more reluctant, were persuaded to contribute by their fellows. The clothiers

made presents of cloth and maintained soldiers at their own expense.
Great men and colleges melted down their plate. Common
people gave trinkets and money to help in the righteous cause
against their King.

Soon Parliament had a presentable and formidable force at their
command. Although less well disciplined than the Royalists, they
made up for this deficiency by an extraordinary religious fervour.
They were only 'old decayed serving men and tapsters and such
kind of fellows', with no recent military heritage, but were held
together by a fierce, ruthless, iconoclastic spirit. Only leaders of their
own stamp were accepted, and one unfortunate, described as a
'Goddam blade and doubtless hatch in hell', was promptly removed—much to the Royalists' amusement. But underlying this
outward appearance of ill-discipline was a fearful determination,
and very soon the King's followers came to respect and even dread
these 'base and mean fellows'.

As the weeks passed, the confused situation clarified itself a
little. The areas of loyalty were still undefined, but in the main the
King was able to count on the support of Wales, the West Country,
and most of the North and North-West. Parliament, on the other
hand, held London and much of South and South-Eastern England,
while some of the manufacturing districts in the North-West came
out solidly behind them. But these were rough geographical
divisions and within these areas private hatreds and antipathies
transcended mere boundaries. In the bitter climate of civil war local
rivalries and personal feuds thrived. Parishes and even villages were
divided amongst themselves, whilst in many a family brother fought
brother and the father his son.

By early September the King felt strong enough to try his hand,
and quitting Nottingham he marched west to join his Welsh levies,
reported gathering near Shrewsbury.

The first skirmish of the campaign took place at Powick Bridge,
near Worcester, where a small force under Prince Rupert confronted a larger one of the enemy as they debouched from a narrow
lane—and routed them utterly. In a moment the Prince was a true
hero, establishing himself by this one small action as a paragon of
valour and dash, and this reputation remained with him to the end
of his days. More important, the Royalists had found in the King's
nephew a born if impetuous leader, who, as the conflict wore on,
established himself as their one outstanding commander. To the

Earl of Essex, the Parliament General, this defeat held a deeper meaning, and he clearly perceived that the real cause of the disaster was the very bad discipline of his army. An edict was sent forth that no time must be wasted 'practising the ceremonious forms of discipline', but that the men were to be drilled 'in the necessary rudiments of war, that they may know to fall on with discretion and retreat with care'. This was a lesson which some of Rupert's own troops would have been well advised to take to heart.

Elsewhere in the country sporadic bursts of trouble broke out. All too often personal quarrels were the motive behind outrages masquerading under a more political banner. This was particularly so in Kent and the outskirts of London, both powerful Roundhead strongholds. As yet, no widespread disturbances had occurred, but isolated houses of the opposing side had frequently been the targets for mischief and plundering forays.

Henrietta Maria had played her part nobly and many seasoned officers and men, paid by her bounty, found their way to the royal army at Shrewsbury. Charles was surrounded by professional, experienced military advisers, and, spurred by their constant exhortation, and encouraged by his success at Worcester, he determined to continue his march on London and the south.

The wisdom of this course was soon apparent. Received with acclaim at Bridgnorth; at Wolverhampton he was joined by the last of the Welsh levies, and with an army now totalling over 13,000 he pressed on towards the capital.

In London the Royalists' impending approach caused near hysteria. Shops were closed, chains stretched across the main thoroughfares to impede attack, and trenches and earthworks constructed on the outskirts of the city. The armed bands exercising under their Swedish officers gave backbone to the resistance of the capital, and encouraged by their example, the citizens helped prepare the defences. But not before an offer to commence peace negotiations had been sent to the King, who was being closely pursued by Essex and was now approaching Oxford from the north.

The King, with the bulk of his army, spent the night of Saturday the 22nd of October at Edgecote, a small hamlet north of Banbury and about thirty miles from Oxford. His pursuers' advance guard was only ten miles away at Kineton, but they had outstripped their main body and much of the artillery, which was labouring a day's march behind—nearly immobile for want of transport and draught-horses for the cannon. In the evening it was decided to send a force under Byron to take Banbury, but that night Prince Rupert's cavalry had a brush with a foraging party of the enemy. Recovering from his surprise and profiting from this opportune Intelligence that Essex was so close, the Prince occupied the high ground of Edgehill with his cavalry. There he was joined in the morning by the King and the remainder of the Royalist army, who had force-marched since before dawn.

They were in hostile country now, for this was the home of the Puritan Lords Saye and Brooke, who had so ostentatiously defected from the King's side many months before at York. To the north lay Coventry and Warwick, which had garrisons detached from the main body of Essex's army. Behind was Banbury, strongly fortified by a local garrison. The nearest haven of loyal sympathies was at Compton Wynates, the seat of the Earl of Northampton, but this was to the west, away from the King's line of march on London.

The Roundhead Intelligence seems to have been as poor as that of their enemies, for information that the royal army had occupied the high ground between his forces and the London road came to Essex only as he was going to morning service at Kineton. The discoverer of this piece of news happened to be a 'Worthy Divine' who quite by chance espied some of Rupert's cavalry on the crest of the escarpment, 'by the help of a perspective glass, from the top of a hill'.

At once the wisdom of the Prince's action was apparent, and with the Royalists astride the one dominating height in the vicinity, Essex's every movement could be clearly seen and forestalled. The rebel troops, many of whom were in the middle of their breakfast or attending Divine service, were hurriedly alerted in their widely scattered quarters in the local villages, and made ready to form for battle in the valley beyond Kineton—those billeted in the nearby hamlet of Tysoe are said to have taken the bread hot from the village ovens on their way to the fight.

The fringe of hills known as Edgehill divides the lush Warwickshire Vale of the Red Horse from the valley of the Thames and the road to London. He who is master of Edgehill is master of the entire country, to as far afield as Cheltenham in the west and Birmingham in the north. Edgehill itself was a precipitous mound with its northern slopes dangerously steep, and far too steep for

N

cavalry charge or manœuvre. Thus the King was in a magnificent defensive position, and could conceal the exact number and position of his own forces, which were hidden from view behind the brow of the escarpment.

But was a defensive position what he wanted? Although virtually immune from attack with the enemy as weak as he was at present, to remain on the hill courted ultimate disaster. Only a day's march away was the rebels' main body, and with their support Essex would outnumber the Royalists and nullify their tactical advantage. Rumours of discontent in Essex's army might or might not be true, but it was an early winter and mid-October was no time to pass the night on a windswept slope in the open. The King's forces, accustomed as they were to seek what shelter they could in barns and outhouses on the line of march, were in no discipline to sustain the rigours of a siege on their frosty hill. Many men had not eaten for forty-eight hours, there were no tents and few waggons and the system of supply was hopelessly inadequate to the task of provisioning the royal army.

To live off the country is no simple matter, and when that country is hostile it is made incomparably more difficult—such was the King's dilemma. With the peasantry hiding what they could, molesting stragglers and in many cases resisting entry, the foraging parties had perforce to be of sufficient strength to fight if necessary and protect what they had procured. Even then there was no guarantee that enough victuals could be found. It was probably this uncertainty above others that determined the King to force Essex to do battle.

The two armies were quite fairly matched in numbers, although the Royalists had more horse. It was in calibre and equipment that the true difference lay: Rupert's cavalry, recruited from magnificent material, was but poorly equipped, while some of the infantry were armed only with weapons borrowed from the Trained Bands. Nevertheless, the Royalists' discipline was superior to that of Essex's forces, who were of a generally poorer quality.

Parliament's true military strength lay in their lavish supply of excellent arms and a fierce, but at times ephemeral, zeal raised to fever heat by the preachers attached to the army. Added to this, many of the soldiers were fighting on their own home ground, and in the parts of the battlefield where they were employed evidence shows that here the fight was particularly fierce.

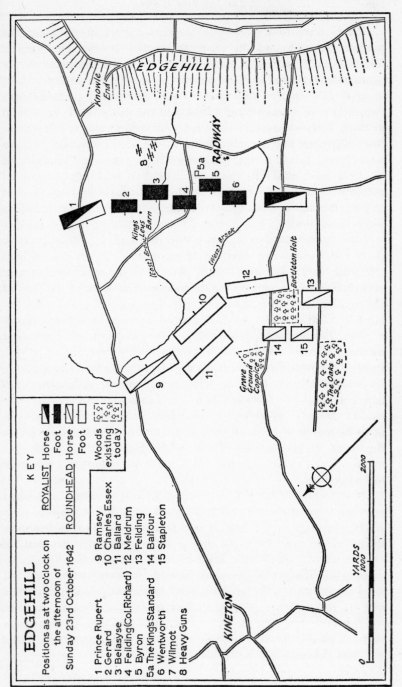

EDGEHILL

Positions as at two o'clock on
the afternoon of
Sunday 23rd October 1642

KEY

ROYALIST Horse
        Foot
ROUNDHEAD Horse
        Foot
Woods
existing
today

1 Prince Rupert   9 Ramsey
2 Gerard   10 Charles Essex
3 Belasyse   11 Ballard
4 Feilding(Col.Richard) 12 Meldrum
5 Byron   13 Feilding
5a The King's Standard 14 Balfour
6 Wentworth   15 Stapleton
7 Wilmot
8 Heavy Guns

EDGEHILL

Knowle End

RADWAY

Kings Leys Barn

(east) Brook

(West) Brook

Battleton Holt

Grave Ground Coppice

The Oaks

KINETON

YARDS
1000   2000

0

The Field of Edgehill

There were two schools of warfare current at the time: the modern Swedish and the more traditional Dutch. The former, founded and practised to perfection by Gustavus Adolphus on the Continent, favoured the use of mixed musketeers and pikemen, supported by cavalry who charged at a gallop and pressed home their attack with sword and pistol. On the other hand, the Dutch method, long in use on the Continent before the revolutionary Swedes appeared on the scene, relied on massed pikemen and cavalry who approached at a trot, discharged their pieces and swerved off to allow fresh ranks to come up. The Earl of Lindsey, nominal commander of the King's army, had been brought up in the Dutch school; the more dashing Prince Rupert advocated the modern Swedish method.

Charles had not learned his lesson on divided command in the short and ignominious Scottish Wars; now, once again, a divided leadership bedevilled the King's plans. On the march the rivalry between Lindsey, commanding the infantry, and Rupert, in charge of the cavalry, had flared intermittently. For reasons known only to himself, Charles had inserted a special clause into Rupert's commission. This exempted him from receiving orders from anyone but the King himself, and can hardly have tended to harmony. Now the Prince's determination to have his way over the conduct of the battle, his tactlessness and obstinacy caused the rupture in the long unhappy relationship between him and Lindsey. Casting down his baton in front of his own troops, Lindsey declared that if he 'was not fit to be a general he would rather die a colonel at the head of his Regiment'. In his place was appointed Sir Jacob Astley, who had at one time been Prince Rupert's tutor, and who doubtless knew how to handle him.

It was nearly noon of a cold and windy day before Charles had completely assembled his forces from their widely scattered billets and had managed to call back Byron, who was just short of Banbury. In the eyes of many it was too late to fight a battle that day, but the knowledge of Essex's main body approaching and the difficulty of keeping his hungry, ill-provided troops together, determined the King on action—he ordered the descent into the valley; doubtless with the full support of the ever-impetuous Prince Rupert.

This descent was no easy task and horses had even to be hitched to the cannon to prevent their headlong fall, but, fortunately, Essex was too preoccupied with his own defensive arrangements to interfere. By early afternoon the forces of both sides lay in full array in the Vale of the Red Horse.

The two armies were deployed with cavalry on either wing, and the light guns and infantry in the centre. Rupert, on the King's right flank, faced a mixed force of Roundhead cavalry and musketeers under Sir James Ramsey; on the left Lord Wilmot's Horse confronted that of Feilding.

The Royalist infantry was drawn up in five tertios or brigades; while their heavy guns were held back on the higher ground northeast of Radway, and probably forward of the existing road out of the village. The Roundhead infantry lay behind the (west) Brook in three brigades: the left under Charles Essex supported by Ballard was probably opposite the junction of the two streams; the right under Meldrum it is now believed lay forward of what is now Battleton Holt and at extreme range from the King's heavy guns below Knowle End. To some extent sheltered by closer ground and Meldrum's brigade of foot, were the two cavalry regiments of Stapleton and that seasoned campaigner and fervent Parliamentarian, Sir William Balfour—they were to play a significant part in the forthcoming battle.

The King was in the centre of the Royalist line surrounded by his gentlemen, including Sir Edmund, his Standard Bearer and Knight-Marshal of the King's Horse who had breakfasted at Edgecote with Charles on that fateful day. By an unfortunate decision, His Majesty's mounted guard had been granted permission to charge at the head of Rupert's cavalry, so the King was undefended except for a small number of his personal footguard.

At this historic moment, if Dugdale is to be believed, an incident occurred which gave a whisper of light relief. For, to the astonished eyes of the two assembled armies, suddenly appeared the extraordinary and incongruous sight of a gentleman with his servants enjoying a day's hunting. This turned out to be a local elderly squire, one Sir Richard Shuckburgh, who declared he was utterly unaware of any trouble between the King and his subjects, and was immensely surprised when he found himself between two armies of some 30,000 men, of whose very existence in his own county he had not known. However, he recovered from his amazement and fought bravely for his King.

While this was happening, Charles summoned his officers and addressed them:

'My Lords and Gentlemen here present,—If this day shine prosperously for us, we shall be happy in a glorious victory. Your King is both your cause, your quarrel, and your captain. The foe is in sight. Now show yourselves no malignant parties, but with your swords declare what courage and fidelity is within you. . . . Come life or death your King will bear you company, and ever keep this field, this place, and this days' service in his grateful remembrance.'

A conspicuous figure in a black velvet mantle, with his Star and Garter over his armour, he rode along the lines of his troops encouraging them: 'Your King bids you be courageous, and Heaven make you victorious'; and, when Essex, hoping to snatch the initiative, opened with his cannon, the King, with his own hand, applied the match that returned the fire. A fire whose terrible repercussions were to be felt throughout the country and beyond for the next eighteen long, weary years.

At three o'clock, at a range of several hundred yards, the guns of both sides engaged in an ineffectual and time-wasting duel—doing little damage, but clouding the air with acrid smoke.

In front of Rupert on the right flank then took place an event that might well have had a more far-reaching effect than it anyway did: amongst the cavalry on Essex's left, confronting the young Prince, was a certain Sir Faithful Fortescue with a small body of Irish horse newly arrived from their native country. Stepping boldly forward, they discharged their pistols at the ground and wheeling round joined Rupert's cavalry, casting aside the distinguishing orange scarves worn by Essex's men. This defection seemed to mesmerize the Parliamentarians—not knowing who might follow suit, neighbours eyed one another apprehensively, and when Rupert's inevitable charge was delivered the entire Roundhead left-wing disintegrated, its remnants thrust back, and in the process disorganizing the infantry nearest them and some of the reserve as well.

With his left in rout and fugitives spreading despondency as fast as legs could carry them, Essex was in a sore plight—a wheel to the left by Rupert's victorious horse and the Roundhead reserve and centre were at their mercy. But it was not to be; once started there was no stopping the Royalist cavalry. The custom then in the King's army was that the infantry were paid in cash for their services, but the horsemen were expected to provide for themselves from the loot and pillage they could collect on their way. This opportunity of plundering the enemy train was too great to be missed and some of Rupert's men set about ransacking the bulging provision carts lying unprotected in the streets of Kineton and beyond.

Of the remainder, their headlong career after the fleeing Roundheads was at last brought to a stop by the guns of John Hampden's main body which was pressing forward with all speed to join the battle. Only then were the frantic efforts of their officers of any avail in restoring discipline to the Royalist cavalry. Meanwhile, Prince Rupert had received word that all was not well elsewhere on the battlefield, and gathering a few followers he hurried back. But by that time his troopers, blown and exhausted, and suffering from that strange lassitude of momentary victory, were too spent to be of much further service.

On the Royalist left Lord Wilmot's horse attacked at the same time as Prince Rupert started his ill-controlled gallop. Initially their charge had some success against the rebels' right-wing, which was 'easily dispersed, and fled the chase fearlessly', hotly pursued by their foes, including even the King's reserve of cavalry under Sir Thomas Aston.

As the cavalry on both wings disappeared from view in glorious chase, Sir Jacob Astley, commander of the Royalist foot and author of the classic battle-prayer 'O Lord, thou knowest how busy I must be this day. If I forget thee, do not thou forget me', led forward his five brigades to close with the enemy.

No sooner had the infantry come 'to push of pike', than the wily Balfour, whose regiment, together with that of Stapleton, had been missed by Wilmot in his wild charge, advanced through the gaps in his own infantry and attacked the centre brigade of Royalist foot. The Cavaliers broke and fled before him. On seeing this, the Royalist left-wing wavered. Exploiting the confusion to the full, Balfour made another assault, taking the regiments of Sir Nicholas Byron's brigade in the flank and rear.

In an instant a situation that had seemed so promising for the King turned to one of the gravest danger to his cause and even to his person.

The Royalist infantry were in no shape to withstand such an onslaught; and, when Meldrum attacked them from the other side, they were very soon fighting for their lives. Lindsey's own Lincolnshire Regiment was overrun, their general fatally wounded and left for dead. Lord Willoughby, Lindsey's son, commanding the King's Red Regiment, moved to the support of his father, but, with his men all but annihilated, he himself was taken prisoner. Sir Jacob Astley himself narrowly escaped capture. Only the most strenuous efforts of their officers kept the remainder in any sort of order.

The two young Princes nearly came in contact with the enemy; the Prince of Wales, much to his delight, found himself involved and shouted: 'I fear them not,' as he prepared to defend himself. This, fortunately, was not necessary, and he and his brother were removed by their servants and tutor. The latter prior to this had distinguished himself by being found alone under a hedge, absorbed in a learned treatise, unconscious of the tumult around him.

The focus of the action was now the King's battle standard, where the struggle was furious 'in the extream'; to and fro swayed the conflict, and the absence of the King's mounted guard was sorely felt. According to one chronicle, Sir Edmund 'adventured' with the Standard amongst the enemy so 'the souldiers might be engaged to follow him. He was offered his life by a throng of his enemies, upon condition that he would deliver the standard; he answered that his life was his own, but the standard was his and their sovereign's, and he would not deliver it while he lived, as he hoped it would be rescued . . . when he was dead; selling it and his life, at the rate of sixteen gentlemen which fell that day by his sword.' The legend goes that he refused to surrender it even in death and eventually they had to hack off the hand that held it. In confirmation of this the ring that Sir Edmund always wore, the gift of Charles and bearing a tiny miniature of the King, was returned and is to this day at Claydon—his body was never found.

The further adventures of the King's Standard were as dramatic —delivered to Essex it was given by him to his own secretary, Chambers, who, it was said: 'Elated by the prize . . . rode about, more proudly than wisely, waving it round his head. Whereupon, in the confusion, one of the King's officers, Captain Smith, of the Lord John Stewart's troop, seeing the Standard captured, threw round him the orange scarf of a fallen Parliamentarian, and, riding in among the lines of his enemies, told the secretary that "it were a shame that so honourable a trophy of war should be borne by a penman". To which suggestion the credulous guardian of this honourable trophy consenting, surrendered it to the distinguished cavalier, who galloped back with it again, and before evening received knighthood under its shadow,'—reputedly the last banneret or recipient of a knighthood on the field of battle.

Elsewhere, the battle fared badly for the King. On one occasion Charles himself was nearly captured and saved only by the timely arrival of some of Rupert's returning cavalry. He was urged to leave the field, but, realizing only his presence held his troops together, he refused.

The Royalist line was in ruins—assailed from both sides, only two regiments remained intact and these slowly withdrew on Knowle End, until rising ground and the close support of the King's heavy guns firing case-shot brought the enemy to a halt.

Night was drawing on. More and more of Rupert's cavalry were returning through the dusk to join the fray. Although these were in no state to fight, their presence alone prevented further Roundhead pressure. The truth of the matter was that both sides were exhausted, and the Parliamentarians were also running out of powder. Royalist training was not such as to fit their soldiers for a lengthy battle, and, although the Roundheads were in better shape in this respect, they were as ready to call a halt as their opponents. So 'horse and foot stood together against horse and foot until night', when this bloody Sunday drew to a close.

That night both armies remained on the field of battle; the Royalists huddled around huge fires on the crest of Edgehill, their only comfort during a particularly severe frost, which, however, saved the lives of many wounded. Essex's men, well provisioned and in better shape, were cared for by the local villagers, who turned out in force to succour the wounded and help bury—and rob—the dead.

At daybreak on the Monday both armies were still in position, but the Parliamentarians, reinforced during the night by Hampden's Buckinghamshire Green Coats, for some inexplicable reason did not attack, and in fact later that day retired northward, leaving the King undisputed master of the field of Edgehill.

Casualties were equally heavy on both sides, although the reports vary according to the political colour of the author. We do not know many details of the losses but there can have been few families in the country who did not mourn the loss of some close friend or relative.

News of Sir Edmund's death shattered all who knew him, and faction was completely forgotten in the almost universal sorrow at his death. Sir Edward Sydenham, his neighbour in Covent Garden, writing to Ralph from 'Ano on the hill' five days after the battle, cannot, however, resist pointing out the extent of the Royalist victory and how sweeping was the defeat of Ralph's own party who had abandoned the field:

'For all our great vycktorie I have had the greatest loss by the death of your nobell father that ever anie freind did . . . he himselfe killed two with his owne hands, whereof one of them had killed poore Jason [Sir Edmund's servant], and brocke the poynt of his standard at push of pike before he fell, which was the last account I could receave of anie of our owne syde of him. The next day the kinge sent a harald to offer mercie to all that would laye down armes, and to enquire for my Lord of Lynsee, my Lo Wyllowby and him; he brought word that my Lord of Lynsee was hurt, your father dead, my Lo Wyllowby only prysoner; he would nither put on armes or buff cote the day of battell, the reason I know not; the battell was bloody on your syde, for your hoorss rann awaye at the first charge, and our men had the execution of them for three miles; it began at 3 a clock and ended at syx. The kinge is a man of the least feare and the greatest mercie and resolution that I ever saw, and had he not bin in the fylde, we might have suffired. My Lord of Essex is retired in great disorder to Warwick, for the next morninge he suffired his connon to be taken away within muskett shott of his armie, and never offired to hindir them; it is sayd ther was killed and run away since, eaygtt thowsand of his armie. This day the kinge tooke in bamberie [Banbury]; our armie dayly increases; god in mercie send us peace and although your loss be as great as a sonn can loose in a father, yitt god's chyldren must beare with patience what afflycktion soever he shall please to laye upon them. . . . My humbell sarvise to your sad wyfe. God of his infinite mercie cumfort you bothe which shall be the prayers of your freind and sarvant who shall ever be reddie to performe anie sarvise in the power of your Ed: Sydenham' and he adds as a postscript, 'Ther is delivered to me fyftie two cornets and colors which was taken; I beleeve ther be manie more.'

Ralph himself was utterly heart-broken; he still had faint hope that his father might be alive, but as time passed and more eye-witnesses related their stories to him, these hopes faded. He pours out his soul to old Lady Sussex:

'Maddam, I never lov'd to bee the messenger of ill newes: therfore I forbore to send you this; which is the saddest and deepest affliction that ever befell any poore distressed man. . . . God's will bee donn, and give mee patience, to support mee in this extremity. there is noe absolute certainty of his Death, that I can yet learne, but sure tis too true. I have sent 3 messengers to both armies to bie informed. On Satterday I expect on of them Back, in the meantime I am forced to make dilligent enquiries after that which (if it proove true) will make mee most unhappy . . . for if hee is gon, I have noe freind in this world but your selfe.'; and again when all hope of finding his father alive had gone: 'Last night I had a servant from my Lord of Essex Army, that tells mee there is noe possibility of finding my Deare father's Body, for my Lord Generall, my Lord Brooke, my Lord Grey, Sr Sam Luke and twenty others of my acquaintance assured him hee was never taken prisiner, neither were any of them ever possessed of his Body; but that hee was slaine by an ordinary trooper. Upon this my man went to all the ministers of severall parishes, that buried the dead that were slaine in the battle, and none of them can give him any information of the body. One of them told him my Lord Aubigny was like to have been buried in the feilds, but that on came by chance that knew him and tooke him into a church, and there laid him in the ground without soe much as a sheete about him, and soe divers of good quallity were buried: the ministers kept Tallies of all that were buried, and they amount to neare 4,000.'

The ghosts of the Battle of Edgehill survived for a long time after the battle itself, for there is a curious pamphlet written in January of the following year which talks of 'Apparitions and Prodigious Noyses of War and Battels seen on Edge-Hill', and goes on:

'At this Edge-Hill, in the very place where the battell was strucken, have since and doth appeare, strange and portentuous Apparations of two jarring and contrary Armies, . . . it being certified by men of most credit in those parts . . . between twelve and one of the clock in the morning was heard by some Sheepherds, and other countryemen, and travellers, first the sound of drummes afar off, and the noyse of souldiers, as it were, giving out their last groanes; . . . but then, on the sudden . . . appeared in the ayre the same incorporeall souldiers that made those clamours, and immediately,

with Ensignes display'd, Drummes beating, Musquets going off,
Cannons discharged, Horses neyghing . . . the alarum . . . was
strucke up . . . and so pell mell to it they went . . . after some three
houres fight, that Army which carryed the Kings colours withdrew,
or rather appeared to flie: the other remaining, as it were masters of
the field. . . . On Sunday, being Christmas night, appeared in the
same tumultuous warlike manner, the same two adverse Armies,
fighting with as much spite and spleen as formerly. . . . The rumour
whereof comming to his Majestie at Oxford, he immediately dis-
patched thither Colonel Kirke and three other Gentlemen of Credit,
. . . who . . . heard and saw the fore-mentioned prodigies, . . .
distinctly knowing divers of the apparitions or incorporeall sub-
stances by their faces, as that of Sir Edmund Varney, and others
that were slaine.'

These 'apparitions' were attributed as 'A sign of God's wrath,
and a proof of the Divills dispersed in the empty regions of the
Ayre'. Recently there was an attempt to exorcize the 'divills' from
the area of Edgehill.

Sir Edmund is an active ghost, for he is still said to haunt
Claydon, where he performs a ceaseless vigil in search of his lost
hand, but he has not been seen there for a number of years now. He
is reputed to come only in times of trouble, doubtless to see if he can
help in any way, so it seems his 'kindness and courtesy to the poorest' lingers even in death.

There is a report from Clarendon of an illuminating conversation
Sir Edmund had with him at Nottingham when the Standard was
raised:

'My Condition', said Sir Edmund, 'is much worse than yours,
and different I believe from any other Man's, and will very well
justify the Melancholick that, I confess to you, possesses me. You
have Satisfaction in your Conscience that you are in the Right;
that the King ought not to grant what is required of him; and so
you do your Duty and your Business together: But for my Part,
I do not like the Quarrel, and do heartily wish that the King would
yield and consent to what they desire; so that my Conscience is
only concerned in Honour and in Gratitude to follow my Master.
I have eaten his Bread, and served him near thirty Years, and will
not do so base a Thing as to forsake him; and chuse rather to lose
my Life (which I am sure I shall do) to preserve and defend those

Things which are against my Conscience to preserve and defend. For I will deal freely with you, I have no Reverence for the Bishops, for whom this Quarrel subsists.'

Such were the old knight's thoughts, and it perhaps explains why he 'would nither put on armes or buff cote the day of battell'.

Thus died Sir Edmund Verney, disillusioned, despairing, but ever mindful of his duty towards his conscience. He was universally loved, 'of a very cheerful, and a generous Nature, and confessedly valiant'. According to Lloyd: 'Of the strictness and piety of a Puritan, of the charity of a Papist, of the civility of an Englishman ... whos carriage was such that he was called "the only courtier that was not complained of".'

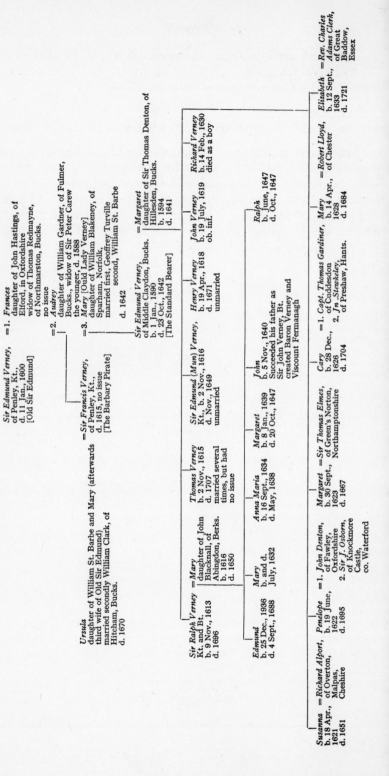

Sir Edmund Verney, Kt., of Penley, d. 11 Jan., 1600 [Old Sir Edmund]

= 1. *Frances* daughter of John Hastings, of Elford, in Oxfordshire widow of Thomas Redmayne, of Northmarston, Bucks. no issue

= 2. *Audrey* daughter of William Gardner, of Fulmer, Bucks., widow of Sir Peter Carew the younger, d. 1588

= 3. *Mary* [Ould Lady Verney] daughter of William Blakeney, of Sparham, Norfolk, married first, Geoffrey Turville second, William St. Barbe d. 1642

Ursula daughter of William St. Barbe and Mary (afterwards third wife of Old Sir Edmund) married secondly William Clark, of Hitcham, Bucks. d. 1670 = *Sir Francis Verney*, of Penley, Kt., d. 1615, no issue [The Barbary Pirate]

Sir Edmund Verney, of Middle Claydon, Bucks. b. 1 Jan., 1590 d. 23 Oct., 1642 [The Standard Bearer] = *Margaret* daughter of Sir Thomas Denton, of Hillesden, Bucks. b. 1594 d. 1641

Sir Ralph Verney, Kt. and Bt. b. 9 Nov., 1613 d. 1696 = *Mary* daughter of John Blacknall, of Abingdon, Berks. b. 1616 d. 1650

Thomas Verney, b. 2 Nov., 1615 d. 1707 married several times, but had no issue

Sir Edmund [Mun] Verney, Kt., b. 2 Nov., 1616 d. Nov., 1649 unmarried

Henry Verney, b. 19 Apr., 1618 d. 1671 unmarried

John Verney, b. 19 July, 1619 ob. inf.

Richard Verney b. 14 Feb., 1630 died as a boy

Edmund b. 25 Dec., 1936 d. 4 Sept., 1688

Mary b. and d. July, 1632

Anna Maria b. 16 Sept., 1634 d. May, 1638

Margaret b. 8 Jan., 1639 d. 20 Oct., 1647

John b. 5 Nov., 1640 Succeeded his father as Sir John Verney, Bt. created Baron Verney and Viscount Fermanagh

Ralph b. June, 1647 d. Oct., 1647

Susanna = *Richard Alport*, of Overton, Malpas, Cheshire b. 18 Apr., 1621 d. 1651

Penelope = 1. *John Denton*, of Fawley, Oxfordshire 2. *Sir J. Osborn*, of Knockmore Castle, co. Waterford b. 19 June, 1622 d. 1695

Margaret = *Sir Thomas Elmes*, of Green's Norton, Northamptonshire b. 30 Sept., 1623 d. 1667

Cary = 1. Capt. *Thomas Gardiner*, of Cuddesdon 2. *Jn. Stewkeley*, of Preshaw, Hants. b. 28 Dec., 1626 d. 1704

Mary = *Robert Lloyd*, of Chester b. 14 Apr., 1628 d. 1684

Elizabeth = *Rev. Charles Adams Clerk*, of Great Baddow, Essex b. 12 Sept., 1633 d. 1721

Letter References

N.B. *For the sake of simplicity, all dates are reckoned according to the modern calendar, taking the beginning of the year as 1st January (not 25th March) and avoiding the double indication of date, i.e. 14 February 1642, not 14 February 1641/2.*

Chapter I

p. 29, l. 21.   Statement by Sir E.V. dated 3 March 1623.

p. 30, l. 22.   Sir Richard Graham to Sir E.V., Oatlands, 30 June 1622.

p. 30, l. 31.   Petition from Whaddon Chase tenants dated 1625.

Chapter II

p. 35, l. 18.   Inventory, 1645.

p. 38, l. 25.   Will of Margaret V., 1639.

p. 40, l. 38.   Sir Thomas Gardiner to Ralph V. from Cuddesden, 1639.

p. 41, l. 2.   Mrs Isham to Mary V. from Claydon, 1640.

p. 47, l. 33.   Sir E.V. to Ralph V. from London, 23 March 1636.

p. 47, l. 38   Sir E.V. to Ralph V. from London, 30 March 1636.

p. 48, l. 2.   Sir E.V. to Ralph V. from London, 22 April 1636.

Chapter IV

p. 70, l. 33.   Mary V. to Mrs Wiseman from Claydon, 2 June 1629.

p. 71, l. 18   Rev. John Crowther to Ralph V. from Newton, November 1631.

p. 71, l. 20   Rev. John Crowther to Ralph V. from Newton, September 1631.

p. 71, l. 31.   Rev. John Crowther to Ralph V. from Newton, October 1631.

p. 72, l. 20   Sir E.V. to Ralph V. from London, 30 March 1636.

p. 73, l. 3.   Sir E.V. to Ralph V. from London, 26 February 1636.

p. 73, l. 13.   Sir E.V. to Ralph V. from London, 23 March 1636.

p. 73, l. 16.   Sir E.V. to Ralph V. from London, 6 April 1636.

p. 73, l. 21.   Sir E.V. to Ralph V. from London, 22 April 1636.

p. 73, l. 29   Sir E.V. to Margaret V. from London, 27 April 1636.

p. 73, l. 34.   Sir E.V. to Margaret V. from London, 30 March 1636.

p. 74, l. 2.   Sir E.V. to Ralph V. from London, 22 April 1636.

p. 74, l. 17.   Sir E.V. to Ralph V. from London, 16 March 1636.

p. 74, l. 21.   Sir E.V. to Ralph V. from London, 6 April 1636.

p. 74, l. 26.   Sir E.V. to Ralph V. from London, 22 April 1636.

p. 74, l. 32.   Sir E.V. to Wm Roades, from Theobalds, October 1632.

Chapter VI

p. 106, l. 3.	Sir John Leake to Sir E.V. from Youghal, 31 August 1635.
p. 107, l. 15.	James Dillon to Ralph V. from Ireland, 13 May 1635.
p. 107, l. 33.	Lady Barrymore to Sir E.V. from Youghal, 18 September 1639.
p. 108, l. 6.	Sir John Leake to Sir E.V. from Youghal, 25 February 1640.
p. 108, l. 14.	Sir John Leake to Sir E.V. from Youghal, 18 August 1648.
p. 108, l. 24.	Sir John Leake to Sir E.V. from Youghal, 25 February 1640.
p. 108, l. 32.	Sir John Leake to Sir E.V. from Youghal, 13 September 1638.
p. 109, l. 4.	Sir John Leake to Sir E.V. from Youghal, December 1640.
p. 110, l. 12.	James Dillon to Ralph V. from London, 12 June 1633.
p. 110, l. 20.	James Dillon to Ralph V. from London, 3 July 1633.
p. 110, l. 27.	James Dillon to Ralph V. from London, 15 October 1633.
p. 110, l. 39.	Ralph V. to James Dillon from London, 12 January 1635.
p. 111, l. 8.	James Dillon to Ralph V. from Ireland, 16 March 1636.
p. 111, l. 16.	Ralph V. to James Dillon from Claydon, 1 April 1636.
p. 111, l. 40.	Sir Richard Hastings to Ralph V. dated 1650.
p. 112, l. 32.	Sir E.V. to Ralph V. from London, 19 May 1638.
p. 113, l. 3.	Ralph V. to Henry V. from Claydon, 3 February 1639.
p. 113, l. 11.	Lady Denton to Sir E.V. from Hillesden, 5 June 1638.
p. 113, l. 17.	Lady Denton to Ralph V. from Hillesden, 29 October 1639.
p. 113, l. 36.	Mun V. to Ralph V. from Claydon, 15 January 1638.
p. 114, l. 12.	Mun V. to Ralph V. from Hillesden, 16 January 1638.
p. 114, l. 21.	Sir E.V. to Ralph V. from London, 26 February 1636.
p. 114, l. 24.	Sir E.V. to Ralph V. from London, 24 March 1635.
p. 114, l. 32.	Sir E.V. to Ralph V. from London, 11 July 1636.
p. 115, l. 1.	Sir E.V. to Ralph V. from London, 5 June 1635.
p. 115, l. 16.	Sir E.V. to Ralph V. from London, 26 February 1635.
p. 115, l. 26.	Sir E.V. to Mary V. from Bath, 20 August 1635.
p. 116, l. 26.	Lady Sussex to Ralph V. from Gorhambury, April 1639.
p. 116, l. 36.	Lady Sussex to Ralph V. from Gorhambury, 19 January 1639.
p. 117, l. 8.	Lady Sussex to Ralph V. from Gorhambury, March 1640.
p. 117, l. 18.	Lady Sussex to Ralph V. from Gorhambury, 25 November 1639.
p. 117, l. 31.	Lady Sussex to Ralph V. from Gorhambury, 1 December 1639.
p. 118, l. 7.	Lady Sussex to Ralph V. from Gorhambury, 27 January 1640.
p. 118, l. 15.	Lady Sussex to Ralph V. from Gorhambury, April 1640.
p. 118, l. 33.	Tom V. to Sir E.V. from London, 11 November 1635.
p. 119, l. 6.	Tom V. to Sir E.V. from London, 22 November 1635.
p. 119, l. 20.	Tom V. to Ralph V. from London, April 1636.

o

p. 137, l. 36.   Ralph V. to Sir E.V. from Claydon, 10 May 1639.

p. 138, l. 17.   Dr Denton to Ralph V. from Newcastle, 16 May 1639.

p. 138, l. 35.   Sir E.V. to Ralph V. from Newcastle, 19 May 1639.

p. 139. l. 12.   Sir E.V. to Ralph V. from York, 25 April 1639.

p. 139, l. 19.   Sir E.V. to Ralph V. from Newcastle, 11 May 1639.

p. 139, l. 26.   Sir E.V. to Ralph V. from 'A Camp Near Berwick', 4 June 1639.

p. 139, l. 31.   Sir E.V. to Ralph V. from Newcastle, 22 May 1639.

p. 139, l. 36.   Sir E.V. to Ralph V. from 'A Camp Near Berwick', 15 June 1639.

p. 140, l. 10.   Sir E.V. to Ralph V. from 'Leslie's Pride', 29 May 1639.

p. 140, l. 20.   Sir E.V. to Ralph V. from 'A Camp Near Berwicke', 4 June 1639.

p. 141, l. 13.   Sir E.V. to Ralph V. from 'A Camp Near Berwick', 9 June 1639.

p. 142, l. 8.   Sir E.V. to Ralph V. from 'A Camp Near Berwick', 11 June 1639.

p. 142, l. 20.   Sir E.V. to Ralph V. from 'A Camp Near Berwick', 15 June 1639.

p. 143, l. 1.   Tom V. to Margaret V. from Barbados, 20 May 1639.

p. 143, l. 9.   Tom V. to Sir E.V. from Barbados, 10 February 1639.

p. 144, l. 21.   Tom V. to Margaret V. from Barbados, 10 February 1639.

p. 144, l. 35.   Sir E.V. to Tom V. from Claydon, June 1639.

p. 145, l. 34.   Mun V. to Ralph V. from The Hague, 28 January 1640.

p. 146, l. 3.   Sir E.V. to Ralph V. from 'A Camp Near Berwik', 21 June 1639.

Chapter VIII

p. 150, l. 38.   Mun V. to Ralph V. from Grimston, 27 July 1640.

p. 151, l. 28.   Mun V. to Ralph V. from York, 10 September 1640.

p. 152, l. 11.   Mun V. to Ralph V. from 'A Campe Neare Yorke', 15 October 1640.

p. 153, l. 23.   Mun V. to Ralph V. from 'A Campe Neare Yorke', 19 October 1640.

p. 153, l. 27.   Mun V. to Ralph V. from North Stanley, 24 January 1641.

p. 154, l. 18.   Ralph V.'s Notes, 3 January 1641.

p. 154, l. 37.   Lady Sussex to Ralph V. from Gorhambury, 11 November 1640.

p. 155, l. 3.   Lady Sussex to Ralph V. from Gorhambury, November 1640.

p. 156, l. 4.   Mun V. to Ralph V. from Ripon, 15 January 1641.

p. 156, l. 11.   Mun V. to Ralph V. from North Stanley, 8 March 1641.

p. 156, l. 36.   Lady Sussex to Ralph V. from Gorhambury, 9 April 1641.

p. 156, l. 38.   Lady Sussex to Ralph V. from Gorhambury, 26 April 1641.

p. 157, l. 7.   Sir E.V. to Wm Roades from London, 3 August 1641.
p. 157, l. 15. Margaret V.'s will dated 1639.
p. 158, l. 36. Ralph V.'s Notes, 13 April 1641.
p. 159, l. 3.   Lady Sussex to Ralph V. from Gorhambury, 19 January 1641.
p. 159, l. 7.   Lady Sussex to Ralph V. from Gorhambury, 17 February 1641.
p. 159, l. 15. Ralph V.'s Notes, 16 April 1641.
p. 161, l. 26. Mun V. to Ralph V. from Claydon, 24 September 1641.
p. 163, l. 25. Lady Sussex to Ralph V. from Gorhambury, 29 November 1641.

Chapter IX
p. 166, l. 8.   Tom V. to Sir E.V. from Barbados, 17 April 1642.
p. 167, l. 30. Tom V. to Wm Roades from Barbados, 21 May 1642.
p. 168, l. 1.   Tom V. to Ralph V. from London, 20 August 1642.
p. 168, l. 21. Henry V. to Ralph V. from The Hague, 16 March 1642.
p. 168, l. 31. Henry V. to Ralph V. from The Hague, 6 April 1642.
p. 169, l. 5.   Henry V. to Ralph V. from The Hague, 28 April 1642.
p. 169, l. 21. Henry V. to Ralph V. from Rotterdam, 18 May 1642.
p. 169, l. 35. Sir E.V. to Ralph V. from London, 6 April 1642.
p. 170, l. 4.   Henry V. to Ralph V. from Breda, 20 June, 1642.
p. 170, l. 16. Ralph V. to Mun V. from Claydon, July 1642.
p. 170, l. 23. Henry V. to Ralph V. from Breda, 15 September 1642.
p. 170, l. 35. Sir John Leake to Sir E.V. from Ireland, December 1641.
p. 171, l. 6.   Ralph V. to Lady Barrymore from Claydon, 2 February 1641.
p. 171, l. 21. Sir John Leake to Sir E.V. from Ireland, 10 January 1642.
p. 172, l. 15. Sir John Leake to Sir E.V. from Ireland, 4 March 1642.
p. 172, l. 39. Mun V. to Ralph V. from Dublin, 2 February 1642.
p. 173, l. 11. Mun V. to Ralph V. from Dublin, 12 February 1642.
p. 173, l. 39. Sir John Leake to Sir E.V. from Youghal, 10 March 1642.
p. 174, l. 9.   Ralph V. to Lady Barrymore from Claydon, 9 June 1642.
p. 174, l. 27. Mun V. to Ralph V. from Trim, 22 June, 1642.
p. 175, l. 10. Mun V. to Ralph V. from Hillesden, 4 October 1641.
p. 175, l. 37. Ralph V.'s Notes, December 1641.
p. 176, l. 5.   Lady Sussex to Ralph V. from Gorhambury, 15 January 1642.
p. 176, l. 6.   Lady Sussex to Ralph V. from Gorhambury, 18 February 1642.
p. 176, l. 17. Thomas Gardiner to Mary V. from Welwyn, 27 June 1642.
p. 176, l. 30. Cary Gardiner to Ralph V. from Cuddesden, 28 July 1642.
p. 176, l. 39. Ralph V. to Cary Gardiner from Gorhambury, August 1642.
p. 177, l. 11. Cary Gardiner to Ralph V. from Cuddesden, 4 September 1642.

Bibliography

Aikin, Lucy, *Memoirs of the Court of King Charles the First* (London, 1833).

Albion, Father Gordon, *Charles I and the Court of Rome*, Burns, Oates (London, 1935).

Ashley, Maurice, *England in the Seventeenth Century*, Penguin (Harmondsworth, Mddx., 1952).

Aylmer, G. E., *The King's Servants*, Routledge and Kegan Paul (London, 1961).

Bagwell, R., *Ireland Under the Stuarts* (London, 1909).

Ball, Rt. Hon. J. J., *The Reformed Church of Ireland* (Dublin and London, 1886).

Barrett, C. R. B., *Battles and Battlefields in England* (London, 1896).

Besant, Sir Walter, *London in the Time of the Stuarts* (London, 1904).

Birch, Thomas, *The Court and Times of James the First* (London, 1848)

Birch, Thomas, *The Court and Times of Charles the First* (London, 1848).

Bradley, Rosa M., *The English Housewife in the Seventeenth and Eighteenth Centuries* (London, 1912).

Brett, N. G., *The Growth of Stuart London*, Allen and Unwin (London, 1935).

Bruce, John, *Notes of Proceedings in the Long Parliament*, Camden Society (London, 1845).

Bruce, John, *Letters and Papers of the Verney Family*, Camden Society (London, 1853).

Brunton, D. and D. H. Pennington, *The Members of the Long Parliament*, Allen and Unwin (London, 1954).

Burne, Colonel A. H. and Brigadier P. Young, *The Civil War*, Eyre and Spottiswoode (London, 1959).

Burton, J. H., *The History of Scotland* (London, 1897).

Carlisle, Nicholas, *The Gentlemen of His Majesty's Most Honourable Privy Chamber* (London, 1829).

Carr, J. A., *Life and Times of Archbishop Ussher* (London, 1895).

Cheyney, Edward P., *A History of England*, Longman (London, 1926).

Clarendon, Lord, *History of the Rebellion* (London, 1826).

Clark, Sir George, *Three Aspects of Stuart England*, Oxford University Press (Oxford, 1960).

Coate, Mary, *Social Life in Stuart England*, Methuen (London, 1924).

Currey, E. H., *Sea Wolves of the Mediterranean* (London, 1910).

Davies, G., *Bibliography of English History 1603–1714*, Oxford University Press (Oxford, 1928).

Dickinson, P. L., *An Outline History of the Architecture of the British Isles*, Butler and Tanner (London, 1926).

Dietz, F. C., *English Public Finance 1558–1641*, Appleton-Century Crofts, (New York, 1932).

Disraeli, Isaac, *Life and Reign of Charles the First* (London, 1851).

Drinkwater, John, *John Hampden's England*, Butterworth (London, 1933).

Dunlop, John, *Memoirs of Spain during the Reigns of Philip IV and Charles II from 1621 to 1700* (London, 1834).

Elrington, C. R., *Life of Archbishop Ussher* (Dublin and London, 1848).

Fisher, G., *The Barbary Legend*, Oxford University Press (Oxford, 1957).

Gardiner, S. R., *Prince Charles and the Spanish Marriage* (London, 1869)

Godfrey, Elizabeth, *Home Life under the Stuarts* (London, 1903).

Godfrey, Elizabeth, *Social Life under the Stuarts* (London, 1904)

Gordon, J., *History of Scots Affairs from 1637–1641* (Aberdeen, 1841).

Gotch, J. A., *The English Home from Charles I to George IV* (London, 1918).

Green, J. R., *A Short History of the English People* (London, 1874).

Guiseppi, M. S., *Guide to the Public Records* (London, 1923).

Hearne, Thomas, *Historia Vitae et Regni Ricardi I* (London, 1729).

Howell, James, *Familiar Letters of Howell* (*Epistolae Ho-elianae*) (London, 1673).

Hume, D., *History of England* (London, 1789).

Hume, Martin, *The Court of Philip IV* (London, 1907).

Huxley, Gervas, *Endymion Porter*, Chatto and Windus (London, 1959).

Inderwick, F. A., *Sidelights on the Stuarts* (London, 1888).

Jesse, J. H., *Memoirs of the Court of England* (London, 1840).

Lane-Poole, S., *Barbary Corsairs* (London, 1890).

McElwee, William, *England's Precedence*, Hodder and Stoughton (London, 1956).

Mackay, Janet, *Little Madam*, Bell (London, 1939).

Mackenzie, R. J., *War Pictures from Clarendon* (Oxford, 1912).

Marriott, J. A. R., *The Life and Times of Lucius Cary Viscount Falkland* (London, 1907).

Mathew, David, *The Social Structure in Caroline England*, Oxford University Press (Oxford, 1948).

Morice, B., *An Essay on the Court of the Marshalsea* (London, 1812).

Nicholas, J., *The Progresses of King James the First* (London, 1628).

Notestein, W., *The Journal of Sir Simon D'Ewes*, Yale University Press, (New Haven, Conn., 1923).

Notestein, W., *The English People on the Eve of Colonization*, Hamish Hamilton (London, 1954).

Notestein, W., *Conflict in Stuart England*, Jonathan Cape (London, 1960).

O'Brien, George, *Economic History of Ireland in the Seventeenth Century* (Dublin and London, 1919).

Palme, Per, *Triumph of Peace*, Thames and Hudson (London, 1957).

Parsons, Daniel, *The Diary of Sir Henry Slingsby* (London, 1836).

Pearl, Valerie, *London and the Outbreak of the Puritan Revolution*, Oxford University Press (Oxford, 1961).

Pegge, Samuel, *Curialia Miscellanea* (London, 1782).

Petrie, Sir Charles, Bt., *The Stuarts*, Eyre and Spottiswoode (London, 1937).

Pevsner, Nikolaus, *An Outline of European Architecture*, John Murray (London, 1948).

Phillips, W. A., *History of the Church of Ireland*, Oxford University Press (Oxford, 1933).

Reade, Hubert G. R., *Sidelights of the Thirty Years War* (London, 1924).

Rennie, James Alan, *In the Steps of the Cavaliers*, Rich and Cowan (London, 1954).

Round, J. H., *The King's Sergeants and Officers of State* (London, 1911).

Ryan, P. F. W., *Stuart Lives and Manners* (London, 1912).

Sands, Mollie, *Garden of Hampton Court*, Evans Bros (London, 1950).

Sheppard, Edgar, *The Old Royal Palace of Whitehall* (London, 1902).

Smith, Charlotte Fell, *Mary Rich: Countess of Warwick* (London, 1901).

Stow, John, *Survey of London* (London, 1623).

Thompson, Gladys Scott, *Life in a Noble Household*, Jonathan Cape (London, 1937).

Townshend, Dorothea, *Life and Letters of Mr. Endymion Porter* (London, 1897).

Trevelyan, G. M., *English Social History*, Longmans (London, 1946).

Trevelyan, G. M., *England under the Stuarts*, Methuen (London, 1949).

Trotter, Eleanor, *Seventeenth Century Life in the Country Parish* (Cambridge, 1919).

Verney, Lady F. P., *Memoirs of the Verney Family during the Civil War* (London, 1892).

Walford, E. A., *Edgehill: the Battle and Battlefield* (Banbury, 1886).

Warriston, Archibald Johnson, Lord, *Diary* (Edinburgh, 1896).

Wedgwood, C. V., *Battlefields in Britain*, Collins (London, 1944).

Wedgwood, C. V., *Civil War Battlefields: 1642–1646*, British Broadcasting Corporation (London 1952).

Wedgwood, C. V., *The King's Peace*, Collins (London, 1955).

Wedgwood, C. V., *The King's War*, Collins (London, 1958).

Wedgwood, C. V., *Thomas Wentworth: First Earl of Strafford*, Jonathan Cape (London, rev. ed. 1961).

Wheatley, Henry B., *London Past and Present*, John Murray (London, 1931).

Williams, Neville, *Captains Outrageous*, Barrie and Rockliffe (London, 1961).

Williamson, Hugh Ross, *King James I*, Duckworth (London, 1936).

Willson, D. H., *James VI and I*, Jonathan Cape (London, 1956).

Wood, A. C., *Nottinghamshire in the Civil War*, Oxford University Press (Oxford, 1937).

Yarwood, D., *The English Home*, Batsford (London, 1956).

PAMPHLETS

Holles, Denzil, *An Extract and The Relation of the Dangerous and Bloody Fight . . . near Kineton* (London, 1642).

Young, Brigadier P., *The Royalist Army at Edgehill* (Journal of the Society for Army Historical Research, Summer 1955).

Young, Brigadier, P., *The Royalist Artillery at Edgehill* (Journal of the Society for Army Historical Research, December 1957).

Index

Essex, Earl of (Robert Devereux), 127, 135, 181, 192 et seq.
Eure, William, 134–5
Evans, Ellen, 104
Evelyn, John, 42

FALKLAND, Viscount (Lucius Cary), 153, 159
Fauconbridge—Thomas the Bastard, 33
Feilding, Colonel Basil, Lord, 197
Feilding, Colonel Richard, 195
Fens, 98–9
Finch, John, Lord, 155
Fortescue, Sir Faithful, 198
Furnishings, 36, 116–17

GARDENS, 42–4
Gardiner, Sir Thomas, 40, 175
Gardiner, Captain Thomas (son of above), 175–6
Gentileschi, Orazio, 91
Gerard (author of *Herbal*), 42
Giffard, John, 23
Giffard, Phillip, 23
Giffard, Richard, 24
Gondomar, Count, 52, 100
Goring, George, Lord, 18, 99, 159, 169
Goring, Colonel George, 159, 169
Graham, Sir Richard, 30, 53
Grand Remonstrance, 163
Grandison, Viscount (William Villiers), 72
Granville (Pirate), 24
Greville, Colonel, 172
Grey, Lord, 203
Gustavus Adolphus, 128, 196

HACKNEYS, 103–4

Hamilton, James, Marquis of, 103, 125 et seq., 162
Hampden, John, 17, 149, 152–3, 163–4, 199
Harrington, Sir John, 89
Harvey, Dr William, 93
Haslerig, Sir Arthur, 164
Henrietta Maria, 53, 88 et seq., 127, 159, 164, 168, 181, 190, 192
Henry Prince of Wales, 18, 26–7, 49, 91, 158
Herbert, Sir Edward, 153
Herbert, Lord, 18
Hillesden, 27
Hobart, Sir Nathaniel, 28, 40, 98–9
Holborn, Sir Robert, 104
Holland, Earl of (Henry Rich), 127, 137, 149
Holles, Denzil, 164
Horses, 73, 115, 146
Hotham, Sir John, 181
Howard, Lord, 134
Howard, Sir William, 59
Howell, James, 49, 60, 66
Huntly, Marquis of (George Gordon), 127, 135

IRELAND, 106–9, 162–3, 170 et seq.
Isham, Elizabeth Denton, Mrs, 40

JAMES I
   Court, 26, 37, 84 et seq.
   naval policy, 21–2
   policy, 21, 49 et seq., 125
Jansen, Cornelius, 110–11
Jermyn, Henry, Lord, 159
Jones, Inigo, 88, 91
Jonson, Ben, 88
Justices of the Peace, 46